# G-D

# ME

## ARE YOU READY TO MEET YOUR MAKER?

# RABBI SHLOMO BEN ZEEV

G-d & Me

Copyright © 2018 by Rabbi S. Ben Zeev



ISBN (978-965-92588-2-6)

Published by Rabbi Shlomo Ben Zeev
DN Nahal Soreq PO Box 148
Beit Hilkiya, Israel 7681500
Core.Emunah@gmail.com

# Contents

## *Introduction*

S I STATED in volume one of the Core Emunah series, the
main purpose of the book was to prime our understanding of
the world and its truth. To come face to face with the reality of
reality. To recognize that this world, in all of its splendor and glory,
cannot exist without the power, the intelligence, and the decision of the
Creator. The more we peel back the layers of existence and the fabric of
reality – the more this truth becomes evident. The more we sift the
science from the science-fiction, the more we see how it is in-tune with
the truth of the Torah. For what is the purpose of science if not to search
for the understanding of the truth in this world? Why would the Truth
(Torah) not be in-sync with the truth (evidence) of this world?

This realization is at the core of all emunah. For if there is no G-d,
then what is the point of pondering the reason for existence in the first
place? An accident, by its very definition, is something that may have a
cause, (this is, after all, a world of cause-and-effect), but it most certainly

has no purpose. However, if there is G-d, then the issue of the cause becomes clear, and the question that we are left with, therefore, is what is our purpose if indeed, there is one?

In addition, once that realization has solidified within our minds, we then should begin the process of making it the core of our reality and understanding. We do not want to miss the point of life among the day to day details of living. We all know that, like all other life forms, if we don't eat – we starve; if we don't have shelter – we are at the mercy of the elements. Indeed, we have many other basic needs, which require work and effort to fulfill. However, let's say that we have already fulfilled them, and we are no longer in need. Then what? What happens when I have all that I need? What happens when I have finished working, and I have made the money that I need to cover the expense of my existence, then what?

If I am a doctor, when I hang up my lab coat at the end of the day, am I still just a doctor? If I am the President, when I go to the bathroom do I continue to be the president? Does it matter whether I live a life of 120 years on this planet or only just a few minutes? Is there any intrinsic difference in the length of my existence? Is there, indeed, a reason *to be*?

This brings us to the second fundamental question regarding life, which I posited at the beginning of volume one. Here is the question: "In the immensity and profundity of this great and complex creation, is it possible for the Creator to know little-old-me"? There seem to be so many things that are so much greater in the world. There are so many happenings that we would, naturally, assume are of greater importance. So that I, being another one of life's details, would get lost in the creation's details! However, if the reality of life is that the Creator, G-d, DOES know me, then there is a reason for my being here, and what I do with my life DOES, indeed, matter. For otherwise, why would He bother?

So, let's start the journey together, you and I, to prove and understand, clearly and profoundly, that G-d really does know each of us, and thereby begin our journey towards question number three, "What is my relationship with Him"?

# Paranormal Phenomenon

## ***Real-life Experiences of the World to Come.***

ONE OF THE GREATEST issues of life, one which lies at the heart of all things, is the matter of the soul. It is the most significant question that mankind deals with because, beyond a shadow of a doubt, if you've got one – it's from G-d.

There is no physical explanation for the soul. It's not chemical, mechanical, or anything else. It is also not energy as is classically defined by science, (i.e. it's not the "E" of $E=MC^2$). Clearly, however, it is that. It is energy. Why do I say that it is not our traditional understanding of energy? Because we all know, and can all say with confidence, that we are not automatons. We have the ability to think, to consider our actions and their consequences, and to act against our base desires and/or drives.

This cannot be explained by a physical phenomenon. Yet at the same time, we are told that we are just like any other animal. We are merely biological phenomena, like all animals, like all plants. We are here today – gone tomorrow!

But if we DO have a soul, that would be something amazing! Isn't that true?


So, do we have one – yes or no?


## **The Body Electric**

Let us first consider the following: We know that the body is controlled by bio-electricity. This bio-electricity is relayed to and from the brain via synapses and neurons. However, we also know that, essentially, the body is a biological machine. Ergo: if it has electricity – it works, and if it does not – it doesn't.

As we mentioned in the previous volume, (in chapters nine, "*In the beginning*" and chapter seven, "*Abraham and Abiogenesis*"), there is no scientific explanation today that can explain how beams of light, atoms, and all their parts, can become a biological machine, (i.e. life). It also cannot explain what makes the trillions of individual cells that make up our bodies into the integral unit that functions in unison to allow for the body's functioning.

We are told that really "I think – therefore I am"! I am a functioning human being and, regardless of how that happened, I am no more than a biological machine. All I need is a little food and water (i.e. fuel), which gets processed in my stomach and is then injected, via the heart and the bloodstream, to all the parts of my body and I'm ready to go! But is that really so? Is that the actual source of the body's life, or is there something else? Am "I" just a physical body that is bio-electrically powered; or is there a much more powerful and invasive presence that is the real "me"[1]?

We all have heard of "Frankenstein", the story of the monster made by "Doctor Frankenstein" in the book, written by Mary Shelly. Essentially the premise of the book behind the monster was as follows: the body is just a biological machine. It remains so regardless of whether it is alive or dead. Therefore, if the only difference between a live and a dead body is whether or not it has (bio-electric) energy, then all I have to do is supply even a corpse with enough power[2] and it will return to life! In reality, even before the body has yet to deteriorate immediately after death, it just doesn't work. If electric shocks don't succeed in restarting the heart to allow for the continuity of the original bio-electricity then further shocks, and/or plugging the corpse into a wall socket just won't do it. Once the real "spark" is gone – so, too, goes the body.

So clearly, despite the electricity that the body creates and utilizes, it's not just an electrical issue. So, what is it in the body that could possibly be "me"?

1 Concerning this issue see Emunot v'De'ot of Rav Sa'adiya Gaon in the second ma'amar part 5

2 1.21 gigawatts perhaps? I mean, in all of the Frankenstein movies lightning was the source of his reanimation.

## Have a Heart!

When our heart is beating, and the bio-electricity is flowing, we are alive. If that's the case then maybe it's the heart, that non-stop engine of amazement, which makes us alive and is the source of said bio-electricity?

Nope! No way whatsoever! We know this conclusively from heart transplants.

During a transplant, the blood-flow to the heart is stopped and as a result, the heart stops pumping. But not only does the guys/girls heart stop, but it is then removed from the body entirely, to be replaced by that of a donor[3]. Meaning, that if it was the heart that gave a person his[4] life, that made a man who he is, then when he gets a *new* heart he should be living someone else's life! But after a transplant – that doesn't happen. When the person gets up off the operating table, he might have a new *lease* on life – but he's the same person. It's the same life that he had pre-operation. Whereas the donor of the heart is now dead.

## It's All in the Blood

A genuinely critical ingredient for life is blood. As is evident during heart transplants, if the blood remains pumping around the system, even via an external source of pumping, the body, and the person can survive.

---

3 http://en.wikipedia.org/wiki/Heart_transplantation#Operative

4 I'm using the masculine to simplify matters and due to the fact that I am a male. If this bothers you, if you consider this not to be P.C. - I guess you'll just have to live with it as that isn't my intention.

It cannot do this indefinitely, as the machinery available today cannot do the heart's job as well as the heart, but for a while it is sufficient.

There isn't a single part of the body that does not require this all-important ingredient called blood. The heart, the lungs, the brain, and all of the other parts of the body are dependent upon the blood to survive. If there is no blood – there is no life[5].

Yet a person who is deathly ill can receive a blood transfusion to replace the entirety of his body's blood and although none of the blood that is presently in his body is actually his own after the transfusion, he still "wakes up" as the same individual. So clearly, it's not JUST the blood that makes me who I am. Nor is it the blood that supplies the bio-electricity that our body so sorely needs. It is most certainly a catalyst for the continued bio-electric activity. It may be the bioelectricity's conduit – but it's not the source[6].

---

5 Clearly not all of a person's blood is necessary to survive, but there is a clear minimum before the body goes into shock from blood loss. Our sages call this bare minimum the "Reviis Dam", a "reviis" being a certain small amount of blood. This amount of blood is what our sages tell us contains the soul. This does not mean that if I would replace a person's blood with that of another he would wake up with someone else's soul. It means that if a person were to lose 25% (=reviis, Hebrew for a quarter) of their blood in the times of the Talmud and even up until recent history, until the advent of refrigeration and sterilization techniques – they were dead men! This is also true today as well, as a person who loses more than 20% of their blood enters a state called "shock". This is an automatic protective mode in which the body, due to lack of enough blood to sustain the entire system, starts shutting down the less important systems in order to protect those systems that are vital. Even today, without blood transfusions, most, if not all people in this state, would die.

6 Rav Saadiah Gaon, in his book "Emunot v'De'ot", Sixth Ma'amar, part 1, in his refutation of the sixth opinion of the soul, addresses those who feel that the Torah states that the blood is the source for the soul. The following is a quote (translated) from there:

> The sixth opinion is he who thinks that it (the soul) is specifically the blood. This is the opinion of Anan (the leader of the Sadducees in RS"G's time) only, as he explained in his book. It was his (simplistic reading of the) Torah (that caused him to make this mistake) which wrote (Devarim (Deuteronomy) 12:23) "for the blood is the soul". But he didn't notice that which the Torah stated previously (Vayikra (Leviticus) 17:11) "For the soul of the flesh is in the blood". It is even obvious that the blood is the dwelling place of the soul and it's source of equilibrium (not the soul itself), and it is via the strength of one's blood we see strength of one's soul, and by the weakness (of lack) of blood that it becomes weakened… but the Torah has surely stated (in the verse quoted by Anan) that the blood is the soul based on the laws of grammar. For sometimes a thing is called by the place that it resides, just as wisdom is referred to as "heart"… for the heart is it's place (but not it's source), and it calls language "lips" (safah in Hebrew) … for it is enunciated with the lips.

## It's a No-Brainer

As we all know, or at least so we have been told, the real source of a person's personality resides in his brain. The assumption, therefore, is that if a person were to undergo a brain transplant, then he would indeed wake up in a strange body. Maybe this is true, but the question is – why?

Well, it's because information regarding all the body's functions and everything from our five senses are all sent to the brain for processing. After the brain processes the information it either sends it to long or short-term storage for later use or sends out orders to the body for immediate response. Since the brain is the receptacle of all a person's experiences, it is therefore assumed that if he were to get a brain transplant, he would no longer "wake up" the same person as he was pre-operation.

But is that really so? I mean it does seem that a person with brain damage has problems accessing parts of his or her memory. It has also been noted that touching areas of the brain during surgical procedures affect areas of memory and personality, but is that really it? Is it all just electrical impulses that are stored in a part of our brain? If so, how? no one seems to know! Is that the be-all and end-all of who and what we are? A lump of cells with stored memories?

Maybe... but then again, maybe not!

Perhaps the brain is just another physical receptacle for something else? Maybe it's just the BIOS for the workings of our amazing bodies, whereas the REAL "me" is something different entirely?

What if it could be shown that there remains something of a person after their demise? If we were to find that a person's persona and memories can live on after their physical death and in that state still have sight and memory, or live on in another body with another brain – then what?

Well, then, apparently, we are not talking about just bio-energy, as we were postulating previously. It must be energy of another kind. It must be an energy that is INDEPENDENT of the body. It must be a soul.

To round out the issue: is the brain the source of the bio-electricity mentioned above? Well, no. But then again, we really don't know what is! Can science today truly account for what the measurable bio-electricity of the body is and where it comes from? No. Once again, it's "I think – therefore I am". The assumption remains that we are here and that our body seems to function OK with some food and water, so it must be a combination of "fuel combustion" that supplies the body with the ever-so-vital bio-electricity. Right?

Nope! It's a soul!


## I'm a Soul Man!

So just what is a soul?

A soul, say our Rabbi's, ob"m, consists of many parts, and there are many types and sizes of souls. In truth, the human soul is so great that it cannot "fit" into the body despite the fact that it has no actual physicality[7].

All things, great and small, have a form of soul. It is, despite scientific ignorance[8], that which makes a pile of chemical goo into living biology. It's what takes a bunch of single cells and makes them into an organism.

The lowest form of soul is the power source that animates a body. All living things have this type of soul. The higher form of soul, called the *neshamah* is possessed solely by human beings. It is the source of our intelligence, our personality, and all that makes us unique. It also is what allows us to speak. Humans, who are intrinsically different than all other living creatures, are in possession of something above and beyond just the rudimentary soul, (called "*Nefesh*" in Hebrew). It is the *Neshamah* that makes man into the pinnacle of creation[9].

As an illustration, imagine that the soul, the real you, are bound upside-down reaching down from the heavens with only the "head", perhaps just the eyes, inserted inside of the cranium. In the cranium, it has only a limited amount of sight (via the eyes) and sound (via the ears) and senses (via the skin and nerves, etc.) because it has been "crammed" into a very limited space. If it is "tied" to the body, all its senses are

---

7 Our sages, ob"m, in Tractate Berachos 10a tell us that it does, however, fill up the entire body.

8 I refer to what I mentioned in the chapters "Abraham and A-biogenesis" and "In the Beginning", in Core Emunah volume 1, that modern science, despite any and all statements to the contrary, cannot account for why a living cell is no more than a pile of bonded chemicals (organic or otherwise) and what it is that subjugates the trillions of individual cells into an organized, structured, well-oiled machine that work in tandem to allow for even the most basic of all multi-celled organisms.

9 This is explicit in the verse in Genesis (Bereishis) 2:7 "...and He breathed into his (man's) nostrils *nishmas chaim*", the breath of life. It is translated by the Targum Onkelos as "He breathed into his nostrils the breath of speech", which is also the source of the qualitative difference between the intelligence of man and that of animals.

limited to those of the body and connected to the body via the fantastic BIOS of the body, the brain.

However, since the soul is NOT part of the body, it is therefore not bound to the body, except during life. Even during life, it is only linked to the conscious mind. But after life, or when speaking to the SUB-conscious mind... well that's a whole other story!

## **<u>Eden</u>**

Before we begin to explore the topic, I would like to point out that there is (or was) virtually no society on the face of the planet that claimed that there is no concept of life after death and no place of final reward[10].

Everyone, until recent history, posited that there was (at least) one G-d, everyone held that we have a soul, and everyone "knew" (=believed) that there was the world to come[11]. This is incontestable.

The scientific method, however, which is based upon skepticism, doesn't like this issue and rejects this clear universal historical truth because... they believed that these people were all primitive, (i.e. they predated the scientific method). We all know that we cannot accept the testimony of primitive people, as there is no way that they could be right!

*... Matter alone appears to be able to carry out all the activities that have been traditionally associated*

---

10 I am not talking about individuals, as there have been many individuals throughout history who didn't accept this premise. I am talking about the basis of all the world's faiths. Socially there was no nation that denied this principle to the best of my knowledge.

11 Check out any of the core beliefs found at http://www.deathreference.com/ see for example http://www.deathreference.com/A-Bi/African-Religions.html and also https://en.wikipedia.org/wiki/Soul#Religious_views

*with the soul. No "spiritual" element is required by the data. The implication that "we" are bodies and brains made of atoms and nothing more is perhaps simply too new, too disturbing, too incompatible with common preconceptions to be soon accepted into common knowledge. However, if we do indeed possess an immaterial soul or a material one with special properties that cannot be found in inanimate matter, then we should expect to find some evidence for it. (Stenger, Failed Hypothesis pg. 84)*

In a nutshell: if I cannot bring observable proof to G-d in a controlled scientific experiment it must be because He doesn't exist!

I will, later in this chapter, address the issues with this ridiculous and hypocritical statement. Please be patient. However, this argument is not the summation of the issue.

So, for the sake of the skeptics – let's add some more fuel to the fire.

I realize that most of the information that I will present here does not necessarily lend itself to scrutiny via the scientific method. I only ask that the reader takes this information under careful consideration. Although possibly unproven scientifically, when looked at in the perspective of all the information presented herein, a clear picture emerges. Don't miss the forest because of all the trees.

In truth, all the information that will be brought in the rest of this chapter should be at least considered as what is called "anecdotal evidence". Anecdotal evidence is not something to be laughed at! There have been many great discoveries that were made using anecdotal evidence. Even if much of what will be presented does not lend itself to scrutiny via the scientific method, this doesn't mean that it is worthless. Having said that, let's get back on track!

As we will see each and every one of us, has a divine soul.

## **NDE – Near Death Experiences**

The topic known as "NDE's", "Near Death Experiences", describes a phenomenon that became popularized in the early 1970's by Dr. Raymond Moody, a forensic psychologist in a Georgia state hospital. He noted that in stories related to him by many of his patients who were resuscitated, there were many key and overlapping concepts that kept recurring. These findings led to his writing the book *Life after Life*, in which he related the results of his study of this phenomenon.

It was not new, there have been many stories in recorded history relating details like those of Dr. Moody's patients[12]. It is also not an isolated phenomenon. A rough estimation is that there are around 8 million Americans alone, (which is likely, a gross under-estimation), who

---

12 For example, the Talmud in Bava Batra 10b brings the story of Yosef, son of Rabbi Yehoshua, who passed away and was revived and related the story of what he witnessed when passing.

have experienced an NDE[13]. Who can indeed tell us just how many have experienced this phenomenon worldwide?

So, what is the NDE?

The typical NDE is an occurrence that happens close to the cessation of the body's functioning. There is no discernible heart or brain activity which could be recorded, and the person is pronounced dead. Yet despite this diagnosis, and despite all evidence to the contrary, the "deceased", either minutes or hours after their demise[14], open their eyes and can relate a fantastic story. Many of the stories contain similarities, binding together those who had the same experience. So, what happens?

Dr. Moody, in his study of 150 of his patients found the following similar characteristics, referred to as the "core experiences" of an NDE:

1. A feeling of peace and painlessness

2. Having an out-of-body experience

3. A sense of traveling through a tunnel

4. A sense of rising into the heavens

5. Seeing people, often dead relatives

6. Meeting a spiritual being such as God

7. Seeing a review of one's life

8. Feeling a reluctance to return to life

---

13 https://en.wikipedia.org/wiki/Near-death_experience#cite_note-13

14 Dr. Melvin Morse, a famed investigator of NDE's in children, relates one story of a child who revived after having been immersed under water for 45 minutes. He then told over his NDE story. This is one story of many. Dr. Morse relates that there are many known cases of people having been "sitting" in the morgue for even up to three days before they revived! See the end-notes for more info.

The out-of-body experience, (OOBE), is a fantastic phenomenon. The reason for this is because almost all those who experienced it can give a detailed account relating what happened to them and their general surroundings during their OOBE while their bodies lay "dead" on the floor. It boggles the mind[15].

Examples of these details includes: conversations between the medical staff, descriptions of what the people were wearing, medical and surgical procedures performed, (all of which were conducted during the time of the person's collapse/demise), and, in at least one recorded instance, the fact that there was a shoe out on the ledge of the building several floors above[16].

Another surprising fact is that the descriptions given were not done from the perspective of the person's line of sight, or point of view (i.e. as if he was viewing the scenario with his or her eyes), but rather as seen from the ceiling or some other type of vantage point. More on this in a moment.

But science is the art of skepticism, and the following three cynicisms were posited concerning the validity of the NDE as a proof of the soul:

---

15 http://www.near-death.com/experiences/research11.html#a02

16 "Maria was a migrant worker who, while visiting friends in Seattle, had a severe heart attack. She was rushed to Harborview Hospital and placed in the coronary care unit. A few days later, she had a cardiac arrest and an unusual out-of-body experience. At one point in this experience, she found herself outside the hospital and spotted a single tennis shoe on the ledge of the north side of the third floor of the building. Maria not only was able to indicate the whereabouts of this oddly situated object, but was able to provide precise details concerning its appearance, such as that its little toe area was worn and one of its laces was stuck underneath its heel. Upon hearing Maria's story, Clark, with some considerable degree of skepticism and metaphysical misgiving, went to the location described to see whether any such shoe could be found. Indeed, it was, just where and precisely as Maria had described it, except that from the window through which Clark was able to see it, the details of its appearance that Maria had specified could not be discerned. Clark concluded, "The only way she could have had such a perspective was if she had been floating right outside and at very close range to the tennis shoe. I retrieved the shoe and brought it back to Maria; it was very concrete evidence for me.". (Ibid)

> *First, the NDE could just as easily have occurred before or after any state resembling brain death. There is no way to verify the timing of memory formation relative to brain scans when the patient is not conscious.*

Meaning: who says the "experience" isn't entirely based on the phenomenon that happened *immediately before or immediately after* the clinical death of the body, not during the "death" state.

This is the weakest of all the arguments raised, as in most cases the NDE's story that is related "occurred" *during* the "death" state. Meaning that the information which was relayed contained details of things that happened during the time that the person was diagnosed as being "Dead". It is, therefore, very difficult to contend that detailed memories of what transpired during the "dead" period could or would be constructed from memories that occurred either before or after the fact.

> *Second, it is very difficult to verify that there was, in fact, no measurable brain activity. There are many types of brain activity, and they require different types of tests to verify them. Most of these types of tests are not typically performed when a patient is undergoing attempts at emergency resuscitation. It is entirely possible, for example, that a patient showing no activity on an EEG scan could still have brain activity that would appear on an*

*FMRI, PET, or catSCAN. In the words of Dr. Mark Cohen, a neuroimaging researcher at UCLA: "The EEG can appear flat, even in the presence of high activity when that activity is not synchronous. For example, the EEG flattens in regions involved in direct task processing. This phenomenon is known as event-related desynchronization."*

Meaning: who says that, despite the other apparent symptoms of death, there was no brain activity occurring during the "death"? Perhaps the brain continues to have some undetected activity during the "death" stage? In which case, the experience wasn't one of "death" but one of life. … Maybe… but maybe not as well! Even if we were to assume that during the "death" stage there is continued brain activity of some sort (even though it's not recorded or noticeable), there still remain two issues. First of all, "activity" occurring in the brain in and of itself isn't enough as a rebuttal. It would have to be demonstrated that it occurred in an area of the brain that controls cognizance. Secondly, who is to say that the conscious mind would have any access to said activity upon "waking" from the "death" stage?

*Third, the experiences reported by NDE subjects have also been reported by other patients whose experiences had known triggers (mostly chemicals of a psychedelic nature.) The chemical processes that happen in a brain under oxygen deprivation are known to share some characteristics with the effects*

*of psychoactive substances[17].*

Meaning: because we have found that there are chemical substances that allow for similar experiences to occur, and similar experiences have been recorded by people who underwent oxygen deprivation (i.e. they couldn't breathe) – who says that these experiences have anything whatsoever to do with death?

Ah, pessimism! It costs you nothing to be pessimistic. But even after the pessimism, the question remains: are any of these claims logical counter-arguments to the above NDE experiences? Are the NDE experiences qualitatively different than those caused by chemical compounds and/or other sources, or are they of the same precise nature? Even after the pessimism, these are questions that still need to be explored!

Furthermore, do the above skepticisms explain why or how the information relayed concerning the OOB experiences are from an entirely different vantage point than the person's body? No.

Do the skepticisms above explain the similarities between the "core" NDE experiences vs. the rather random experiences of the other types of patients? No.

So, what we DO have are many documented cases, in almost all of which the attending medical teams diagnosed the patient as dead, and

---

17 https://en.wikipedia.org/wiki/Near-death_experience#Criticism_of_NDE_as_proof_for_.22afterlife.22_or_.22a_soul.22_outside_the_brain

the detailed descriptions of what transpired took place immediately *after* that prognosis.

However, that is not all there is to say about the skepticism above.

Let's just stop and consider for a moment: just how "dead" is the "Death" of the NDE? A prime example of this is the experience of singer Pam Renolds-Lowery from Atlanta, Ga.

> *In 1991, Ms. Reynolds Lowery was diagnosed with an aneurysm at the base of her brain. Informed that it was inoperable, she chose to try a novel procedure developed by Dr. Robert Spetzler, chief of neurosurgery at Barrow Neurological Institute in Phoenix. To prevent a rupture of the aneurysm during surgery, her body temperature was lowered to 60 degrees Fahrenheit, and blood was drained from her brain. Her heart was stopped, and brain activity ceased. Clinically, she was dead.*

> *Afterward, Ms. Reynolds Lowery was able to describe the procedure in minute detail -- including the little dent in the device the surgeon used to open her skull -- even though her eyes were covered with surgical pads and plugs were inserted in her ears.* [18]

---

18 http://www.ajc.com/news/news/local/pam-reynolds-lowery-noted-for-near-death-episode/nQgP3/ (This is the webpage of the Atlanta Journal and Constitution. A local newspaper). Although there have been some counter-arguments posited to "explain" the phenomenon described in her NDE, as can be seen at http://en.wikipedia.org/wiki/Pam_Reynolds_case#Critical_analysis the arguments, when looked at analytically, are weak and don't really address the core issues of the NDE stated above.

Effectively, even if she were not as dead as the above description portrays, even assuming that there was continued brain activity the eye-pads and the ear-plugs almost certainly would have prevented her from seeing and hearing what transpired during her surgery. But when you top that off with the fact that there was no brain activity, (indeed, there was no blood in her brain!), no heartbeat and that the body was basically in a state of hypothermia[19] – what could the brain have picked up on? Although the hypo-tension prevented her from reaching the finality of absolute death – it's clear that there was nothing going on in there!

Another issue that isn't really addressed is the transformative nature that is reported relating to NDE's. A large percentage of those who had an NDE stated that they came back from the experience a changed person. To what degree and how long this lasted aside, this is something that most people don't recall. However, this is not something that we find about drug trips and oxygen deprivation that brought about the "NDE-like" phenomenon.

The truth is that the results of a 5-year study into the reported phenomenon of NDE's as compared to those experienced under other circumstances showed conclusively that they are not really comparable at all[20].

*The conclusion of the study is that the NDE phenomenon remains "unexplained when considered*

---

19 Hypothermia (from Greek υποθερμία) is a condition in which core temperature drops below the required temperature for normal metabolism and body functions which is defined as 35.0 °C (95.0 °F). https://en.wikipedia.org/wiki/Hypothermia

20 http://www.nderf.org/NDERF/NDE_Experiences/sartori_study.htm

*from the current scientific perspective of consciousness being a by-product of neurological processes. The fact that clear, lucid experiences were reported during a time when the brain was devoid of activity (Aminoff et al., 1988, Clute and Levy 1990, de Vries et al., 1998), does not sit easily with current scientific belief."*

Furthermore: death aside, no one ever claimed that the only way one can experience the soul is to kill yourself and hope that you come back to claim an NDE! The soul can be experienced through contacting the subconscious mind as well, as it is the conscious mind that prevents us from sensing our soul. We will explore this later in the chapter.

Does this mean that all of the above repeats itself in every single NDE? (Meaning that every time that someone has an NDE it occurs with the same details and fidelity?) No. It does not. Each and every individual experience a different NDE, some of which are highly detailed and others not. Some with fantastic descriptions of what transpired and some with flights of fancy. Does that mean that we should assume that the NDE's are not a spiritual phenomenon? No.

Why? Very simple: it depends on the amount that the soul has left the body. IF the soul is entirely removed from the body, then the experience is detailed and high-fidelity. If the soul is not fully removed from the body, then it is influenced by the human mind which is prone to flights of fancy[21]. In all likelihood, the phenomena experienced under oxygen deprivation were the beginnings of an NDE even though the subjects didn't die. It's even quite possible that psychedelic drugs, which affect a person's conscious mind, also allow for NDE-like phenomena. How is the observer to know which is which? He can't. It's wholly dependent on the soul's relationship and connection to the body and the extent of the damage that the body has undergone.

(See more resources for further in-depth exploration at the footnotes[22].)

But not all the people who die come back to tell us their experience and present us with living testimony as to their experience with their real self, their soul. Many remain dead. In fact, most do. Yet despite that... we still find that we have the ability to continue and experience the soul even in the land of the living by contacting the spirits of those who are already deceased. Which brings us to the next topic:

## Séances, Mediums and Other Forms of After Death Communication[23]

Talking to the dead is not a newly discovered phenomenon, it has been done for centuries. The Holy Torah itself relates that this practice

21 This is akin to what our sages, ob"m, tell us in Tractate Berachos that there is no such thing as a dream without *devarim betailim*, "nullified things", (meaning whimsical, nonsense aspects). This despite the fact that dreams contain within them an aspect, (according to our sages, ob"m, its 1/60th), of prophecy.

22 There is a plethora of important information which can be easily accessed through the internet. Examples of which are http://www.nderf.org/, http://iands.org/home.html and http://spiritualscientific.com/home

23 Sites with information on this topic http://www.adcrf.org/, http://www.after-death.com/Default.aspx, http://www.islandnet.com/~sric/, and http://www.medicine.virginia.edu/clinical/departments/psychiatry/sections/cspp/dops/case_types-page#Crisis

was performed by the Canaanite and other nations. The Torah forbids any member of the Jewish people from performing such practices[24]. Despite this, we find in the book of Samuel (I 28:7-25) that the prophet related that King Saul utilized the magic of the time to speak to the soul of the deceased prophet Samuel. There are also many stories in the Talmud of talking to the dead in various forms and through dreams. This phenomenon was widespread throughout the ancient world as well.

The result is all the same: sensing and communicating with the spirits of the deceased. The scope of the communication varies from vague sensations to actual conversation. The 12 Most Frequent Types of After-death contacts are:

1. Sensing their presence.

2. Hearing their voice.

3. Feeling their touch.

4. Smelling their fragrance.

5. Seeing their apparition.

6. Seeing a flat vision of them like a photo.

7. Experiencing one of these types while half-asleep.

---

24 As it says in Exodus 22:17 "A practitioner of witchcraft – should not be allowed to live". It also says in Deuteronomy (*Devarim*) 18:9-12 that we are forbidden from practicing necromancy in any form, as all forms of communication with the dead or divination of the future by magical means is forbidden.

8.  Having a visitation dream.

9.  Having an out-of-body experience and meeting them.

10. Receiving a telephone call. (Two-way conversations have actually been reported.)

11. Experiencing physical activity such as lights, TVs, and radios going on and off.

12. Receiving a symbolic message, sign, meaningful coincidence, or synchronicity.

I remember when my grandfather, ob"m, was in the last stages before his passing, and he would have conversations with his deceased relatives and friends. Science tells us that this is due to the deterioration of his conscious mind and his accessing his stored long-term memories. Tradition, however, says that those that are about to pass are visited by the deceased, who come to both prepare them for the transition and/or to accompany them on their journey to the next world[25].

Skepticism aside, this is one of the most well-known of all paranormal phenomena.

> *"The truth is that over 60% of the population reports that they have felt some connection, some communication, with someone that has passed on.*

---

25 See, for example Tractate *Berahchos 28b*, where the Gemara gives a detailed description of Rabbi Yochanan Ben Zakai's passing. One of the things that the Gemara relates there is that Rabbi Yochanan tells his students to prepare a chair for King Hezekiah, who is coming to escort him to the next world.

*And as results-based and empirical as I am, I have to say I'm among that 60%, but it certainly wasn't through a psychic.[26]"*

However, as I mentioned earlier, it costs us "nothing" to be skeptical and to dismiss this phenomenon as being rational-irrationalities of the mind and psyche. But I'm asking you, the reader, to take a look at the information as a whole and not just as scattered bits of "maybe". When we consider the entire gamut of information, lack of capability to perform controlled experiments aside, what does the information seem to be saying to you?

## Past Life Regression and Reincarnation

Aside from sensations, apparitions and the like, there are many other types of experiences through which we can see the soul.

The issue of reincarnation is not a new one, it has been around for a very long time now and is addressed by almost every major religion of ancient history. This goes for Jewish tradition[27] as well.

Although there aren't people walking around trailing their own spiritual history for all to see – it is still possible to connect with and

26 Dr. Phil on The Dr. Phil Show on December 20, 2004

27 The concept of reincarnation is not discussed directly in the Talmud. However, the concept of the revival of the dead is discussed. This does not preclude, however, that the Talmud doesn't hold of reincarnation, rather it means that it is not a topic of outright discussion. Reincarnation is discussed clearly in the Kabbalah. It should, however, be noted that Rav Sa'adiah Gaon, in his book *Emunot v'Deot* states clearly that he doesn't believe in reincarnation. However, it should be noted that the books pertaining to the Kabbalah were unknown in his time.

discover this "other you" via hypnosis. You can access this by doing what is known as "past life regression".

This is a field of study that is not run by quacks and lunatics. Its adherents include the University of Virginia's Division of Perceptual Studies in the School of Medicine, heads of departments of Clinical Psychology, Anthropology, Social studies and more[28].

During Past-Life Regression therapy the patient is "regressed" via hypnosis to a point beyond his or her birth and asked to relay information about what is either being seen or experienced.

*The most famous case of past life regression through hypnosis is that of Ruth Simmons. In 1952, her therapist, Morey Bernstein, took her back past the point of her birth. Suddenly, Ruth began to speak with an Irish accent and claimed that her name was Bridey Murphy, who lived in 19th century Belfast, Ireland. Ruth recalled many details of her life as Bridey, but, unfortunately, attempts to find out if Ms. Murphy really existed were unsuccessful. There was, however, some indirect evidence for the truth of her story: under hypnosis, Bridey mentioned the names of two grocers in Belfast from whom she bought food, Mr. Farr, and John Carrigan. A*

28 https://en.wikipedia.org/wiki/Reincarnation_research#Researchers

> *Belfast librarian found a city directory for 1865–*
> *1866 that listed both men as grocers[29].*

However, "Bridey Murphy" and similar stories are skeptically postulated as the result of the susceptibility of the patient to hypnosis, their inbred belief in reincarnation, and to suggestibility of the patient towards false memories contrived under the "guidance" of the therapist. The Scientific consensus is that the "memories" are the result of *Cryptomnesia,* which are narratives created by the subconscious mind using imagination, forgotten information, and suggestions from the therapist[30].

In simple language: if the patient didn't, in their subconscious, make it up themselves – it's because the therapist helped them to create the "false memories".

But is that all the information that we have available concerning the topic of reincarnation? Absolutely not!

> *Psychiatrist Ian Stevenson, from the University of*
> *Virginia, investigated many reports of young*
> *children who claimed to remember a past life. He*
> *conducted more than 2,500 case studies over a period*
> *of 40 years and published twelve books, including*
> *"Twenty Cases Suggestive of Reincarnation" and*
> *"Where Reincarnation and Biology Intersect".*

---

29 http://paranormal.about.com/cs/reincarnation/a/aa081103.htm

30 http://en.wikipedia.org/wiki/Past_life_regression#Sources_of_memories

> *Stevenson searched for disconfirming evidence and alternative explanations for the reports and believed that his strict methods ruled out all possible "normal" explanations for the child's memories[31].*

Stevenson concluded that reincarnation was the "best possible explanation" for the following reasons:

> *The large number of witnesses and the lack of apparent motivation and opportunity, due to the vetting process, make the hypothesis of fraud extremely unlikely.*

> *The large amount of information possessed by the child is not generally consistent with the hypothesis that the child obtained that information through investigated contact between the families.*

> *Demonstration of similar personality characteristics and skills not learned in the current life and the lack of motivation for the long length of identification with a past life make the hypothesis of the child gaining his recollections and behavior through extra-sensory perception improbable.*

> *When there is a correlation between congenital deformities or birthmarks possessed by the child and*

---

31 http://en.wikipedia.org/wiki/Reincarnation_research#Reincarnation_research

*the history of the previous individual, the hypothesis*
*of random occurrence is improbable[32].*

What are the real objections that science has with the issue of reincarnation?  They are these:

*Objections to claims of reincarnation include the facts that the vast majority of people do not remember previous lives, and there is no mechanism known to modern science that would enable a personality to survive death and travel to another body, barring the idea of biocentrism (more on this later). Researchers such as Stevenson have acknowledged these limitations. (ibid.)*

Meaning that there are two main reasons for the skepticism: the more important of the two being "I don't know", (how that would work in physical terms), and the other being the fact that not all people "recall" past lives.

So, in reality, what the scientific consensus is saying, is that if we could find a theoretical framework that would explain these two things – We really *shouldn't* have a problem at all! So, for the sake of science let's posit the following two things:

---

32 http://en.wikipedia.org/wiki/Twenty_Cases_Suggestive_of_Reincarnation

1. Let's call the soul a theoretical model. The *real* part of "man" that makes him "man" is precisely this thing: the soul. It has no physical manifestation[33] other than the presence of bio-energy, which is readily perceivable in almost all forms of modern scanning techniques. Without this bio-energy, the body is just a sack of meat and bones.

2. Why don't all people experience "recall" of previous lives? For one of two reasons: either, (the more likely), they are not so receptive to hypnosis and the like, in which case they cannot "get in touch" with their soul due to interference from the conscious mind; or – they are not a reincarnation at all[34]. Although few in number, many are not "reincarnations" rather they are "incarnations" or "new souls". They, therefore, have nothing to remember!

Let's take a look at some more "anecdotal" evidence, shall we?

## Facilitated Communication with Severely Disabled Children

Although it has not been proven in scientific studies, there remains much more than just anecdotal evidence to back up the issue of reincarnation in severely disabled children.

---

33 This is also stated clearly by our sages, ob"m, in Tractate Berachos 10a that "Just like HKB"H sees, but is not (Himself) seen, so too the soul sees but is not (itself) seen".
34 http://hebrew.grimoar.cz/vital/saar_ha-gilgulim.htm see ו הקדמה (introduction no. 6) that speaks about this issue.

I have had the merit of personally knowing Rabbi Yehuda Serevnik, one of the staunchest proponents of FC (facilitated communication). I know him to be a steadfast, G-d fearing man. Rabbi Serevnik and many other people have had scores of meetings with such children, during which information was revealed which could only have been known from a divine source. Detailed information about people in past lives, detailed information concerning thoughts and actions of the individuals who came to speak with these children and in some cases predictions of what will happen in the immediate future. All of these are topics that are claimed to be revealed via the means of FC.

While not a widespread phenomenon, I mention it only as one more example that is "fit to be joined" with all the information which has been presented so far. For if the aforementioned is true: if personal information can be revealed at the time of facilitation that can only be verified by the persons themselves, then it can never be scientifically verified. However, if it IS true information, then it cannot be based on the influence of the facilitator! It must emanate from something that can see beyond the flesh of the body, and that can see that which is only visible to the soul: another soul (or another facet of one's own soul).

It is also possible to add the issue of possession as well, however, for the sake of brevity I will leave the issue open.

## Biocentric!

Recently there has been much talk about the conclusions of the renowned Dr. Robert Lanza. In his book entitled "*Biocentrism: How Life and Consciousness are the Keys to Understanding the True Nature of the Universe,*" Dr. Lanza concludes that:

> *Biocentrism shatters the reader's ideas of life, time and space, and even death. At the same time, it releases us from the dull worldview that life is merely the activity of an admixture of carbon and a few other elements; it suggests the exhilarating possibility that life is fundamentally immortal*[35].

What, you might ask, is "biocentrism"? Well, it's the following:

> *...biocentrism – a new theory of everything – tells us death may not be the terminal event we think. Amazingly, if you add life and consciousness to the equation, you can explain some of the biggest puzzles of science. For instance, it becomes clear why space and time – and even the properties of matter itself – depend on the observer. It also becomes clear why the laws, forces, and constants of the universe appear to be exquisitely fine-tuned for the existence of life*[36].

In short: "bio-centrism" means that the "bio" (=life), or rather a biological observer, is at the "center" of everything. Dr. Lanza, in his

---

35      http://www.robertlanza.com/biocentrism-how-life-and-consciousness-are-the-keys-to-understanding-the-true-nature-of-the-universe/

36 http://www.robertlanzabiocentrism.com/is-death-an-illusion-evidence-suggests-death-isnt-the-end/

attempt to make sense of many scientific phenomena that demonstrate conclusively that the world is tied to the observer, concludes that therefore there is no - and there can be no - world without an observer. As a result of this conclusion, he says that it must be that the consciousness of the human is not wholly tied to the physical world. If it were otherwise, how could human consciousness have had the "creation" effect on the world? Ergo: there must be something metaphysical to the human.

Of course, Dr. Lanza in no way ties this to G-d, for to do so is not scientific. However, it would seem that even science is slowly beginning to acknowledge the existence of the soul. (A soul by any other name...)

## **The Skeptics Say:**

*... However, if we do indeed possess an immaterial soul or a material one with special properties that cannot be found in inanimate matter, then we should expect to find some evidence for it. (Failed hypotheses, Stenger pg. 84)*

*Well-understood physical and chemical processes, the same that occur in all materials, whether dead or alive, are sufficient to account for the observed interactions between various parts of living*

> *organisms. The physics and chemistry of living cells is basically the same as the physics and chemistry of rocks, just a bit more complicated. (Ibid, Stenger pg. 85)*

> *...living organisms emit no unique radiation that can be detected by our best scientific instruments. (Ibid, pg.86)*

> *We need not go any further into these unconfirmable speculations (at least unconfirmable in this life). The scientific question is whether there is any evidence for life after death. As with ESP and other proposed superpowers of the mind, despite numerous claims over the years, no claimed connection with a hereafter has ever been scientifically verified. And, as with those special powers, we can easily see how a connection should have been verified in controlled, scientific experiments. (Ibid, pg.103)*

So basically:

1. The soul cannot be confirmed in scientific studies. And:
2. Biology can account for all workings of the human/biological bodies.

First of all, please remember: this is not a new topic! It is one concerning which there seems to be a universal consensus in all of the ancient world, all of whom agree that there is a soul and that many times it is "reprocessed" and comes back to this world in a new body! Why do we reject this once universal truth? Because *they* weren't scientists! *They* were backward! *They* were primitives! OK! Fine! SO:

This issue of "I don't see no G-d anywhere!" and its blatant hypocrisy was addressed in the first volume in the chapter entitled *Abraham and Abiogenesis*. There have been, are, and always will be things that science believes in despite not being able to see them. Why should G-d and anything relating to G-d, such as the soul, be the exceptions to the rule? The answer: because it's the only thing that would actually have repercussions in my life and I don't want that!

Furthermore, as we discussed in the previous volume, the observable sciences are only as good as the observer. "Didn't find it" doesn't mean it's not there! Maybe you aren't looking in the right place? Maybe you have the wrong equipment? Maybe your eyes need to be checked? But maybe, just maybe, (as it so clearly true in this instance) it's plainly visible in front of your face, but you are ascribing it to "biological processes"? Just where does the bio-energy, which is readily visible in a plain-old EEG, come from? Firing Synapses? Is that really all we are?

Biological workings "explain" the human being? Tell me then, Professor Stenger, just where DOES the bio-energy inherent in the body come from? Is it simply the product of the "combustion" of the foodstuff in our gut? Is that scientifically verifiable? Or are those only the processes needed for the sole purpose of sustaining the cellular biology of our bodies, whereas the bio-energy is inherent in and of itself? If you tell me that it's part of the biology alone, then on a cellular level there is no difference between a living being and a dead one, (obviously I'm talking about before the body begins to degenerate on the cellular level)! So why can't we just plug him right in to bring him back to life? The only real difference is the presence of some energy? Right? Is the problem that he's 110 volts and here, in Israel and Europe, we use 220? Is biological life really so easy to explain?

What, truly, is the *real* me? The brain? Do we really have any voracious proof to that end?

Is it the fact that by touching/stimulating certain areas of the brain somehow affects the body's function and/or access to memories and the like? Is there any clear evidence that that is because the brain is you or is it possible that by such stimulation we are preventing, stimulating or accessing "my" access to the body's function and/or connection to that body, and *that* is what is causing that phenomenon?

The answer: no. There is no such evidence. All there is, (once again), is the claim that "I don't see something else, so it must be…".

Does science have a genuinely plausible explanation as to the biological workings of the human/animal body that make it only "slightly" more complex than that of a rock? Or is it that the scientific community tends to quickly and quietly over-simplify processes that are truly so complex that they – to this day – totally stagger our frail human minds?

But if there is an energy that "dwells" within the human body and is not really part and parcel of the biology of the body – then according to the laws of physics, like all energy it cannot be destroyed[37]! So, what? Why did the guy die? Was his energy used up? Transferred to a different type of energy? If so, what type?

The real question is: does something so blatantly obvious actually require scientific verification?

## In Conclusion:

As we said at the beginning of this chapter: if you've got a soul – it's clearly from G-d. As the tradition of the entire ancient world and Jewish tradition throughout the ages teach us: the real "you" *is* your soul!

Virtually all of the people who reported having, during their NDE experience, a visitation with a Deity, (regardless of who they claim Him to be[38]), relate that they had never experienced a feeling of all-encompassing love like the love that they felt from this Being. I don't know, what do you think? Does it sound like G-d would like a relationship with you?

All actions that we take in this world have either a positive or negative effect on us, on the REAL us, on our soul. And after 120 years, (give or

---

37 See the Law of Conservation of Energy (1st law of thermodynamics). Even though this law states that this is only true for closed systems, that does not mean that in an open system, it can be destroyed!

38 I would assume that this should be clear to all. However, to make sure I will explain quickly. The lowest common denominator among all the claims is that the individual met a Divine being. This does not mean that I would believe any further claims as to who/what that being actually IS, as that would imply that each and every individual has no personal bias or the ability to misconstrue or prescribe information. This is inherently not true. But we CAN still assume that the common denominator is true.

take), on this earth, it is that "I" that will either go to its heavenly reward or... not.

Why would that be? Why reward or punish the soul? Unless... G-d knows who we are and has expectations of us? If you have an immortal soul, which is akin unto G-d himself, (which is why, Dr. Lanza, the observer affects the observed physical world), then you, my friend, are linked to G-d, and we begin our journey down question number two out of the three basic questions that a thinking person asks themselves in life:

1. Does G-d Exist? (If it's not clear to you as of yet – go read, (or re-read), book 1!) Yes, He does! So now:
2. Does G-d know me? Let's explore this issue more fully!

# Chosen!

## *How do we differ from all other religions?*

LMOST ALL RELIGIONS in the world today claim – with one voice – that G-d, the Creator of all, desires a relationship with you and *these* are the laws and the directives that you should follow to achieve that lofty goal: a relationship with the Living G-d!

However, one of the most difficult things that we deal with in the realm of Emunah is the issue of how does one contend with the plethora of faiths that exist in the world today? If there are: Christians, Muslims, Buddhists, Hinduists, Shintoists and a plethora of other -ist's and -ism's, how are we to know which one is correct? Which one are we supposed to follow?

After all, they are all claiming to have THE TRUTH and that all other faiths and beliefs are incorrect, (unless you happen to be a pluralist, in which case everyone is right! Good luck keeping that one!). I mean, if you're a Christian you are convinced that you are going to that Heavenly reward, whereas the Jews, the Muslims and everyone else are all going to be taking that fiery bath; and if you are a Muslim, then only you are going to get the pleasures of the hereafter[39], whereas everyone else is going to burn in the fires of hell along with all of the other infidels. As long as you are not a member of my "club" - you're in for it!

However, there is a common denominator/consensus among everyone, and that is that there is something called "the Truth" and that there is something called "the world to come", call it "Heaven", call it whatever you want! There is something called "reward" that will be given in that heavenly place, and there is something called "punishment" that will be dispensed in the other one. How does one get to the one or the other? By following the "rules" laid out in [X].

The only commonality between them is that G-d, whoever He, (or She[40]), may be, wants a relationship with YOU. (Thus, answering Question number 2: "Does G-d know you?" YES, He does. Does He want a relationship with you? YES!)

---

39 I have always wondered, though: If the men, in the Islamic "next world" get 70 virgins – what do the women get? I can only assume it's a better husband… (It's just a joke! Don't take it too seriously!)

40 I'm just doing this to be P.C., not that I really care to be. By the way: G-d technically has no real sex, He is neither male nor female. (No, He's also not a hermaphrodite!) We use the masculine to describe Him for two reasons: 1> Because we ascribe to Him a masculine attitude towards the world (i.e. one in which He takes an active role in the shaping of all things which was, classically, a male role); and 2> Because a male, unless gender confused, will always ascribe masculinity to anything that he is talking about unless it's clearly feminine! I'm a male, by the way.

So, if we are going to gamble our world-to-come on this, we had better take a good close look and know which one is the right one! After all, it seems that we all agree that there can be only one truth and one path to the world to come! So, which one is it?

The truth is that the above search for truth and the questioning which must be undertaken to establish which religion is the truth is neither new nor original! As a matter of fact, there is a very famous legend in history, upon which a very basic, very famous *sefer*[41], "*The Kuzari*" by Rav Yehuda HaLevi ztvk"l, was based. This book is about the spiritual journey taken by the king of the Khazars some 1900 years ago, which ended with his conversion to Judaism.

It starts out saying that the king of the Khazars was a very religious, very pious, very active person in his people's religion. Yet, despite his efforts and his devotion he had a recurring dream that greatly troubled him. In his dream, an angel would come to him and say, "Your intentions find favor in the eyes of the Lord, but your actions do not!" Well, after several nights like this the king of the Khazars decided to go on a spiritual journey to try and discover what the correct way of worshiping G-D was!

The book– even to this day – is an excellent introduction to all of the major religions and all of the philosophies that existed in the ancient world, and despite its age, its precepts are as valid today as they were way back then, when it was written almost 1000 years ago!

---

41 Hebrew for "Book".

The King began his search with a Philosopher, moved on to a Christian and then to a Muslim. In all of their explanations, he divines an essential motif: that G-D made the universe and all of its complexities, and it is that self-same G-D that they worship[42].

Ever notice how things never change?

During the time that I was working with the IDF, I decided to compile a video library of amazing wonders of the world so that the soldiers could watch them and grow during their off-time. During my search, I discovered two films related to the topics that I covered in volume 1 "Hello? G-d?". (Of course, in all modesty, I did a *much* better job...) Both of these videos brought proofs of G-D's existence using science to show that the only real explanation for the existence of our universe is G-d. The only difference between them was that one of the films was developed by devout Christians, whereas the other was the product of devout Muslims. Amazingly enough, they had the exact same commonality:

"Now that I have proven to you that there is a G-D you now must accept that that G-D is [Allah/Jesus] and that the [New Testament/Koran] is the word of the living G-D".

WHAT?????? How did we jump from point A to point B[43]?

---

42 Or according to the philosopher's creed doesn't worship, as G-d has no connection with you anyway. This philosophy is called "Deism", meaning that the universe is a Divine construct, but the creator is oblivious to His creation.

43 Personally, I feel that the Muslims did a better job of selling this point. Not because they brought better, or even different, proofs, but because they interwove the above argument into the proofs themselves. It was more like subliminal advertising! "See the complexities of the DNA molecule? That's Allah at work!" and then they would bring a verse from the Koran, which sounds (vaguely) connected to the point.

When you think about it, if we want to explore and understand something for which we have no prior knowledge, there are really two ways to go about doing so: either by using *induction* or by using *deduction!* The difference between the two is as follows:

In induction, I take a look at and try to quantify, the thing itself. Therefore, all of the information that I gather tells me something about what the thing is. Whereas in deduction I gather all the information that tells me what the thing is not. In using deduction, I can get an inverse picture which limits my understanding, by the process of elimination of all information that the thing isn't, to the thing to all information about what the thing is... yet it tells me nothing about what it actually is. Sir Arthur Conan Doyle's character, Sherlock Holmes, was famed for having said to his sidekick, Watson, concerning deduction, "*When you have eliminated the impossible, whatever remains, however improbable, must be the truth*".

That's true, and it was these two methods of investigation that were utilized to show the Divine-ness of the universe, as I, myself, did in the first volume. However, the conclusions that one can reach using purely investigative devices is limited. These two devices, when used in tandem, tell me something about what G-D is NOT, (limited or stupid), and they can tell me something about what He IS, (Powerful and Intelligent), but it's one thing to prove to me that there is a G-D, but it's an entirely different thing to show to me *who that G-D is!* Even using the methodology of profiling, an investigative method employed by major investigators when trying to apprehend a felon or to figure out how to catch him, doesn't tell you *who* he is, it just gives us an idea as to what makes him/her tick!

G-D didn't sign off on this universe "made by Allah", He also didn't send us via radio, x-ray or satellite "G-D, the Father, here! For more info speak to my Son". In short: if that's all we have... then we don't really know G-D very well at all!

How do all organized religions deal with this issue? Very simple. They tell us that we know Him... because we met Him! Not only did we meet him, they say, but he also gave us His Holy Word in the form of a written Torah/Bible/Koran/Whatever.

Ahh! If you MEET Him, that's a whole other story!

The point is that if I/him/they/someone met Him, (in which case I don't need "faith", as I met Him), and He told me/him/them what He desires of me/him/them then we surely know two things. A> He knows who I am, and B> He cares enough about me to tell me how to live my life in a meaningful way.

However, if, as all religions claim, we met Him, then we are back to square one! Can it be that He met with so many different faiths, gave each of them the absolute truth and yet each and every one of them claims that their truth is entirely different than everyone else's? They can't all have the absolute truth yet be so very different at the same time!

Then we need to ask: How can we divine the truth? In this regard, we also need to ask is the Torah, and therefore the Jewish people, different from any other Holy law and therefore any other nation?

What's interesting in this regard is that both Christianity and Islam agree on this one crucial issue. The Jews and their Torah ARE different than everyone else! If we were to have a frank conversation with representatives of both religions and we were to ask them: before YOU came around[44], who was it that had the Heaven Breathed, True Word of G-D in their hands? Both would agree on this one issue: it was the Jews. Before Christianity, before Islam – the Jews were the sole possessors of the True Word of G-D.

So, what is it about the Jews, and our claims concerning our Holy Torah, that makes it different than any and all other "holy books" in existence in the world?

In a word: Prophecy.

Prophecy? How can we say that is what makes the difference? Jews have Prophets, Christianity has prophets, Islam has their prophet, and Mormons have their prophet[45]. Prophets seem to be a dime-a-dozen! How in the world can you tell me that what sets us apart from all other nations is that we – also – have a prophet? Or, to coin a phrase, "How is this Prophet different than all other prophets?", (or perhaps "Why is it that Jews know how to make a prophet?")

Let me illustrate with the following question: (That's us Jews! Always answering a question with a question!)

---

44 According to Christian tradition, as of this writing, the religion is 2016 years old, (see, for example https://en.wikipedia.org/wiki/History_of_Christianity) and Islam, according to everyone is only 1394 years old (see, for example, https://en.wikipedia.org/wiki/Timeline_of_Islamic_history). According to everyone Judaism has been around WAY longer! According to our countin 3330 years. We were the founders of Monotheism.

45 Joseph Smith Jr. gained a small following in the late 1820's as he was dictating the Book of Mormon, which he said was a translation of words found on a set of golden plates that had been buried near his home in western New York by an indigenous American prophet.

What is our special place among the nations? Why is it that we are different from all of the other nations?

Is it that we are successful lawyers?        No.

Is it that we are prosperous businessmen?     No.

Great doctors?   …..                          Maybe.

NO. No, that's not it. It's because… we know how to make money!

Yep! That must be it! Jews just know – intuitively – how to make oodles and oodles of money!

Does anyone want some advice on how to make a lot of money[46]? Open your own religion! THAT'S how you make a lot of money!

So, let's say we are opening our new religion: how do we go about building its foundation?

Well, as any business course would tell you: first do your due-diligence! Historically how did all of the religions in the world begin?

The answer: using prophecy. Therefore, the first item of business is to get a prophet! Clearly, all religions of the world have this one ticked off.

However, history and logic also show us that the prophetic experience can happen in only one of two ways. Either a single person or a small group of people witnessed an event or experienced a prophetic vision, or an entire nation did.

Now, which of these two do you think is the better claim? Even more so: *why* is it a better claim?

---

46 Although Rabbi's, in general, are not very successful in this respect, I'll assume that my Jewish genes will help out in this regard.

Let's explore the two possibilities:

I would like to use a parable that I heard from HaRav Noach Weinberg, ztvk"l, many years ago. There was a great Chassidic Rebbe who for many years led his flock with all of his abilities and for G-D's honor. When he passed, he left behind two children who were fit to take his place. In the manner of almost all inheritances almost immediately a dispute erupted. There were those among the Chassidim who said that the older son should be the Rebbe. There were those among the Chassidim that said that the younger son should be the Rebbe. (There were those among the Chassidim who said, "*I* should be the Rebbe" and also "We don't really need a *live* Rebbe").

In any case, it's clear to all of us that the situation was desperate.

One day the younger son goes running through the village saying "Come qvick! (Yiddish for "quick", or is it Yinglish? Anyway…). Come qvick! I have the solution to all of all of our struggles!" and of course, eager to have this dilemma solved, all of the people came.

Once everyone was gathered together the younger son stands in the middle of the village square and turns to them and says "Last night I vas so troubled by the situation that ve find ourselves in that I prayed to G-D vith all of my heart that a sign should be sent to solve this long-standing conflict. I then went to sleep and had a dream. And then, in the middle of my dream – Lo and Behold! – our father, the Rebbe, appeared to me and told me as follows. 'My dear son! Your prayers and the plight of my holy Chassidim stirred the Heavenly Host so much! … [at this point he went off on a lengthy and profound *derasha* (sermon), you all remember the Rebbe! So, even in my dream I promptly fell asleep until he got to the end] … so... anyway I'm here to resolve the dispute", he said. He then looked at me and said "'You're the new Rebbe!' So that's it! Problem solved!"

What do you think? Does that solve the Rebbe issue? … Of course not!

What do you think the other brother is going to say to him? "If Father wanted us to know that you are the next Rebbe... *he would have told us all*."

This is the principal difficulty with the prophet model of "I had a vision… now believe me!". If I believe him it's usually because I trust him or have been influenced by his charisma, but it's not because I know that what he is saying is true.

However, in the National prophecy model, where mass-revelation occurs, there we most certainly do not have this issue! Why is that? Because the National prophecy model only works if the prophecy actually happened!

Imagine we have opened up our franchise religion, we printed up the pamphlets, and we have rented the hall where we are going to be holding our new religion's first meeting. Our "prophet" has prepared his "prophecy" and now all that is left to do is for us to do is a bit of advertising to get people to come. So, we send out our volunteers from door to door, and we try really hard to get them to come.

According to the first model, the approach is as follows:

"Hello! My name is [X] and I am a member of the First Church of the M.Q.B. (that's **M**ake a **Q**uick **B**uck, but they don't have to know that). I want you to know that our prophet, the holy Reverend Ca$h, had a prophecy concerning you (*and* your financial future) ... and it doesn't look good! If you want to know the power of Rev. Ca$h's prophecy, please come to [X] at the time [Y] and *YOU WILL BELIEVE!*"

Well, I would assume that if you said it with enough charisma and feeling and if the guy is gullible enough then there's a good chance that he will believe in the prophetic powers of the good Rev. Ca$h. However, there's also an excellent chance that he won't!

OK! Let's try model B: the national revelation model.

Once again, going door to door on our sales mission. We knock on the door, and the guy opens, and we say "HI! How are you doing? My name is [X], and I am a member of the first Church of the M.Q.B.! Today we all had a prophecy – you included! – concerning your financial future, and it really didn't look good! Isn't that so?" The chances are that he's going to look at you sideways and say, "You know, before you came I was in my den, watching the fight on TV, and during the commercials... nothing happened!" There is no logical, rational way for me to utilize this model of prophecy in a way which would or should convince you that you saw something when you are equally sure, or even moderately sure, that you didn't!

Therefore, it would seem to me that to make the claim of a national revelation – it actually had to have occurred!

Yet when we look through history and make a comparison between the various religions we find that, without exception, they all took the road of model A!

Christianity, for example, began when Paul, (a Jew, his real name was *Shaul*, Saul), was walking along on the road to Damascus, some 30 years after Jesus's demise. Suddenly, Jesus appears! He relates to Saul his whole life story, describes for him in detail all the miracles that he performed and explains to him the point of it all. Saul immediately converts to Christianity and starts going around teaching the Gospels and proliferating the new religion to the world.

Islam also followed this method.

Mohamed drops to the ground, looking for all the world as if he is having an epileptic fit, (he probably was), after which he gets up, wipes the foam off his mouth and says, "I just received the word of G-D". (He then picked up his sword, pointed it at the throat of the guy next to him and said, "Wouldn't you agree?"). From which point he starts dictating the messages that he received in his head and inscribing them for posterity in the suras of the Koran.

Buddhism also follows the same model. It began when Siddhārtha Gautama, a Nepali prince, was sitting under a Bodi tree. All of a sudden, with no previous preparation, he transcended to the eighth state of enlightenment and became a Bu-d-d-ha[47]. Upon returning, he

---

47 As this is the name of a foreign god – it is forbidden for a Jew, as explicit in the Holy Torah, to pronounce or to cause others to pronounce its name.

immediately sets out to teach the machinations of Buddhism, saying that he is not the only person to reach this state of enlightenment, there have been many others as well. Not that anyone has ever met anyone else who has reached this state. How do we know this? Well, because he told us so!

The Mormons? Yup! Them too!

Joseph Smith Jr. went out on a hike in the wilderness. During his trip, he discovered golden tablets from the angel Gabriel, written in Reformed Egyptian, a language known only to Joseph Smith. Of course, he only understood it because right next to the golden tablets was the only known dictionary of Reformed Egyptian in existence. He then proceeded to write down the authoritative translation of the tablets which he brought back with him upon his return home. However, for reasons unknown to all but Joseph Smith, the tablets themselves and their dictionary "disappeared".

Does anyone here know how many Nations there are in the world that claim to have experienced a National revelation? There are two!

That's right! Two! There are the Jews, as written explicitly in the Holy Torah, the world's all-time best-seller, and it has been taught publicly as we have been passing down for generations from father to son, according to all opinions for well over 2000 years; and then there is a group of Hindus in India, a sect of the Har-e Krish-na. Do you know what the difference is between the claim of the Jews and the claim of the Hindus? The difference is three-fold. First of all, ours is stated explicitly in the Holy written Torah (Deuteronomy 4:33) (Meaning that we have always openly publicized it). Secondly, as is described explicitly in said verse, we lived to tell the tale! Thus, sayeth the Torah:

*"Has there (ever) been a nation who heard the voice of G-D speaking (with them) from the midst of the fire, as you have, and lived?"*

Whereas the Hindus claim, is from a little-known oral tradition, that 4000 years ago there was a major war amongst two major clans. In the heat of battle, there was a Divine revelation witnessed by the gathered millions from amidst the fire and then... they all died... and stayed that way. So... how does anyone know about this? There was no one left to tell the tale! Oh, no! Wait. There were a few people who weren't there and didn't experience the Divine revelation, but they heard about it! Or they were there, but it's just a couple of individuals claiming to have witnessed the whole thing.

Thirdly, the mass-revelation was not just a one-time thing. It was ongoing for the entire 40-year sojourn in the desert. There were clear, incontestable miracles that occurred every single day. Whether we are talking about the manna that the people collected and ate. Whether we are talking about the pillar of cloud/fire that led the people for the entire 40 years in the desert. Whether we are talking about the miracles that were constantly on display in the Tabernacle (the *Mishkan*, in Hebrew). Or even if we are talking about the random miracles that were performed by Moses at different times. All of these were done for a very specific purpose. All of them filled the needs of the people as they were needed.

The Sinai Revelation was special because of its intensity and because of the special significance that it held for us (as will be explained in the following chapter, wG"h (with G-d's help).

So, in reality, there is only ONE nation in all of the world who claims a National Revelation and that nation happen to be the Jews!

When did this super special Revelation occur? At Mount Sinai, around 3328 years ago[48], (as of this writing). The Holy Torah in Exodus, and again in Deuteronomy, describe to us in detail the occurrence. Today we commemorate this special day with the Holy Day known as *Shavuos*, (The Festival of Weeks).

I would like to describe to you what that day looked like to the Children of Israel as it is outlined in the Holy Torah in Exodus chapter 19-20 and in Deuteronomy chapters 4-5 with the pertinent additions of our sages. I will address specifically the day of this experience even though the Torah gives a lot of detail about the days leading up to it as well.

On the day of the national Divine experience, the people of Israel awoke to the sounds of lightning and thunder. From their encampment, which was close by, they turned to look at the mountain, and they saw that it was on fire! Not fire like a match, not like a flamethrower, but a fire that burned from the base of the mountain all the way up to the heavens! And smoke! Thick smoke was billowing up from the mountain all the way up to the sky!

---

48 According to Jewish tradition as of this writing today is 5776 years from creation. Our tradition teaches us that the Torah was given at Sinai 2448 years from the creation. Do the math!

As they watched, they saw an incredible thing: the mountain was torn out of the ground and began to levitate in the air! As the mountain began to rise, the people looked towards the skies and watched as all of the heavens, the entire universe, begin to condense above the mountain. The heavens themselves folded-up until it appeared like a blanket. It then descended upon the mountain, gently covering it with its folds[49]. Upon this mountain, covered with the Universal blanket, some of the Hosts of Heaven, the angels themselves, descended in all of their glory.

At this point, a great *shofar*, (ram's horn) began to blow. In contrast to a *shofar* blown by man, which, the longer it is blown the weaker the blast becomes, here the *shofar* blast slowly climbed to a crescendo and kept getting louder and louder until... the people witnessed the "Chair of (His) Honor[50]", (*kissey hakavod* in Hebrew) descend upon the top of the "Heavenly spread and Hosts" and came to a rest on top of the Mountain. From there the Divine Presence of HaShem, Himself, beckoned from the mountain to the children of Israel to come near. Moses gathered the people and sent them forth towards the mountain, warning them not to go beyond the boundary that was set for them not to pass.

The children of Israel then gathered at the base of the mountain and stood under the mountain's expanse[51]. It was from this vantage point that

---

49 This is learned from our sages in the Midrashic commentaries on these portions of the Torah

50 According to Rav Sa'adiya Gaon, in his work Emunot v'De'ot this is a construct that HaShem makes to lend power to the prophetic vision, as HaShem, Himself, has no physical form that would require a place to sit. The issue of "sitting", however, signifies a lack of change. It is apropos to HaShem, as the verse says "*I am HaShem, and I do not change*" (*Melachi* 3:6 )

51 This is learned from the verse (Exodus 19:17) which says that the children of Israel stood betachtit hahar, which translates literally as "underneath the mountain".

the people heard the 10 commandments, which was the "giving of the Torah" National Experience. All opinions agree that the first two commandments were heard directly from G-D, with no intermediaries whatsoever[52]. When G-d told us the first commandment, *"I am the Lord, your G-D, who took you out of Egypt, from the house of bondage"*, the 7 levels of the Heavens were torn asunder and along with the 7 levels of *Gehinnom*, (commonly translated as *Hell*), and the people could see and grasp simultaneously all of existence and they knew, with no room for doubt, that there is no other like G-D in all of the existence. That He is One and that there is no other Singularity like him anywhere. It was evident to all assembled that He was The Truth, (*Emmet* in Hebrew) and that there was nothing else comparable to Him in all of the existence in any shape, way or form. The force of The Voice threw the bodies of the people twelve *parsang* and their souls left their bodies from the immensity of the revelation. The angels then gathered their bodies back together under the mountain, and the people were revived using the "dew of the revival of the dead"[53]. They were now ready to receive the second commandment.

You could understand why, after two such commandments, that the people begged Moshe to hear the rest of the commandments from him and not from G-d.

---

52 There is some controversy among our sages as to whether or not G-D said all of the 10 commandments to us there or only the first two. But even the opinion that holds "first two" agrees that at first G-D related all of the 10 commandments to the children of Israel as one, "that which the (human mind) cannot hear, nor grasp" and then afterwards they were reiterated one at a time.

53 This is explicit in Tractate Shabbos on page 87a

It is for this reason, (the national revelation of Sinai and the miracles of the desert for 40 years) that all of the major world religions agree that the Jewish Torah is Divine.

Furthermore, based on the above it should be clear that we are not looking at "Faith" here, nor are we looking at "Belief". No faith or belief is involved what-so-ever!! We met HIM. We spoke WITH HIM. We have no doubts concerning the authenticity of the commandments which HE gave us. This brings us back to our definition of Emunah[54]: when G-D tells me something explicitly in the Torah, do I trust HIM that if He said it He'll also keep His word? THAT is Emunah! The practical application of what we know in our day to day life. The strengthening of my trust in G-d.

Now there was this one time that I gave over this lesson, and after I had finished, I looked at the audience, and this one guy in the back was shaking his head back and forth, (usually not a good sign), so I asked him "is there a problem?"

SO, he looks at me, and he goes "Rabbi! You haven't proved a thing here this evening!"

I then asked him "Why not?" So, he says to me "Rabbi, couldn't it be that the people only thought that they were having a National revelation when in reality they were not? You know everybody knows that the Jews had close connections with the Chinese, from whom we made an order, (and what an order it must have been!), of fireworks. If you believe the

---

Discovery Channel in their programming, (see Ancient Bible Discoveries, who claim that we had superconductors to facilitate the levitation of the Ark of the Covenant and other such nonsense), we had electricity and a speaker system going off in the background, Moses and Joshua passed around a little weed and some Chivas, so the people were a little tipsy and … Presto Chango! … instant National revelation!"

So, I looked at him, and I said "Let's say you're right, (about the Sinai revelation, not about the rest of the 40 years in the desert, all the plagues done to Egypt, and all of the other phenomena which occurred during the sojourn in the desert, none of which could be covered by a "National Drug Trip"). Let's say, Moses, Joshua, and Aaron pulled it off! The only instance in all of history of a "National Revelation" that was orchestrated, and it went off like clockwork! The next day they then must build off of their success. They then sit down, make a little *"LeChaim"*, and begin the writing of the Written Torah.

Obviously, as our minds are still involved with our successful performance yesterday, we decided to codify the "Mount Sinai Caper" into the Torah for posterity, so as to ensure its centrality.

At this point, Joshua turns to Moses, and he says "Moses! How about we write *This is a one-time event in history and it will never ever be repeated?* What do you think?". Would that work? Could we write that?

Well, of course, we COULD… but it really wouldn't make sense to do it!

I mean, the Torah DID write it, as it says (Deuteronomy chapter 4 verses 32-35):

*(32) For ask, please, concerning the first days which were before you, from the day which G-D created man on this land, and from one end of the skies to the (other) end of the skies. Was there ever something like unto this great thing, or has a similar thing been heard of? (33) Has a nation ever heard the voice of the G-D speaking to them from amidst the fire as you have and lived (to tell about it)?*

Why are you such a pessimist, Rabbi? What's wrong with writing that in?

Well, in my opinion, assuming Moses is "Moe" of the three stooges, he would bap Joshua (Larry) on the head and say to him "You knucklehead! Didn't *we* just pull it off? Well if we can do it... so can someone else! What will we do if another person, in the future, also succeeds to do it? The basis of our entire religion will fall apart! Come on! Keep thinking!" he would say. "Does that sound about right?" I asked him.

Please take note: the Torah begs us – that's right! BEGS US, in the above verses *shaal na,* "ask please" – don't take my word for it! Don't even take your father's word! Check it out! Don't even limit yourself to your own people, your own country, or even your own continent. Is there even one other nation on the face of the planet or anywhere under the skies[55] that have a similar claim of revelation as you do? PLEASE CHECK IT OUT! That's what the Torah said! Well, guess what? When you challenge someone to do something many (most?) times – they take you up on your challenge! Guess how many similar cases have been found? …

But that's not even the biggest problem. (We'll come back to that later)

Let's get back on track:

Now the real hard-core skeptics of the world rise up at this point, and they say, "Really Rabbi? You want us to believe that the Jewish people really had a National Revelation? *Narishkeit*! (Yiddish for "stupidity", *farshteit?*) WE ALL KNOW, (from where, nobody seems to know!), that the Torah is a document put together by either a brilliant person or a group of brilliant people (the more prevalent opinion) and then a very charismatic person came along and "sold" the tribes living in Judah the whole *shpiel*, (Yiddish for "tall-tale")"! In reality, they say, there never WAS a revelation, but we succeeded in selling it to the Jewish people anyway.

Well, what do you say? Does that sound convincing to you?

Well, it certainly does not to me! Why? Because only the truly gullible would accept this at face value! My reasons are as follows:

---

55 Please note that the verse doesn't say from one end of the land to the other, but rather from one end of the sky to the other. Why did it say it that way? It must be because this very, very old document knew of the existence of other land masses which were not connected to the main land-mass of Europe-Asia-Africa but were under the same skies!! Hmm! How is that possible? Check out my article related to this topic at my blog www.rabbibz.com entitled "Noah and Tectonic Movement".

1> First of all: Torah by committee. The madness of the methodology.

Biblical literary criticism, which is used by Bible critics to form the basis for the "multiple authors" claim, is based on the assumption that any written document is authored by a human being. Therefore, the document can be studied utilizing the knowledge-base of modern psychology to assess the mind and outlook of the author. This implies that the subconscious mind of the author will affect the wording and structure of the written word to the extent that the authorship of the document can be divined from literary devices and sentence structure patterns.

Even we agree that the person who actually wrote the Torah was a man. However, when the writer isn't the author, but rather a stenographer, and the words and phrases are not his own: then whose mind and whose authorship are we going to sense? Certainly not the one who was only the implement of writing! Obviously, it's the one who dictated it. The Torah never said that Moses authored the book. The Torah says only that Moses wrote it and passed it on to the people.

Having said that we come to a theological and philosophical divide: because according to Jewish tradition, this that means that Bible critics when scrutinizing the Bible, are looking to the divine and decipher the subconscious mind... of a being whose mind has no subconscious! But this divide aside – what other problems are there with this screwball opinion?

It also relies on comparing other existing historical documents, of which we only have fragments or incomplete texts, to the present-day Bible. The *assumption* that is made is that today's document (the Bible, not the new testament) is a whole manuscript that was made-up from the fragments. This is due to the fact that we do not have complete Torah scrolls that are older than a few thousand years, nor a full set of the Bible from earlier times.

This issue of "I haven't found one" takes us back to the basic problem of proof based on "I haven't found X". As our sages, ob"m, teach us "I haven't found is not a proof (of anything)". This is due to several issues.

a) Much of the ancient artifacts, especially Torah scrolls and their like, were destroyed at varying times and places throughout history[56]. The land of Israel was pillaged and raped many, many times, just as the holy Temples were.

b) This assumes that there has been a complete and thorough excavation of all possible sites. There hasn't been[57]. If you don't look very well – you also don't find anything.

c) Finding parts of a whole doesn't mean that there isn't or wasn't ever a whole that existed before the part/fragment.

2> Secondly: The Jewish timeline of our history.

---

56 For example, during the pillage of Jerusalem by the Babylonians (first Temple period) and later by the Romans, (second Temple period) both of whom destroyed the holy Temple in Jerusalem. During the Middle-ages in Europe, where the Torah and the Talmud were publicly burned by the wagon-full in France.

57 I recall reading sources for this. I haven't found a clear source for this yet.

Jewish tradition today, and Jewish history as far back as we can search, all claim that we are in possession of this Holy document since Sinai. This was not only an uncontested fact up until the days of the "enlightenment", it is also spelled out for us – quite clearly – within the pages of both the written and the oral Torah's. It's not just the claim, it's the existence of historical documents and the ability to reconstruct not only many a family tree throughout history, all the way back to the Bible, but also the existence of a chain of learning from Rebbe to student which can also be traced all the way back to Moses. (With the documentation to back it up! We are one of the few people on the planet that have a documented chain of transmission from teacher-to-student that extends throughout known history!)

3> The Practical Problems of "introducing" a Torah.

But for the sake of argument, let's presume that this claim is correct. Let's assume that the Torah was introduced at a "late" period of time and that Moses didn't write it. Practically speaking – how do we do it? How could we introduce it to the people in a way that makes a shred of sense?

To come out of nowhere and plop a "holy" book down on a people without any prehistory leads to many problems – all of which need to be addressed – to solidify the logic-base of our new religion! We now should ask: at what point in time was it that this "committee sponsored" book was put into circulation?

a)   The Nitty-Gritty: How would it work?

Practically speaking, upon introducing this new book to the masses, what would be the selling "catch-phrase"? Would the claim be that this is an old book or that it is a new one? The text itself clearly states that it was given to the people by Moses, who lived almost 800 years before the reign of Josiah, who is commonly cited as being the one who "introduced" the Torah to the people during his reign[58] (more on this later). If that's the case, how do you deal with the question of "where has it been up until today"?

If I would follow the advice laid out in the book itself, (as quoted above) and asked the previous generations, my father, and grandfather, whether they had heard anything like that which was described in the book, would they verify the information within? Of course not! If the stories inside were unknown, there is no way that any of it could be verified! The fraud would have eventually come to the fore.

How would George, (the guy who is now selling us this previously unknown book), explain the revelation story to us? Did it: already happen, happened sometime today, or will happen sometime in the future?

If it were sold to us as "It hasn't happened yet, but don't worry! It will!", then why haven't the entire Jewish people been saying "It hasn't happened yet, but don't worry! It will!"?

---

58 The Exodus from Egypt took place 480 years before the building of the first Temple in Jerusalem, as is described clearly in the book of Kings 1 (6:1) at the time of King Solomon's consecration of the Temple. As the first Temple stood for 410 years, and King Josiah was king towards the end of the first Temple period there was, therefor, somewhere around 800 years between Moses and Josiah.

If it were sold to us as "It happened just now!" or "It is happening right now!", well – that would bring us back to the information laid out at the beginning of the chapter! "Sorry! I didn't see it! Did you see it? No? I guess it didn't really occur".

The only possibility that makes sense is to say that it happened a long time ago. So… where has it been all this time? Why haven't I ever heard of it or anything that is written in it before today?

If it really did occur that we were "sold" a revision of our own national history, and that the explanation as to why we haven't ever seen or heard of the book before is "it was forgotten (for some unknown or forgotten reason) and I'm just setting things back to the way they were by giving you back the long-forgotten book" (a common "answer" to the above), then why do we find no record of such a gap in the transition of the book in the annals of Jewish, or even world history? Why are there no folk tales telling us of the time that we didn't know any better, but now we do? There would have had to have been an extensive amount of lore built up to explain to the masses why it is that we forgot about it in the first place so that we had to reacquire it again at a later point in time! Yet there isn't, nor has there ever been, any of the above.

b)   The Historical Timeline of The Book problem:

Jewish tradition places the Torah as having been given to us a little over 3327 years ago. 1273 years after that Christianity became a religion and 500 years after Christianity – Islam was born. But at the time that Christianity became something, the Jews already had a full set of scriptures[59] and an entire religious infrastructure in place. So, it's certainly at least 2100 years old, even according to our most fervent skeptics. However, it must be even older than that, as well.

The second Temple in Jerusalem stood for 420 years, according to Jewish tradition. For almost the entire second Temple period, we have plenty of archaeological remains and documentation to verify, clearly, the existence of not just the Jewish worship at the Temple, but the prevalence of vibrant Jewish life throughout the land, both in Israel and abroad[60]. During this entire time, public readings of the Torah were carried out on a regular basis, on the Sabbath day (morning and afternoon) and at least twice weekly on Mondays and Thursdays[61]. (Guess what? You can't publicly read a book that doesn't exist!) Jewish communal life and their adherence to the laws of the Torah during their exile in Babylonia also are well documented, as is the return of the Jewish people to the land of Israel at the behest of King Cyrus and King Darius. This tacks another 490 years[62] onto the timeline bringing us to a total of 2590 years ago.

---

59 This is undeniable because of the Septuagint, the Greek translation of the entire Bible from the original Hebrew. The Septuagint, meaning "the (translation of the) seventy", as it was translated by seventy of the Jewish elders – against their will – under the auspices of Ptolemy II, (*Talmai* in the Talmud), at around 250 BCE. It is impossible to translate a document that does not exist.

60 This is especially true for the Jewish communities in Babylonia, in Egypt (Alexandria especially), and during the times of the Greeks and the Romans as well.

61 As the Gemara in Tractate Bava Kamma tells us (82a) that the readings of Shabbos Mincha (afternoon) was established by Ezra the Scribe. The readings of Mondays and Thursdays was made at an even earlier time. Jewish tradition teaches that it was Moses himself who established this. For more on this topic – check out my blog www.rabbibz.com

62 The combined amount of the 420 years of the second Temple and the 70 years of exile in Babylonia.

However, in addition to the above information, there is plenty of archaeological evidence as to the religious observance of the Jewish people dating even earlier than that! Recently archaeological evidence has been found of first temple artifacts showing clearly the existence of organized religion dating to that time[63]. The excavation of the Old City tunnels shows that the standing walls, from the time of the second Temple, are built on the foundation of walls dating back to the date of the first temple[64]. There is consistent Jewish historical and archaeological evidence as to the existence of flourishing Jewish communities, both in Israel and abroad, up until that time period[65]. This means that we can tack another 410 years of the first Temple period, for a total of 3000 years of religious observance! So, at what point, exactly, are we supposed to believe that the "new" Torah was introduced to the people?

The "late"-ness of the Torah becomes particularly challenging given the sorts of archaeological findings that keep popping up, showing us that the Torah is older than "we" thought. Take, for example, the recent (2010) discovery on the Temple mount of an inscription that matches the words of the prophet in Kings (first temple period).

*The inscription is the earliest example of Hebrew writing found, which stands in opposition to the dating of the composition of the Bible in current*

---

63    http://en.wikipedia.org/wiki/Solomon%27s_Temple#Related_archeological_artifacts    and
http://www.israelnationalnews.com/News/News.aspx/128174#.Tm4BMalUXZt
64 See http://www.generationword.com/jerusalem101/37-western-wall.html for more on this.
65 See http://science.jrank.org/pages/7629/Diasporas-Jewish-Diaspora.html for some examples of Jewish life during the first Temple period.

*research; prior to this discovery, it was not believed that the Bible or parts of it could have been written this long ago[66].*

Or the discovery of silver encased scrolls that contained within them the priestly benediction as written in the Torah of today[67]!

Bible critics, being the wonderfully, woefully misinformed people that they are, like to claim that it was introduced in Bible times, during the reign of King Josiah (*Yoshiahu*, in Hebrew). The reason they do this is based on the simple understanding of some verses ... when read without any context or any exploration as to whether the reading is correct. The implication of this overly simplistic reading is that a/the sefer Torah was "found" during Josiah's reign. There are many clear problems with this. Let me enumerate a few.

First of all, that explanation dates the written Torah at around 2700 years, which is when Josiah ruled. Secondly, it relies on the interpretation of a word, (*vayimatzeh*, "and it was found") according to its literal meaning, while ignoring the details of the surrounding verses. It also ignores how the word *vayimatzeh* is used throughout the Bible. Thirdly, it doesn't even bother to try and understand the issue within the context of any historical background. Lastly, it precludes that everything said in the book of Kings before that about the people worshiping G-d (or not)

66 Read more: http://www.foxnews.com/scitech/2010/01/08/bible-really-written#ixzz1XkCsPETw
or http://www.itsgila.com/highlightspriestly.htm  or http://www.itsgila.com/highlightspriestly.htm

and of them following His Torah (or not) isn't true! (For a more detailed refutation of this stupidity – please look in Appendix III).

It also doesn't really address the practical issues that arise from the relatively "late" introduction of such a Torah! (But it sure does lead us into them!)

c)  The Performance of *Mitzvos* issue.

Were the *mitzvos* (commandments) prescribed in the "new" Torah first introduced and then afterward the people began to follow its precepts; or were they already keeping the precepts when the "new" Torah was introduced to them? If they were keeping the precepts already[68]: where, exactly, did they come from? Some vague religious fanaticism?

Let's propose that the Jews *weren't* keeping the mitzvos listed in the "torah". They ate pork and lobster, wore *sha'atnez* (clothes made with both wool and flax), worked 7 days a week, and enjoyed disco dancing on Friday nights. Life's good. At least, as good as it can be under the circumstances of yesteryear.

Then, all of a sudden, out of the blue, George comes to the people of Israel and everything changes. George says to everyone "I know that you don't know what is written in this book", which he then proceeds to show them. "I also know that you have never heard of any of the things that I

---

68 They were. Despite the civil-war that divided the kingdom into two, (the Northern and Southern kingdoms), they still worshiped the same G-d (albeit, many times, along with other deities) and had many other religious commonalities. For more on this – see Appendix I.

am about to tell you", he says. "However, know … that they are the absolute truth"! "This book is the word of G-d. It was given to our people, your ancestors, a long time ago (in a galaxy far, far away!) and it was lost to the ages. I'm here to set the record straight! From now on – you may no longer live your life the way you have been for many generations now. The pork and all of the utensils that you used to cook them? Throw them all away! No more lobster! No more… (a very long list ensues). All of that, from this day forth – no good! You're done with it!

Shopping seven days a week – finished! You can no longer shop or do all sorts of constructive labor on the … seventh day! (That sounds good? Right?). Oh, yeah! Also, once every seven years, you know all of the farming that you all do in order to survive on a daily basis? Yeah, that's all forbidden now. No more of that"!

"Is there anyone here", said George, "who has a problem with any of these restrictions?" he asked. "Ok! Those are the ones (that I just thought of) for today! I'll come back tomorrow with *even more of them*"!

What do you think? Would the people, especially the Jewish people, turn to each other and say "Well, that sounds perfectly reasonable! Don't you think? I think I'll just accept all of these restrictions from this book, that I have never heard about, thereby making my life so much more difficult. After all, George is clearly a reliable source of all things that affect my personal life"!

Nah! I don't buy it.

Even if we were to suppose that it was imposed upon the people by one of the kings that thought it up (as someone suggested to me during a lecture on the topic), guess what? It would survive for the length of time that the king did. (Which most of them didn't really succeed so well at doing!) It would then have been relegated to the trash-bin for being another piece of trash that was served-up over the course of history.

This is, of course, assuming that the people were *not* living in accordance with the mitzvos commanded in the Torah.

However, is there any reason to assume that the practices of history were *different* than those of "today"? Is there any proof, other than the words of the Bible itself, that suggests that the performance of "religious ritual" in those days were any different than they are today? The Bible tells us that they *did* worship idols and did other atrocities, however, there is no place where it says that that was the only religion that they practiced. Idol worship is always described as being the result of the Jews *straying* from the Torah given at Sinai by Moses. Is there any evidence of a point in time where the practices of the people underwent radical change, so as to "fit" the "stage" for giving a new "torah"? My logic in this is as follows:

If they were the same, and they were *already* doing the mitzvos before the supposed "introduction" of the Torah – then we are stuck with the question of why they were doing them in the first place? Why were they keeping them? A new "torah" doesn't explain that.

But if it could be demonstrated that they were doing something essentially different and that at a certain time in our history there was a significant change in the religion as opposed to that which was practiced at an earlier point in time, (not by a splinter group, but by the masses), then there would/could be room to argue that a source of significant change (such as a new "torah") was then introduced.

But to the best of my knowledge – there is no proof of any kind to substantiate such a claim.


d)   Where's our *hakoras hatov* (gratitude)?

Even more so: If there really was such an event, a late "introduction" of a relatively new, human-made Torah, then why do we not find the name of the person responsible for "re-introducing" our heritage back to us recorded in Jewish tradition, along with all of the other people who relayed new aspects of Torah through history? We should have a list looking something like this: Moses (Torah), Joshua, ... Samuel (Naviim)... Rabbi Judah the Prince (Mishna), Ravina (Gemara)... and George, (the guy who reminded us of what we forgot).

But it ain't there!


4> The Redactionary issue

Why are there no records of any kind as to the convening of the committee that came up with the (first, second, third and) final version of the written Torah?

The Mishna and the Gemara (Talmud), both of which comprise the Oral Law (Torah), and also the compilation of the "Old Testament", (TaNa"Ch in Hebrew, standing for Torah (Pentateuch, the "Five Books" of Moses),  Nevi'im (Prophets) and Cesuvim (Writings)), all have documented histories in Jewish tradition as to who it was that finalized their compilation[69]. Why is it that the Five Books, if they also were also a "Communal Project", have no such documented histories?

*L'Havdil*, (Hebrew for "to note a distinction"), it's a well-known fact that the Christian Bible went through many revisions and has differing versions numbering in the tens or hundreds. The Muslim Koran also has well-documented differences and versions to it, but only the Jewish Torah has no such variants! (More on this, G-D willing, when we discuss Torah from Heaven, in the chapter entitled *Celestial Words*).

5> The Zeroth Law of History

There is not today, nor has there ever been, a documented case of a nation being fed a cock and bull story about something important in that nation's history that never actually happened which the people accepted. So why should we assume that the "One True Case" would start with the Jews?

If you think about it, just the opposite should or would be true! If there are one people on the face of the planet today who are the most

---

69 Regarding the issue of the redaction of the oral Torah, the Mishna and Gemara, and why they are not proof as to a late redaction, I refer the reader to the blogs that I wrote on the topic at www.rabbibz.com labeled "The Torah, the Massorah and the ???"

difficult, stiff-necked people, just incredibly difficult to convince about anything – it's the Jews! What really is the likelihood that we would buy it?

If there truly is a "natural" explanation as to how the transition from Sinai could have happened through logical, plausible mechanisms, then the Zeroth Law of History applies: "What goes around... comes around", or in other words "History repeats itself". (Those who don't learn from history are destined to repeat it!). A truly historical event, one which has natural causes and is subject to human foibles, will reoccur or be repeated over the course of human history. The only exception to this is if the event isn't "historical" but rather "miracle".

I remember as a child growing up, my father took out neckties from his youth and showed them to me. They were these big, clunky, paisley ties, and I looked at them and said "Dad, did you actually wear these things?" to which he answered "Yep." I then asked him "So now that they are out of style, what are you keeping them for"? To which he answered, "Because that's the way fashion (=history) goes, what's out of fashion today will come back into fashion tomorrow". And they did.

Yet, for some unknown and unexplained reason, as opposed to every other historical event this one, which is supposedly a natural, regular historical event never repeated itself.

By every other religion and every cult throughout history when we scrutinize their origins and compare them one to the other, we find that in almost all regards, if not in all of the details they are basically the same except for the Torah. Except for Judaism.

Why? The only plausible answer: because it wasn't a natural occurrence. It was, indeed, as described clearly in the book, a miraculous occurrence.

But even all of that is not all.


Going back to the Kuzari: In the opening dialogue between the King of the Khazars and the Wise Jew, ("*chaver*" in Hebrew, a euphemism for a wise man or a rabbi), the king asked the *chaver* "In what do you believe?" The *chaver* answered, (paraphrased, of course), "I believe in the G-D of Abraham, Isaac, and Jacob, who took my people out of Egypt and led them into the desert for 40 years and brought them to the land of their forefathers and gave them his Torah in a public display of His glory".

When the king heard this, he turns to the *chaver* and tells him "That's not a G-D! (He says while pulling out a statue from behind his back, "Now THIS! THIS is a G-D"! …) A G-D is all-powerful, world making and universe shaking! (Now THAT'S a G-D!) Of what use is your little pocket "save my people" type G-D?"

So, the *chaver* turns to the king, and he says, "Let me answer with a question..." No! Just kidding! He actually answered with a parable[70]. He

---

70 Which is, of course, the next best type of Jewish answer!

then says to the king "King! Let me answer you with a parable, (keeping in mind that this is greatly paraphrased):

Let's say that you hear about the King of India that he is super smart, savvy, rich, suave and any other positive-type description that you can think of. Let's say you meet up with one of your friends, and he says to you "So, King-y baby! What do you feel about the King of India? Isn't he just the coolest cat? Sounds amazing, no?" How would you answer?

The king answered, "I would say 'Yes, he does'".

"And if your friend would tell you "You know, I think we should erect a statue, maybe dedicate a University library in his honor. What do you say?" what would you say to him"?

"Well", said the king, "I would tell him that he should check his medication! I mean – come on! Sure, I've heard about him, but I'm not about to honor him unless I either get to meet and know him or if I get some sort of proof that he actually exists and that everything everyone is saying about him is true!"

"AHA!", said the *chaver*, "My point exactly! It's very easy to speak about "the great and powerful G-D! Earth-shaking, ocean-crashing, super-duper... G-D" but I wouldn't expect you to honor or respect Him unless you actually know He exists. Unless you actually met Him!

SO how do you go about knowing that He exists? How do you know that all that was attributed to Him is true? Well, if he comes to you, publicly acts on your behalf, and shows you proof of his brilliance by giving you Written and Oral instructions which you then research, experiment on, and experience. Then – and only then! –not only will you

KNOW that there is a G-D, but you will also know what you are talking about, as you will know a little bit about who He is and what His true greatness is!"

"THAT," said the *chaver*, "is why I told you that I believe in the G-d who took us out of Egypt and publicly gave us his Torah. All of which occurred publicly, in front of the entire nation: men, women, and children"!

But it is not the Sinai event alone that forms the basis for our faith, our *emunah*, in *HaKadosh Baruch Hu*. As the *chaver* first answered the king of the Khazars – G-d, quite publicly, did so much more for us. He took us out of Egypt with signs, wonders and 10 miraculous plagues, (which we commemorate yearly during the festival of Pesach (Passover)). He tore the sea asunder, and led us through on dry land, (also accompanied with miracles, as described in the Midrash on Exodus), and then proceeded to utterly destroy our enemies by drowning them in the sea (Which we commemorate yearly on the festival of the seventh day of Passover). He also fed us with miraculous food (the *manna*) daily, gave us to drink from a miraculous wellspring which traveled with us throughout our sojourn in the desert (called "Miriam's Well") and did many other obvious miracles for us over the course of 40 years in the desert, (which we commemorate yearly during the festival of *Sukkot* (Booths)). All of the above forms the basis of our emunah. All of the above is referred to generally as "*yetzias Mitzrayim*" (Leaving Egypt) because we never truly finished leaving Egypt until we finally settled on our land. That all of the above forms the basis of our emunah is stated explicitly in the full Torah passage from Deuteronomy chapter 4:

> *(32) For ask, please, concerning the first days which were before you, from the day which G-D created man on this land, and from one end of the skies to the (other) end of the skies. Was there ever something like unto this great thing, or has a similar thing (ever) been heard of? (33) Has a nation EVER HEARD THE VOICE OF THE G-D SPEAKING TO THEM FROM AMIDST THE FIRE as you have and lived (to tell about it)? (34) OR HAS THERE EVER BEEN (A CASE IN WHICH) A G-D CAME IN ORDER TO TAKE OUT A NATION, (that's any nation, especially not a conquered one), from amidst another nation, with trials and signs and wonders and war and with a mighty hand and an outstretched arm and with great fearful (acts), as all of the things which HaShem, your G-D, has done for you in Egypt for you to see, (lit. "to your eyes")? (35) You have been shown all of this so that you know that HaShem is the G-D, there is none other than Him.*

All of the above miracles are referred to collectively as "The Removal from Egypt" (in Hebrew *Yetzias Mitzrayim*) as the removal of the Jewish people from Egypt didn't end until they entered into the Promised Land, Canaan.

Looking back in history, from today to as far back as we know, the Jewish people – daily – have reminded ourselves of these historical events. In the regular prayer services, there are many statements made about the removal from Egypt. In the *Kiddush*[62] on Friday night and on all of the Jewish festivals we mention that this is "*in remembrance of the departure from Egypt*". The entire Pesach *Seder*, (the festive meal on the first night of Passover) and the eating of the *matzah*, *maror*, (bitter herbs), and in the times of the Temple in Jerusalem the Pascal lamb, are entirely in remembrance of these miracles. We sit in booths on the festival of *Sukkot* in remembrance of our sojourn in the desert during the removal from Egypt. We celebrate the giving of the Torah at the Festival of Weeks, *Shavuot*. All of this as a living testimony that these events actually occurred.

There is no other nation on the face of the planet and throughout all human history that has or even can begin to make a similar claim[71].

There are only the Jewish people and the heavenly instructions for living known as the Torah that have this claim and has proudly attested to this throughout all known human history.

---

71 I write this because there are people who like to search for, and have found, instances of mass "revelations" or "sightings" of unexplained phenomena who like to compare them to the Sinai Revelation and say "See! This was also a mass revelation"! To which I say, "While that may be true, it is still not relevant or in any way comparable to the above". For although some phenomena have been witnessed in human history by multitudes – there is no other case in history of: a> revelation on a personal level (i.e. everyone spoke directly with the Deity); b> Clear instructions given at the time of the phenomena; and c> a long-enduring phenomena of a clearly miraculous nature, yet with a clear and abiding purpose (redemption from Egypt, destruction of enemies by miraculous phenomena, provision of basic needs, miraculous guides (pillar of cloud/fire), and the list goes on and on! All of the above are the criteria that the Torah (in the verses quoted above) spells out clearly. There has never been anything comparable. Ever.

## **In Summary of this Chapter:**

⅄ It's not enough to prove that there is a G-D as the basis for a religion because anyone can create a religion based on the same premise and one would be just as "truthful" as the next.

⅄ Prophecy is the litmus test for the validity of a religion's claims, as the religion's relationship with G-D is based solely on the power of prophecy.

⅄ Since all religions claim to have prophecy the only way to differentiate between them would be based on both the quality, but more especially the quantity of those founding members who experienced the prophecy itself.

⅄ The only religion in the world which claims that the entire nation as a whole experienced prophecy is the Jewish people, as described in detail in the Written Torah. There is no one who makes a claim even remotely similar to this. This is not our only claim of having met our Deity, just our most powerful one. This is in addition to the outright miracles of Egypt, those of the Red Sea, those we experienced during our 40-year sojourn in the desert and also those encountered in the subsequent conquest of our land, Canaan, the modern land of Israel.

⋏ The only religion in the world concerning which both Christianity and Islam agree, (probably the only thing upon which they agree), was in possession of the True Word of THE One True G-D before them is Judaism.

⋏ Jews and Judaism are the only nation in the entire world who claim prophecy on a national level WHICH CANNOT BE FAKED as I cannot convince someone who didn't witness it that he or she saw it!

⋏ The claims that such a national revelation can be faked make about as much sense as building a space shuttle out of spaghetti.

In a nutshell: What makes us unique? Why are the Jews different than all other religions in the world?

Because we are the only nation in existence, who met G-d together, as one, face-to-face and lived to not only tell the tale but to live it throughout our generations. And tell that story we have! From generation to generation, every single year since we first became a people.

It was at this public revelation that we met the Living G-d and heard Him say, through the commandments "I know you and want a relationship with you. Let me tell you how that works". He then taught us His Holy Torah.

But the Revelation aside. A real die-hard skeptic might ask "OK, so the revelation was G-d. The outright miracles? Also, G-d! But who says that that is true of the Torah is as well? Perhaps the Torah really IS the product of man, (i.e. Moses)?" And even if we do say that it is, in fact, prophetic so why should we listen only to the Torah when later prophets came along and told us that it is no longer relevant?

Let's explore these issues in the next few chapters, shall we?

# Supernatural!

## ***Prophecy, Witchcraft and the Role of Moses, our Teacher.***

I N THE PREVIOUS CHAPTER we discussed the difference between the Torah and other world religions known as the National Revelation. We discussed that when looked at from all sides, the claim of National Revelation would seem to be the strongest, most persuasive, and most correct of all possible foundations of religion. If we all experienced it – it requires no explaining or convincing whatsoever!

However, some 3328 years have gone by since then, and during that time there have been many prophets that have come and gone. Lots of water under the bridge!

Islam claims that they had a prophet, Mohammed.

The Mormons claim that they had a prophet, John Smith Jr.

The Christians… well, it depends on who you speak to. They either believe that they had – at the very least – a prophet; or at the very best – better than a prophet. The next best thing to G-D in fact! His name was Jesus.

In fact, every single religion of G-d is based upon the claim of prophecy.

Judaism too is no exception to this rule. We don't find that the Jews had just the one prophet. The Bible, TaNaCh, comprises 24 books, all of which were written with prophecy. Within their pages, we count many, (at least several tens), of prophets-at-large during Biblical times. Our sages, ob"m, tell us in Tractate *Megilla14a* that in reality during biblical times there were somewhere around 1.2 *million* prophets living in Israel. The reason that we have only 24 books in the TaNaCh is that only those prophecies that had ramifications for future generations were encoded into the Bible. All of the other prophecies and any books of wisdom that were written without any prophecy were winnowed out by the men of the Great Assembly. This occurred during the time of the redaction of TaNaCh.

In addition to the issue of the quantity and quality of the people who experienced the "foundation prophecy" of any religion, there is something else that needs to be addressed. That is the question of whether all prophets are created equal? If I've got a prophet and you've got a prophet are we, as they say in Hebrew, *"Teko-Teko"*, ("even-steven"). Does my prophet cancel your prophet? Do prophets have rankings? Is one greater/stronger than another one?

But before we can even begin to ask ourselves this question we have to ask an even more fundamental question: Just what is a prophet in the first place?

Is a prophet just a person who goes down the street yelling "Repent you, sinners!"? No.

Is a prophet a guy who walks up to you and hands you his card, which has emblazoned on it in gold lettering "John K. Mooney – prophet at large"?

Is there a special handshake?

So how in the world are we supposed to know the difference between a Prophet and a profiteer? Remember: If you want to make a lot of money – make your own religion and all religions start with one!

So, in this regard, the Torah tells us clearly that if one day you are standing around in the market, buying vegetables, and a guy walks up to you and says "Hello there, young man. I'm a prophet!", and you don't know this guy from Adam, what are you supposed to do?

Well, the first thing you are going to do is give the guy (or gal![72]) a look-over to see if: a> you have some clue as to who s/he is, and b> that after evaluation it seems that he or she is not a whack-job! The reason for this is because prophecy, like all professions, is something that not

---

72 G-d is an equal opportunity employer. There are at least 7 women who our sages record as having been prophetesses, (see Tractate Megilla 14a). This number doesn't take into account the ones that weren't recorded, as well.

just anyone can get into. You can't just simply apply for a course online, do moderately well, and hang out your shingle. Not all people are candidates for the prophet's power, known as *Nevuah*. If a person wants it – he or she has to prepare for it, and not just any candidates are eligible for Nevuah-U!

Candidates for prophecy are called *Bnei HaNeviim*[73], (literally "the sons of prophets") because they sat before the Prophet and learned the ways of the prophets from him for many years. This is how they tried to prepare themselves to be prophets.

Let me tell you: Fools were NOT eligible to be prophets.

If you look at this person and he or she looks like they are either going to drool on you or that something there just isn't right – hands-down that's not a prophet!

Second of all: Evil men, and by "evil" I mean Jews who know the Torah's laws, but DON'T keep them, or non-Jews who don't keep the seven Noachide laws[74] are also not eligible. Every day, ordinary type people, those who are not exceptionally pious, are also not qualified to be prophets[75].

Regarding the issue of piety, we find an interesting statement by Obadiah, (*Ovadiah,* in Hebrew), a prophet whose prophecies are recorded in the "12 prophets" segment of THE Testament, (again, there

---

73 See, for example, Kings 2 6:1 or Kings 2 9:1

74 Our sages, ob"m, tell us that since Moshe's time HaShem has never again given prophecy to non-Jews. It was one of the things that Moses requested of G-d and the request was granted. (See Berachos14a).

75 This idea goes against the general understanding of the Christians, who seem to hold that a prophet can be anyone. G-d sort of just picks a name out of a hat randomly and says "Guess what? You're a prophet!" whether the guy wanted it or not.

is only one and its old). The following story is from the book of Kings regarding a supposedly unnecessary statement that Obadiah makes upon meeting with Elijah the Prophet. The story is as follows. The evil king of Israel, Ahab, has been looking for Elijah for two years. During this time, the land has not seen a drop of rain as Elijah had prayed to G-D that the rains stop until the people living in Israel repent their sins. So, Obadiah met up with Elijah and Elijah told him to go back – by himself – to King Ahab and tell him to come and meet him (Elijah). At this point, Obadiah begged Elijah to come with him and not to send him alone, for fear that Ahab would kill him for not bringing Elijah with him. This is how he presented his case in Kings 1 chapter 18 verses 9-14

> *(9) And he (Obadiah) said "What is my sin for which you are giving your servant into the hand of Ahab to kill me? (10) By the Living G-D, your Lord, if there is not a Nation or Kingdom to which my Master (Ahab) did not send to in order to ask of your whereabouts, and they said to him "(he) is not (here)", and he (Ahab) forced the Nations and Kingdoms to swear that you are not to be found. (11) And now you say to me "Go to your master and tell him 'Here is Elijah!'"? (12) And (what will be) if I go from you, and the Spirit of G-D will take you to a place that I do not know, and I will come to tell Ahab and he will come and won't find you, and he*

Why did Obadiah say this to Elijah? Well, first and foremost because he wanted Elijah to know that he was not a worshiper of *Ba'al*, the Idol. Of almost equal importance was that he wanted him to know that he was a pious Jew and a student of the *Neviim*! He then told Elijah how he saved and sustained (at *great* personal expense, I might add!), 100 prophets of G-d who Isabel, Ahab's evil wife, tried to kill off.

It's not enough to *presently* be a righteous person to receive prophecy. One has to strive to be a vessel since his youth and to be known as such!

Let's say that we find such a person. He's normal, is known to be a righteous, G-D-fearing person, and is known as a student of the prophets. He walks over to us in the market during our vegetable shopping and announces, "I have a prophecy for you!" Do we start speaking in Shakespearean English with him "Speak, O' Prophet, for thou knowest best the ways of the Lord and thou are right in my eyes?"

No.

We Jews are a skeptical people. We look him or her in the eyes and we say: "If you really *are* a prophet, give us a sign or a wonder!"

This is something that the Holy Torah states explicitly in *Deuteronomy 13:2*

> When a prophet or a dreamer of dreams will arise
>
> from amongst you and he will give unto you a sign
>
> (ot) or a wonder (mofes).

Now by a "sign", I don't mean "yield" or "stop", and by a "wonder" I don't mean a statement starting "I wonder..." These things mean "something out of the ordinary." Classically, by studying the Bible, we find that there are two types of signs and wonders: 1. An *ot-* something that is spectacularly against the tide of reality as we know it, (think "splitting of the red sea"). 2. A *mofes-* something that is mostly within the flow of reality, but was related to us in detail ahead of its occurrence. Either is acceptable. The more common of the two, however, is the *mofes*: foreseeing the future.

So, our guy (or gal!) comes over to us in the market and s/he says to us "Listen! I had a prophecy concerning your financial future, *and it didn't look good!*" is that good enough?

Again: No.

In this regard, we run into a little trouble because of two things: Horoscopes and Madame Fortuna.

Do you know that there are many people out there who won't step out of their door without first checking their horoscope? What is a horoscope you ask? Well depending on the constellation, (sign of the Zodiac in which you were born), there are certain forces of the Universe that act upon you at certain times of the year. As of this writing, my horoscope says (courtesy of horoscope.com, not that I ever check it)

*"Social events or group activities may prove draining today, as a lot of people might want to take advantage of your talents. Your kind,*

*accommodating nature might cause you to try to make everyone happy, Pisces, but this isn't realistic. You might stress yourself to the point of not caring what gets done. Be discriminating about what you commit to doing".*

I must say in looking at this, that a lot of it is relevant to things that I have to deal with in my near future.

Madame Fortuna? She's the woman in the psychic tent at the local fair with the crystal ball and tarot cards. She palm-reads and can relate your future based on tea leaves and other such things.

The question that we need to ask is: how is the "future" predicted by the prophet different than Horoscopes and Madame Fortuna?

This, too, is stated explicitly in the Holy Torah in Deuteronomy 18:18-22

*(18) I will raise a prophet from amongst their brothers, like you (Moses), and I will place My words in his mouth, and he will relate to them all that I shall command him. (19) ... (21) And if you say in your hearts "How is it that I am supposed to know what thing was not commanded by G–D to be said?" (22) That which the prophet will say (will come to pass) and it doesn't happen, and it doesn't come – that is the thing which G–D did not say. The*

*prophet has intentionally (mis-)spoken in my name,*
*and you should not fear from him (to kill him).*

Now, what could the Torah be talking about here? My horoscope? Obviously not! Why? Because there really is *no accurate information in my horoscope which clearly will or will not come to pass.* I mean, in my horoscope above it states that "Social events or group activities *may* prove draining today......", well, they also may not be draining in the end. It could be that no one will try to take advantage of my skills. Either outcome is covered in the words of the horoscope!

Same goes for Madame Fortuna. "I see great disappointment in your future!" ... OK. About what, per se? Will I lose my favorite pencil and become disappointed? Stub my toe? Run over the neighbor's dog? It's all kind of vague.

Prophecies, on the other hand, are not vague. Let's take a look at an example of prophecy explicit in the Holy Torah. Let's take one of the prophecies of the prophet Jeremiah (*Yirmiyahu*).

Jeremiah was called to prophesy in 626 BCE, a few years after Josiah, king of Judah, became king. However, because of the people's flagrant disregard for the Torah's laws, Jeremiah was burdened with the task of rebuking them and foretelling the upcoming conquest of Judah by the Nation of Babylon. His words came to pass in 587 BCE, about 40 years after he began to prophesy. This is when the King of Babylon exiled the people of Judah to Babylon. In addition to this prophecy of exile, a prophecy of woe, Jeremiah also merited to prophesy the destruction of

Babylon and the redemption of the Jews from that exile. As it says (Jeremiah 25:11-12):

*And this whole land [of Israel] shall be a desolation, and an astonishment; and these nations [Judah and several of her neighbors] shall serve the king of Babylon seventy years. And it shall come to pass, when seventy years are accomplished, that I will punish the king of Babylon, and that nation, says G-D, for their iniquity.*

These are not vague words of something that "might" be. This is a detailed, definitive statement of fact describing precisely what will happen using clear and accurate information[76].

In 534 BCE, the kingdom of Babylon fell to Cyrus, king of Persia, and at some time between then and the following year (533 BCE) Cyrus passed an edict allowing the Jews to return to Israel and rebuild the Holy Temple in Jerusalem. However, this edict was disallowed, and the temple lay half completed for another 22 years, until the 2nd year of Darius II when a new decree was issued allowing all those who wanted to return and rebuild the land to do so. This is stated explicitly in the books of Ezra and Chronicles.

---

76 In truth, there are two prophecies of 70 years in the words of the prophet above. The more famous refers to the return of the Jewish people to their ancestral land after 70 years of exile in Babylon. The second refers to the punishment of the kings of Babylon that will be meted out after 70 years as well. See the Gemara in Tractate Megilla 3b for more details.

So, the timeline is[77]: (Please don't get confused by the backwardness of the BCE timeline. It's not a Jewish or a practical contrivance…)

586 – Destruction of First Temple.

536 – Belshazzar errs and believes that the 70 years of Jewish exile that were prophesied have passed without salvation.

534 – Cyrus conquers Babylonia and allows Jews to begin returning to Israel to rebuild the Temple, but recants the permission

529 – Achashverosh errs and believes the 70 years of exile have passed without salvation

517 – First year of the reign of Darius II —Daniel prays to G-d for salvation

516 – During the Second year of Darius II he allows the Jews to return to Israel and to complete the rebuilding of the Temple.

586-516= 70 years of exile of the Jewish people after the destruction of the first Temple in Jerusalem.

This is one example of many of the prophecies in the Bible, which came to pass exactly as the prophet foretold.

Many, many aspects detailing both the first and second temples and exiles can be found in prophecies both in the 5 books of Moses, (the Pentateuch) and also in the Prophets[78]. For more on this topic, the reader should see Maimonides, Laws of the Foundations of the Torah chapter 7.

---

77 http://www.jewishanswers.org/?p=891

78 See http://www.daat.ac.il/encyclopedia/value.asp?id1=2253, for example, concerning the destruction in the first temple period. Or http://www.arachim.org/ArticleDetail.asp?ArticleID=13882 concerning the second Temple period and its destruction.

How do the skeptics look at this and explain it away?

"Very simple!", they say. They then proceed to claim that the scriptures were written *after the fact*. After all, "Hindsight is 20/20".

Of course, this goes hand-in-hand with the assumption that we mentioned in the previous chapter, that the National Prophecy of Israel never actually happened in the first place, but rather it was "sold" to the people at a later time.

However, the Jewish tradition of both the chronology and the history of events, what happened, to whom, and when is living testimony as to its authenticity. You cannot sell a people their own history.

One of the reasons that Bible critics love this claim is because *it is clearly true concerning the canonization of the New Testament*. Jesus himself, having lived[79] sometime towards the end of the second temple period is not a great source of prophecy. His words were written down some 30 years after his death by his disciple, Paul, who apparently never met Jesus[80] during his lifetime. More on this in a moment.

But do you know what? Let's play devil's advocate. Let's pretend that their presumption is correct. OK! Babylonian exile and destruction and return to the land of Israel – we wrote it afterward. Fine! Let's assume they are right. Those prophecies are not explained away. Does that now mean that there are no other real prophecies in the Torah except for those of antiquity? Absolutely not! There are, in fact, many prophecies

---

79 If indeed, he ever did exist, there are many differing opinions in this regard!

80 See http://evidenceforchristianity.org/how-can-paul-be-an-apostle-if-he-did-not-meet-jesus-why-is-his-teaching-so-different-from-the-twelve/ or https://www.thisisyourbible.com/index.php?page=questions&task=show&mediaid=1266 as examples concerning this issue.

in the written Torah that have only come to pass in recent history! This despite the fact that even our most vehement antagonists agree that they were written during ancient history and not after the event!

## *I'm Still Standing!!!*

Let's take something a little more basic and much easier to handle: the modern-day existence of the Jewish people.

Over 300 years ago King Louis XIV of France asked Blaise Pascal, the great French philosopher, to give him proof of the supernatural. Pascal answered: "Why, the Jews, your Majesty—the Jews."

Mark Twain (aka Samuel Clemens) the great American writer, who was an agnostic and a self-acknowledged skeptic, penned the following in 1899 for Harper's Magazine:

> *"The Egyptian, the Babylonian, and the Persian rose ... then faded to dream-stuff and passed away. The Greek and Roman followed, made a vast noise, and they are gone. Other peoples have sprung up and held their torch high for a time, but it burned out, and they sit in twilight now or have vanished. The Jew saw them all, beat them all, and is now what he always was ... All things are mortal, but the Jew. All other forces pass, but he remains. What is the secret of his immortality?"*

But it's not just that we, as a people, retained our identity. It's not just that there are people walking around today claiming to be descendants of the Jewish people. It is also our religion, based as it is on the holy Torah, which exists today as it did 2000 years ago at the time of the Roman exile. It is as viable and vibrant today as it was then. This despite the many trials and tribulations that we had as a people over those many years[81].

## *Jews Go Home*

Not only that, but one of the Torah's prophecies is that we will one day return to the land of our forefathers, a land that for many centuries lay desolate. It was based on this prophecy that we have prayed, every day since time immemorial for the return of our people to our country[82]. In addition the land, in spite of its fertility, and despite all of the efforts that were made trying to settle it, remained in its state of desolation until the return of its people. The Jewish people returned to our land despite the fact that at the time of the dispersion, we were literally spread to the four corners of the globe. We were a downtrodden and despised people. We were sold into slavery and worse. Yet today, over 2000 years later, we are still here! We are as vibrant a people today as we were so long ago in history, when we were living in the land of our forefathers. We still

---

81 More on this in a later chapter.

82 We say this a minimum of three times a day in the shemoneh esreh (eighteen benedictions) / amidah (standing) prayer. If we eat bread and need to make the prayer after eating another prayer for our return to our land is made as well.

direct our lives by the very same Torah that our forefathers had, just as they did during their lifetime!

## *__And now, on to the Prophecy__*

Are all the above events prophesied explicitly in the Torah? Of course, they are. As it says in Deuteronomy, chapter 30:

> *(1) And it will come to pass, after all of these things shall come upon you, the blessing and the curse that I have placed before you, and you shall return it unto your heart amongst all of the nations that HaShem, your G-d, has exiled you there. (2) And you shall return unto HaShem, your G-d, and you shall listen to His voice, according to all that I am commanding you this day (i.e. keep the Torah), you and your children, with all of your heart and all of your soul. (3) And HaShem, your G-d, will return your remnant (back to the promised land. i.e. we're still alive and kicking) and have mercy on you and come back and gather you from all of the nations that HaShem, your G-d, dispersed you to.*

How could the Torah have known and "prophesied" Jewish survival so many years ago if it were written by man? Even the most skeptical of opinions agree that the Torah is well over 2000 years old and that the Jews were a small fraction of a conquered people at that time. What usually happens to a small minority within a vast majority? Very simple: give them 100 or 200 years... and they are gone. Does anyone know a Hittite today? How about an Acadian? Babylonian? Where are all the ancient peoples? They are gone, having been swallowed into the societies that came after them[83].

Is there any rational human explanation that can account for the clear and detailed prophecies that the Torah spelled out to us those thousands of years ago? No. There isn't. Yet everything that the prophets said has either come to pass, exactly as they wrote, or will. Just wait a little while longer. That's prophecy!

## *In this Corner... Weighing...*

For argument's sake let's say that we found two prophets meeting all the above-listed criteria for real prophets. Both of them give us a sign or a wonder, and then each of them proceeds to give two completely different prophecies. Who do I believe then? Let's assume that Mohammed and Jesus were two tried and true prophets, (they weren't). Let's assume that they had all of the qualifications that the Torah asked of them (they didn't) and that it would seem to all involved that they spoke with the voice of G-d. This last assertion has some truth to it. After all, there are many people who bought what they were selling. What am I to do now that they both come and tell me that I don't have

---

83 This is not to say that there are no traces of their genes in the gene-pool. But there is no one today who identifies as a member of these once great societies.

to keep the laws that Moses our teacher, wrote down in his five books? Its prophet vs. prophet in a winner takes all battle! Who am I supposed to trust?

Well, first of all – relax! The Torah, itself, has you covered! As it says in Deuteronomy (13:2-6)

> *(2) When a prophet or a dreamer of dreams arises among you and he will give you a sign or a wonder. (3) And when that sign or the wonder come (to pass), that which he said unto you, (and he would then speak again) saying "Let us go after foreign gods, which you have not known, and worship them". (4) Do not listen to the words of that prophet or a dreamer of dreams, for HaShem, your G-d, is testing you to know if there are those among you who love HaShem, your G-d, with all of your hearts and all of your souls. (5)… (6) And that prophet or that dreamer of dreams should be put to death, for he spoke words of upheaval on HaShem, your G-d, who took you out of the land of Egypt and redeemed you from the house of servitude (to foreign masters), (and the aforementioned false prophet did this) to sway you from the path that HaShem, your G-d, commanded you to follow. And you should burn the evil from amongst you.*

It seems very clear in the holy Torah that there is no room to listen to even a tried and true prophet if s/he comes to change or negate the Torah dictated to Moses, our teacher. *Kal va chomer* (even more so) we should not believe anyone who was not proven to be so.

Why is this?

The answer is two-fold: because of the greatness of Moses, our teacher, and because of the extreme clarity of the truth of the Torah of Moses. Let's explain what I meant by that.

## *Regarding the Greatness of Moses, our Teacher.*

The Torah itself tells us, in several places and in several ways, that the prophecy of Moses is not to be compared with that of other prophets.

First, here is what the Torah tells us about Moshe at the time of his death: *"...and there will never arise another prophet like Moshe, who was known to G-d face to face*[84]*"*. This is because the power and quality of Moshe's prophecy were both qualitatively and quantitatively different than that of all other prophets.

This issue is also mentioned in the Torah during the rebuke of Moshe's sister, Miriam, (who was also a prophet). She was punished for having doubted Moshe's sincerity and motives when he divorced his

---

84 Deuteronomy 34:10

wife[85]. The Torah tells us that Moshe's prophecy is intrinsically different than that of all other prophets (Miriam, the prophetess, included).

*"(From My) mouth to (his) mouth will I speak to him, with a clear vision and not with riddles and he saw the visage of HaShem[86]".*

The extent of the quantity and quality of Moses's prophecy is something that we know not only because it was written in the Torah. If that were all he had, then anyone can do it. All you have to do is write it down in your "torah" and - done! (Of course, you then have a lot of convincing to do to sell others your torah). The real power of Moses's prophecy is an extension of the Sinai revelation.

## *There, All was Revealed (Clarity of the Truth?)*

During the revelation at Sinai, the Jewish people themselves experienced first-hand what it is to have prophecy at the level of Moses. At Sinai, the entire nation of Israel bore witness to the fact that Moses was appointed as the messenger of G-d to teach the Jewish people His Torah. Here is what is written in the Torah regarding Moshe's role as a

---

85 Our sages, ob"m, explain that Moshe didn't do this out of ideology or piety. He didn't do so because he felt like it. He divorced her as he was given a personal command from G-d to do so. This occurred in the first year of the children of Israel's departure from Egypt. The people were told to separate from their wives in preparation for the giving of the Ten Commandments. This was done because a seminal emission is a cause of impurity and after sexual intercourse a woman can retain "live" semen from her husband for up to 72 hours (3 days) before her body rejects it or the semen die. A woman becomes impure as a result of the aforementioned emission. Once the semen is dead, they no longer cause impurity. After the 10 commandments Moses is commanded to tell all of the people "Go and tell the people 'Return unto your tents!' (to your wives), but you, here should stand with Me", i.e. you shouldn't return to your tent, rather remain separate from your wife. For Moses this was necessary so that he should be ready for prophecy all of the time.

86 Numbers 12:4

intermediary between G-d and the Jewish people in Deuteronomy 5:1-5

> *(1) And Moshe called unto all of Israel and he said to them "Hear Israel the statutes and the laws, those that I am speaking into your ears today! And you should learn (about) them and you should guard (carefully) to do them! (2) HaShem, our G-d, cut with us a covenant at Horeb (another name for Sinai). (3) Not with our forefathers did HaShem cut this covenant, rather with us, all of those of us who are here today, as we are all living. (4) Face to face HaShem spoke with you at the mountain (Sinai) from amidst the fire. (5) I was standing between HaShem and you, at that time, in order to relate to you the word of HaShem, for you were afraid of the flames, and you did not go up to the mountain in order to say (it, referring to the Ten Commandments, which the Torah then immediately begins to reiterate).*

Moshe was basically telling them is that it was their fear of the flames that prevented them from receiving the Torah (in its entirety) directly from HaShem's own mouth, on Moshe's own level of prophecy.

It also says in Exodus 19:19 that at the time of the Sinai Revelation *"...Moses would speak, and The G-d would answer Him (with a) loud (voice)"*, to which all of the Jewish people were a witness.

However, not only were they all witnesses to the appointment of Moses as THE prophet, to bring back the word of G-d, they were in fact partners, in that decision! This is stated clearly in Deuteronomy (5:20-25):

> *(20) And it was when you heard the voice from amidst the darkness, and the mountain was blazing with fire up unto the skies and you all approached unto me, all of the heads of your tribes and your elders. (21) And you said to me "It's true that HaShem, our G-d, has shown us His honor and His greatness, and we heard His voice (speaking to us) from amidst the fire. On this day, we saw that the Lord does speak unto man and (he can) live. (22) And now, why should we die, that we should be consumed by this enormous fire? If we continue to hear more of the voice of HaShem, our G-d, and we shall die! (23) For who among all flesh has heard the voice of the living G-d speak unto them from amidst the fire, as we have, and has lived (to tell about it)? (24) You should approach (the fiery mountain in our stead) and hear all that which HaShem, our G-d,*

*will say, and you will come and relate to us concerning all of the things that HaShem, our G-d, has told you. And we will listen and we will do (them). (25) And HaShem heard all the voice of your speaking (the conversation of the people) as you were speaking to me, and HaShem said to me 'I have heard the voice of the speech of this people, that which they said to you – all the things that they have said are fine'.*

In this regard, Moshe is intrinsically different from all other prophets. We do not believe in his prophecies because he did a sign or wonder, (or even because he did many, as clearly he did). We believe in his prophecies because the nation was witness to his appointment as the messenger of G-d's word, and as the teacher of Torah to Israel. There was no room for any doubt concerning this matter[87]. There is no other prophet (or "god") in history concerning whom we have such testimony. For more on this topic, the reader is urged to read Maimonides, *Laws of the Foundations of the Torah* chapter 8.

It is for this reason, and this reason alone, that prophecies of the Torah (the five books of Moses, i.e. the Pentateuch) hold more authority than those of any other prophet in history. EVER. So much so, that the only way to negate a prophecy of this magnitude would be if the next prophet were to establish his prophetic ability and credibility in a similar

---

87 Which, of course, never stopped a Jew from finding a reason to argue. Korach, for example.

fashion. (I.e. the authority of his prophetic powers was solidified by a mass revelation during which the prophet was given clear instructions by the deity, which were heard by all of the thousands/millions present witnessing the event).

It is for this reason that many people only mention the Revelation at Sinai in regard to the foundation of our emunah, as it was the one-time source of "super prophecy" ever to have been chronicled in history. However, with regards to our emunah in HaShem, it remains one, (albeit a very BIG one), of the *many* reasons why we have absolute emunah in Him.

I think that I may have mentioned that there have been – to date – no other such prophets in history? I did say that, right?

## <u>In Summary</u>

In this chapter, we have explored the following issues:

- Not just anyone can be a prophet. Only individuals with a history of piety throughout their days, and who have trained for the job are eligible to receive it.

- Prophecy is intrinsically different than all other forms of "future divination". All forms of future divination are vague and apologetic, whereas prophecy is clear, detailed and precise.

- Not all prophets are created equal. The exception to the rule – according to all of the major religions – is the prophecy of Moses.

- Moses's prophecies were substantiated by the Sinaic "Ten Commandments" event, where all of the children of Israel attained prophecy on the level of Moses and were witnesses to his appointment as THE prophet of Israel.

- It is for this reason that the Torah, (aka "the OLD (=only) Testament"), is recognized as the certified word of G-d by all of the major monotheistic religions. It, therefore, has a level of authority that is unparalleled by all future prophets, all of whom are not believed to negate its commandments.

- This is true even if the prophet establishes his/her authenticity with signs or wonders that they performed (and even more so if you have never witnessed them but were told about them by people of questionable credibility???).

But this leaves us – still – with a question. How do we know, (outside of all of the information thus far), that the "testimony" of yesteryear belayed in the Torah can be trusted? How can I, living thousands of years after the fact, know that what the Torah tells me is true? Well, let's deal with that issue now… in the next chapter.

# The Scattered Treasure

## ***The Miracle that is the Jewish People.***

When we talk of emunah, another issue that must be considered is the existence of the Jewish people. In so many ways we defy all aspects of human logic. So much in fact, that when King Louis the 14th asked Blaise Pascal for a proof of the Divine, his immediate response was "The Jews, my Liege! The Jews"!

Let's explore in what ways, we defy logic and prove the Divine.

## ***The Eternal Jew***

According to all opinions, the Torah is ancient. We have been around for a very long time. Even our skeptics acknowledge that the Jewish people have been in existence for more than 2000 years. According to Jewish tradition itself, however, we have been around for more than 3300 years. (For even longer if we go all the way back to our forefather, Abraham).

As opposed to all the other nations of the world, we have a detailed history that connects us from today all the way back to our illustrious past. We are still here despite the trials and tribulations which we have undergone. However, we don't credit our survival to our meticulous bookkeeping, our heroism, or our financial savvy. The only reason that we as a people have survived is because of HaShem and His Torah.

However, this is not just a concept that has come down through our history. It is also prophesied in the Holy Torah itself! As it says in Deuteronomy 4:25-31:

> *(25) When you will have children and grandchildren, and you become old in the land, and you will become destructive and make an idol, an image of anything and you will do evil in the eyes of HaShem your G-d to anger Him. (26) I bring as witnesses today the heavens and the earth that you will surely be destroyed quickly from on the land which you are (now) crossing the Jordan to go there and inherit it. You will not have length of days on*

*it for you will surely be destroyed. (27) And HaShem will disperse you among the nations, and you will remain a small remnant among the nations unto whom HaShem will lead you. (28) And there you will worship foreign gods, the work of a man's hands, wood, and stone, which will never see and will never hear and will never eat and will never smell. (29) And you will request from there HaShem your G-d, and you will find Him if you search with all of your heart and all of your soul. (30) When it is difficult for you and all of these things find you at the end of days, and you will return unto HaShem your G-d, and you will listen to His voice. (31) For He is merciful, your G-d HaShem, He will not release you and will not (utterly) destroy you and He will not forget the covenant of your forefathers, to whom He made an oath:*

This is a very ancient prophecy[88]. Did it come true? (It's rhetorical. You don't need to answer it!)

## **The Wandering Jew**

---

88 As we explained in-depth above, even according to the clear majority of our skeptics the 5 books of Moses, the Pentateuch, is around 2600 years old. Therefore, this prophecy was made long before the destruction of the second Temple. It's even older than the destruction of the first Temple.

Based on a Christian legend, the term "Wandering Jew" has come to symbolize the Jewish nation as a whole and every Jew individually. There's a very simple reason we were given this name. Since the destruction of the second Temple by the Romans, the crushing of the Jewish resistance, and consequent exile of the majority of the Jewish people from the land of Israel, we have never really had a place to "hang our hat." We truly have wandered from country to country for thousands of years.

This was as clearly prophesied in Deuteronomy 28:63-65

*(63) And it will be just as HaShem rejoiced concerning you to give you bounty and to multiply you, so too will HaShem rejoice concerning you to make you perish and to destroy you. And you will surely be removed from the land to which you are being brought to inherit it. (64) And HaShem will disperse you amongst all of the nations, from the edge of the world to the edge of the world and there you will worship foreign gods of wood and stone which you didn't know, neither you nor your fathers. (65) AND AMONG THOSE NATIONS, YOU WILL FIND NO PEACE, NOR WILL YOU FIND REST FOR THE HEEL OF YOUR FOOT. And*

*HaShem will give you there a trembling heart, and*
*failing of eyes, and languishing of the soul.*

Of course, our wandering was not usually our own fault. There have been no less than 109 countries[89] from which the Jews have been expelled since the Roman destruction of the Temple in Jerusalem. There is no other nation in recorded history to have survived any such similar treatment. In truth, there isn't even one that can claim to have survived half, a third, a quarter or even 1/100th similar treatment.

In addition to the expulsions, just imagine the state of the Jews when they were brought at the point of the sword to the farthest reaches of the world! Their national religious base was destroyed. Their homeland was destroyed. Their brothers were spread to the far corners of the earth and the vast majority of them were sold into slavery. What hope was there for their future, both as a people and a religion?

None!

Yet despite all of that, we persevered. Everywhere that the Jews settled they remained for the most part, separate and different. They clung with all of their might to their great and holy Torah

---

89 For a nice list see http://www.biblebelievers.org.au/expelled.htmhttp://www.biblebelievers.org.au/expelled.htm or http://www.eretzyisroel.org/~jkatz/expulsions.html

and tried their utmost to live their lives as prescribed within its pages.

But the life of a Jew was not without trial and tribulation. Our numbers and the strength of our faith were tested numerous times. The rise and fall of Jewish observance may have changed with the times and with the attitudes of our gentile neighbors, based on their friendliness or ferocity, throughout history. Yet despite it all, we are still a strong and vibrant people today.

As recently as the turn of the 20th century many people were convinced that we Jews – finally – were at the end of our rope. Our structure as a people and as a religious entity was weak, and "Orthodox" Jews were few in number. This was the result of both the enlightenment/reform movements and the holocaust. On the one hand the enlightenment wreaked havoc with Jewish adherence to the laws of the holy Torah, and on the other hand, the holocaust resulted in the decimation of most of religious Jewry in Europe. Because of these factors at the beginning of the 20th century, many people were sure that Judaism and Jews were on the verge of going the way of the Do-Do Bird[90], we were on the verge of extinction.

---

90 For an example of this see https://books.google.co.il/books?id=cgMCSrDxKGAC in the introduction (page 3) describing American Judaism at the beginning of the 20th century. See also http://www.simpletoremember.com/articles/a/jewish_life_in_america/

But Judaism didn't die! Instead, it grew and got stronger and revitalized. Today the infrastructure of Jewish religious life is incredible! *Kashrus*, (permitted foods), available almost nation (if not world)-wide, Jewish schools and *yeshivas*, (places of actual "higher learning"), all over the world, Orthodox *shuls*, (Yiddish for "Temple"), in every city!

Yes, my friends, despite all of our expulsions and wanderings, despite the fact that we were a small and weak minority among a majority of non-Jews, that we were broken both nationally and otherwise – the Jews are still here today! …But that's not all!

## **Hate the Sin – not the Sinner**

Despite the truth of the above, it would seem, from a quick perusal of Jewish history that we have been confused with the sin, which one should hate[91]! There truly is no real way to gauge the true extent of the hatred that the non-Jewish world has shown towards the Jewish people over the centuries.

To quote Tom Lehrer in one of his songs[92]:

---

91 Of course, this is in-sync with Christian theology which holds that the Jews are the spawn of Satan and are thus like sin itself!

92 http://www.sing365.com/music/lyric.nsf/National-Brotherhood-Week-lyrics-Tom-Lehrer/625DBDA1F04F231148256A7D0025A2FC

*Oh,      the      Protestants      hate      the      Catholics,*

*And     the     Catholics     hate     the     Protestants,*

*And     the     Hindus     hate     the     Muslims,*

*And everybody hates the Jews.*

This concept of Jew hatred is included in the Torah verses previously quoted which stated that we would never find a place to rest amongst all of the nations where we were dispersed.

*This print shows an attack on Jews in Frankfurt am Main, Germany, in 1614. In those days Jews had to wear a yellow ring on their clothes.*

Suffice it to say that several tens, if not hundreds, of millions of Jews, have been persecuted and massacred over the past 2000 years[93]. To give us an idea as to the ramifications of said persecution, sociologists say that 2000 years ago there were two million Chinese in the world and that there were also two million Jews in the world. How many Chinese are there in the world today? About 1.5 billion. How many Jews? 16 million…

There is no rational explanation as to why the Jews were singled out to be so despised by all of the other nations. Regardless of religion, race, language or any other demographic, the Jews were – and ARE – hated. Hated WITH a passion. (Many times, with the passion of Christ…)

*Of all the extreme fanaticism that plays havoc in man's nature, there is none as irrational as anti-Semitism. The Jews cannot vindicate themselves in the eyes of these fanatics. If the Jews are rich, they are victims of theft and extortion. If they are poor, they are victims of ridicule. If they take sides in a war, it is because they wish to gain advantage from the spilling of non-Jewish blood. If they espouse peace, it is because they are scared and anxious by nature or traitors to their country. If the Jew dwells in a*

93 This is a poor estimate of the extent of the persecution, because there truly is no way to put an actual number on the extent of the destruction. The Holocaust, in which 6 million of our brothers were lost, is only the most recent tragedy. It could very well be that many more lives than that were lost during the times of the Roman occupation of Israel. For a partial list of the Roman and Christian persecution of the Jews over the past 2000 years CE take a look at this site    http://www.religioustolerance.org/jud_pers2.htm, http://www.religioustolerance.org/jud_pers3.htm and http://www.religioustolerance.org/jud_pers4.htm. This site also does not take into account the persecution of Jews under Sephardic/Islamic lands as well.

*foreign land, he is persecuted and expelled. If he wishes to return to his own land, he is prevented from doing so.* George Lloyd, 1923

Rich or poor, fat or thin, religious or not, capitalist or socialist, integrated into or separated from non-Jewish society – every nation found their "calling" to hate the Jews. Even the presence or lack of presence of a Jewish population does not affect the antisemitism factor. This is evident in the antisemitism of Ethiopia and Japan, which flourishes despite the incredibly small number of Jews in either place[94].

Only we Jews know the secret behind antisemitism. Its source is Sinai. Our sages tell us in the Midrash on Exodus that one of the reasons that the mountain upon which the Torah was given is called "*Sinai*" is because on it "*Sinah*" (hatred) came down to the world.

It is the Jewish Torah and the Jewish destiny that is the source of antisemitism. It's one more notch in the uniqueness of the Jewish people in the world. …But this, too, is not all!

## A Sheep Among 70 Wolves

94 For an interesting article on the topic of antisemitism see http://www.aish.com/sem/wtj/82875402.html?s=mpw

Our sages in the Midrash compare Jewish survival among the nations to the survival of a lone sheep among 70 wolves (or Daniel in the lion's den?). Just as it is clear that for one sheep to walk out unscathed from amongst a pack of hungry wolves would be a miracle – so too the fact that the Jews have survived until this day as a vibrant living nation, is a testimony to the miracle that is the Jewish people.

As we read and say every year during the Passover Seder

> *"For in every generation there are those who rise up against us to destroy us, and the Holy One, blessed be He, saves us from their hands."*

How many nations have risen against us over the millennia? Let's consider:

Egyptian Empire,

Chaldean Empire,

Babylonian Empire,

Greek Empire,

Roman Empire,

Byzantine Empire,

Spanish Empire,

Ottoman Turkish Empire,

British Empire,

Austro-Hungarian Empire,

German Empire,

French Empire,

Russian Empire,

Soviet Empire,

Nazi Empire

But that isn't quite the end of it. OH no! The above list only enumerates the countries that have waged war against Jews as an agenda. In addition to the above, the Jewish people were hated and killed throughout history by our various neighbors as well.

The result was always the same, whether the antagonism came from the Christian church bringing the masses to a frenzy over such claims as the blood libels[95] throughout Europe, or whether it was due to the Christian theology that the Jews – knowingly and with premonition – killed "J", thereby rebelling against the will of G-d and choosing evil over good. In the eyes of Christianity, we are therefore the sons of Satan. Or perhaps it's just because the

---

95 A blood libel was the accusation that Jews used the blood of a child (preferably a Christian child) as an ingredient in the baking of matzos for Passover. This is and was entirely false. Altogether, there have been about 150 recorded cases of blood libels (not to mention thousands of rumors) that resulted in the arrest and killing of Jews throughout history. Most of them occurred in the Middle-Ages. In almost every case, Jews were murdered, sometimes by a mob, sometimes following torture and a "trial". A blood libel was the accusation that Jews used the blood of a child (preferably a Christian child) as an ingredient in the baking of matzos for Passover. This is and was entirely false. Altogether, there have been about 150 recorded cases of blood libels (not to mention thousands of rumors) that resulted in the arrest and killing of Jews throughout history. Most of them occurred in the Middle-Ages. In almost every case, Jews were murdered, sometimes by a mob, sometimes following torture and a "trial".

Bubonic plague broke out and the best scapegoats were the Jews. (It was claimed that we were poisoning the wells[96]).

Moslems were also no exception in this regard[97].

To this day we still have plenty of antagonists which includes the entire Arab world AND the United Nations. To date, there is no nation on the face of the planet which has consumed more of the UN's time or has had more UN resolutions condemning them, than the state of Israel[98].

But that's still not all!

All of the above was prophesied in the Holy Torah explicitly in Deuteronomy 28. As it is a very long chapter, (the reader is urged to read it in depth), I will just say that it deals with what will happen to the Jewish people if we don't listen to the commandments of G-d as listed in the Torah. Here are the relevant highlights from that chapter:

> *(36) HaShem will forcibly bring you and the king that you appoint over you, to a land which neither you nor your fathers know, and there you will worship wood and stone.*

---

96 This despite the fact that Jews were also dying from the plague, (although not quite as much, due to hygienic ritual laws), and despite the fact that the Jews were drinking from the very same wells!

97For a full account see http://www.jewishvirtuallibrary.org/jsource/anti-semitism/Jews_in_Arab_lands_%28gen%29.html http://www.jewishvirtuallibrary.org/jsource/anti-semitism/Jews_in_Arab_lands_%28gen%29.html

98See http://en.wikipedia.org/wiki/List_of_the_UN_resolutions_concerning_Israel_and_Palestine for an incomplete list. See also http://www.unwatch.org/site/c.bdKKISNqEmG/b.1359197/k.6748/UN_Israel__AntiSemitism.htm

*(45) And all of these curses will come upon you, and they will chase after you and catch you until you are destroyed because you did not listen to the voice of HaShem your G-d to guard His commandments and statutes that He commanded you.*

*(62) And you will remain with a small number (of people) as opposed to being as the stars in the heavens in multitude, for you did not listen to the voice of HaShem your G-d.*

*(64) And HaShem will scatter you amongst all of the nations, from one end of the land to the other end of the land and you will worship foreign gods of wood and stone that neither you nor your fathers knew. (65) And amongst those nations you will have no calm, nor will there be a place for you in which to rest your feet…*

But even all the above still doesn't cover the special place of the Jewish people in world history.

## **The Protocols of the Elders of Zion**

To really understand this issue, consider the manifesto known as *"The Protocols of the Elders of Zion."*

"The Protocols of the Elders of Zion" or "The Protocols of the Meetings of the Learned Elders of Zion" is an anti-Semitic hoax purporting to describe a Jewish plan for global domination. It was first published in Russia in 1903. It was then translated into multiple languages and disseminated internationally in the early part of the 20th century. Henry Ford funded the printing of 500,000 copies that were distributed throughout the US in the 1920's[99].

This book, although relatively new, is really only a print form of an ancient concept that holds that it is the Jews who secretly run the world. It's truly amazing, when you think about it, that the most persecuted nation on the face of the planet should be considered said planet's decision makers and rulers! And yet... when you think about it... it makes a bit of sense! Throughout history Jews were used as emissaries, in times of good-will we served in high offices of government and in almost every country in the world we have (and still do) hold a place of prominence in the running of the world's economies. All this while being persecuted, at the very same time!

99 http://en.wikipedia.org/wiki/The_Protocols_of_the_Elders_of_Zion

Yet despite everything that was and is stacked against us, we have not only survived – we have thrived. Just as was prophesied by the Holy Torah explicitly so many thousands of years ago. Deuteronomy 30:1-5

*(1) And it will be when all of these things come upon you, the blessing and the curse that I have placed before you, and you return it to your heart among the nations to whom HaShem has dispersed you. (2) And you shall return unto HaShem, your G-d, and you shall listen to His voice, according to all that I have commanded you this day, you and your sons, with all of your hearts and with all of your souls. (3) And HaShem, your G-d, will return your remainder and will have mercy on you, and He will return and gather you from among all of the nations to whom HaShem, your G-d, has dispersed you there. (4) If your scattered ones will be (even) at the ends of the skies – from there will HaShem, your G-d, gather you and from there will He take you. (5) And HaShem, your G-d, will bring you to the land which your fathers inherited, and you will inherit it, and He will make you bountiful and multiply you more than their fathers.*

Not only will we survive as a people, that's a given, but also as a religion we will survive. This despite the fact that we, ourselves, may not have been such great adherents to its principles. We will ignore them and go to the polar extreme, we have even worshiped idols, but eventually, we will come back. If we haven't yet, says the Torah, be patient. We will.

And when we do – then it's time for the redemption from the exile to begin. More on this in a moment.

## *Everyone's Just Got to Have One!*

Although there are those who hate 'em, and there are those who love 'em – almost everyone agrees that they need 'em!

Out of the 109 countries from which the Jews were exiled all of them practically, (if not *actually* all of them), allowed the Jews back into their countries to bolster their economies! A prime example of this is England, who expelled the Jews for 350 years and yet we were invited back under the auspices of Oliver Cromwell, (while ignoring the royal edict evicting the Jews, which was still in place!), to fix England's failing economy[100]. Another prime example is the Jews who were allowed by the emperor of Japan to enter his

---

100 See http://en.wikipedia.org/wiki/Oliver_cromwell#The_Protectorate:_1653.E2.80.9358 for more on this. Although it also talks about the hopes of hastening the second coming – that was a secondary, personal goal of his.

country during World War 2 to aid their failing economy. They did this despite the fact that the Japanese were German allies. They even did it in direct defiance of the Germans orders[101]!

## *Water and Oil – don't mix!*

Jews are to be found everywhere on the globe (almost). We comprise less than 1/5th of 1% of the world's population[102] and despite this fact, there is no one nation that has had as great an impact on the world as much as the Jews have! All things considered, there is not one area of human endeavor in which the Jews have not had a profound effect: politics, finance, sciences, arts, humanities... you name it! We've been there and done that!

*"He is as prominent on the planet as any other people, and his commercial importance is extravagantly out of proportion to the smallness of his bulk. His contributions to the world's list of great names in literature, science, art, music, finance, medicine, and abstruse learning, are also way out of proportion to the weakness of his numbers.[103]"*

101 For more on this see http://www.jewishvirtuallibrary.org/jsource/Holocaust/japan.html

102 Assuming world population is 8 billion people and the Jews count at roughly 16 million worldwide so that's 16,000,000 / 8,000,000,000 = 0.002 or 1/5th of 1 percent.

103 Mark Twain in Harper's Magazine, March 1898

Jewish impact has, (and remains), so great that the 3 most prominent people to have influenced world thought during the 20th century, according to the Wall-Street Journal, were all Jews[104]. Almost 40% of all Nobel Prize winners since 1901 have been Jews and Jews have made many, many other significant contributions to mankind in virtually every way[105].

Above and beyond all of that, however, we have also had the most significant **religious-moral** impact on the world as well. Virtually all, (or, at least, the great majority of), the world's religions are based on the principals of Judaism, assuming they have not also taken our Holy Torah to call it their own!

## Jews Go Home

During the Yom Kippur war in 1973, there was an oil embargo against America. Oil prices sky-rocketed as the Arab world was punishing America for supplying Israel during this crucial war. If America had not done this, Israel might have fallen! Due to the lack of supply of oil to the USA people could sometimes wait in line for hours to fill their gas tanks.

---

104 Carl Marx, Albert Einstein and Sigmund Freud.

105 For more information concerning Jewish contribution to world society via the sciences see http://www.jinfo.org/

As a result, bumper stickers began to appear reading, "We don't want Jews! We want oil!" Antisemitism was flaring dangerously.

At this point, a gentile name William Ikon wrote the following letter to the editor of the Colorado Springs Gazette-Telegraph 1973. It was subsequently published in 250 dailies throughout America[106].

*Jews go home! Well now, this is nothing new. Never in the past have you ever taken this gentle suggestion to move on. But – heaven forbid! – suppose just this once you think that this expression of a few sick people expresses the convictions of all the people in this wonderful land of ours, and all of you start to pack your bags and leave for parts unknown!*

*Jews go home! We don't want Jews, we want oil! But before you leave, can you do me a favor? Would you leave behind your formula for the Salk vaccine with me before you leave? You wouldn't want to be so heartless as to let my children contract polio, would you? And would you please leave your knack for government and politics and persuasion and literature and your good food? And would you please*

---

106 The above is a transcript of the article read by Rabbi Tuvia Singer in one of his dynamic lectures. See his site www.outreachjudaism.org for more information.

*leave me with your secret for your desire to succeed? And please have pity on us! Please show us the secret of how to develop such geniuses as Einstein and Steinmetz and so many others who have helped us all? After all, we owe you a lot for the atomic bomb. Most of our rocket research and perhaps the fact that we are alive today! Instead, we could have been looking up from our chains and from our graves at Hitler, old but glad, driving slowly by in one of our Cadillac's having succeeded in reaching the atom bomb and not us!*

*On your way out, Jews, will you do me another favor? Will you please drop by my house and pick me up too? I'm not sure that I could live very long in a land in which you are not to be found! For if you have to leave love goes with you, democracy and morality go with you and everything that I and my buddies fought for in world war 2 goes with you. And more than that: G-D goes with you.*

*Just pull up in front of my house slow down and honk, because, so help me! I'm going with you too!*

Let me quote one of the founding fathers of the United States of America **John Adams,** who said, and I quote:

*I will insist that the Hebrews have done more to civilize men than any other nation. If I were an atheist and believed in blind eternal fate, I should still believe that fate had ordained the Jews to be the most essential instrument for civilizing the nations. If I were an atheist of the other sect, who believe or pretend to believe that all is ordered by chance, I should believe that chance had ordered the Jews to preserve and propagate to all mankind the doctrine of a supreme, intelligent, wise, almighty sovereign of the universe, which I believe to be the great essential principle of all morality, and consequently of all civilization[107].*

Yet none can say it so succinctly as the Holy Torah itself, which says in Isaiah (42:6),

*"I, the Lord, have called you in righteousness and will hold your hand and keep you. And I will establish you as a covenant of the people, for a light unto the nations."*

107 Amazon.com: Roots of American Order (9781882926992): Russell Kirk, Forrest McDonald: Books

## A Light Unto the Nations

Well, to what DO we owe this primacy? It is the conclusion of the Korean government that we owe this… to the study of the Oral Torah, the Babylonian Talmud! It is due to this conclusion that Talmud is a mandatory subject in school for South Korean children[108].

Although there certainly is much truth in this, however, most of the examples that were the impetus behind the Koreans search for even more advancement in learning, were irreligious Jews. Many of whom probably have never studied Talmud in their lives! Also, the sheer presence of Jewish students in universities boggles the mind[109]! However, this is true despite the fact that the majority of these Jewish students come from irreligious homes. Yet we are told that it's simply due to our historic adherence to Torah learning which has genetically programmed us to seek out knowledge!!?

No. It's more than that. It's because, whether we uphold the laws of the Torah or we don't, we still are Jews. Our sages, ob"m, sum this up stating "*Yisroel,* (a child of our forefather Israel), *even if he has sinned he is still* (called) Yisroel"[110].

---

108 http://www.aish.com/jw/s/South_Koreans_Learning_Talmud.html

109 See http://www.inlikeme.com/jewish-students-at-colleges-universities that lists Jewish student percentages at major universities around the US.

110 Tractate Sanhedrin 44a. It should be noted, however, that the actual status of "Jewish" is not transferred by the father. Our sages in the Oral Torah have passed down to us that Judaism is passed on via the mother. If the mother is Jewish – so is her child. If only the Father is Jewish the child is not Jewish.

There is something extraordinary about us Jews.

## *It's a Local Phone Call*

There's an old Israeli joke that goes as follows:

Once upon a time, the President of the US was on an official visit to the Vatican. While in conversation with the Pope in the Pope's offices he notices that in the office is an ornate red phone. Asking what it was, the Pope tells him that it is a direct line to G-d. "Only 10,000$ a minute," says the Pope. So, the President gets on the phone and has a short conversation with G-d that costs him only 100,000$.

On a similar trip to Israel, the President is meeting with the Chief Rabbi and notices that he, too, has an ornate red phone. Upon inquiry, he is told that this also is a direct line to G-d. "Only 10 cents a minute," he is informed. Upon hearing that he says incredulously "Why by the Pope, it cost me 10,000$ a minute"! "Here" responded the Rabbi, "it's a local call."

In truth for Jews everywhere a conversation with G-d is a local call.

I remember as a child when I was still living in the US in Atlanta, GA, my father – he should live and be well! – had opened the first walk-in emergency room in the southeast and he was in the middle of seeing patients. I was about 10 years old at the time and despite the cold weather I had decided that I was going to ride my bicycle to Toco-Hills, where the medical center was situated. I was wearing cycling gloves that didn't give much in the way of protection and during the ride my fingers got frostbitten. I was in agony. What did I do? As soon as I arrived at the center, I went crying in the waiting room – which was full – stormed into the back and demanded to see my father so that he could take care of me… which he did!

I'm sure that all the people in the waiting room, who were waiting, were genuinely upset at this upstart kid that demanded – and received – immediate attention while they were waiting around to see the doctor!

But when you are the doctor's son – it's different.

When you are The King's son – it's different as well.

The reason why we Jew's are so different from the rest of the world is that of our close relationship with The King. *"You are children of the Lord your G-d,"* says the Torah[111]. It is due to this close relationship that we Jews have with HaShem, the Creator, that our prayers are more readily answered than those of any other nation. It doesn't matter what field of endeavor you are in, nor

111 Deuteronomy 14:1

whether you are religious or not – there is no one on the face of the planet that at some time does not whisper a prayer to G-d asking for help to succeed in their endeavor. This is the reason that we Jews are so much more successful in all fields than all the other nations. It has nothing to do with brain power, nor the fact that Talmud study does, in fact, improve our minds and thinking capabilities.

## ***Going Home!***

Despite all of the above, the final issue that we as a people have been witnessed is the fulfillment of the prophecy which we have been waiting for so expectantly.

For the past 2000 years, we have been praying, daily, three times a day, for our return to the land of our fathers and to the city of Jerusalem, to the Holy Temple. Only in recent history has this begun to occur as prophesied so very long ago. As it says in Deuteronomy 5:5

> *And HaShem, your G-d, will bring you to the land which your fathers inherited, and you will inherit it, and He will make you bountiful and multiply you more than your fathers.*

Take a look at recent history, a really close look, if you dare.

Until the mid-1800's the land of Israel was a desolate land. There was only a minute Jewish presence and despite the many attempts to settle it – no one succeeded to do so. Not even the supposedly "indigenous" Palestinian people… who didn't exist at all back then! The original settlers of the land, the students of the Ba'al Shem Tov and the Gaon of Vilna[112], came not to build the land, but rather to utilize it to achieve greater holiness and closeness to G-d. Those who didn't keep the Torah, the students of Reform and Socialist Judaism, were willing to trade the land of our forefathers for the proposed country of Uganda[113]. Yet despite all this, we find that when the time came for the Jewish people to return home – it is the homeland of our forefathers that we found ourselves. Just as was prophesized by the Torah so very long ago.

We came back … and the desert began to bloom!

In the short span of some 60-odd years as of this writing we have taken a land with no agriculture and very few natural resources and turned it into one of the major agricultural and financial centers of today's world[114]. Just as the Torah prophesied so many years ago.

112 http://en.wikipedia.org/wiki/Vilna_Gaon#Influence
113 https://www.jewishvirtuallibrary.org/jsource/Zionism/Uganda.html
114 http://en.wikipedia.org/wiki/Israel#Economy

In addition, we have seen incredible growth over the past 60 years, unprecedented in Jewish history. If the statistics are correct, then today there are more Jews in the world than there ever were in history. This, too, in fulfillment of the above prophecy

*…and He will make you bountiful and multiply you more than your fathers.*

Although we have not yet witnessed the final part of the redemption, the rebuilding of the Holy Temple in Jerusalem, as we have been witness to so many of the prophecies so far, can there be any doubt as to rest?

## **In Summary:**

I cannot think of a better summary than the words of Mark Twain[115]:

*"If the statistics are right, the Jews constitute but one percent of the human race. It suggests a nebulous dim puff of star-dust lost in the blaze of the Milky Way. Properly the Jew ought hardly to be heard of, but he is heard of, has always been heard of. He is as prominent on the planet as any other people, and his commercial importance is extravagantly out of*

---

115 *"Concerning the Jews"* an essay by Mark Twain published in Harper's Magazine March 1898

*proportion to the smallness of his bulk. His contributions to the world's list of great names in literature, science, art, music, finance, medicine, and abstruse learning are also away out of proportion to the weakness of his numbers. He has made a marvelous fight in the world, in all the ages; and has done it with his hands tied behind him. He could be vain of himself and be excused for it. The Egyptian, the Babylonian, and the Persian rose, filled the planet with sound and splendor, then faded to dream-stuff and passed away; the Greek and the Roman followed and made a vast noise, and they are gone; other peoples have sprung up and held their torch high for a time, but it burned out, and they sit in twilight now or have vanished. The Jew saw them all, beat them all, and is now what he always was, exhibiting no decadence, no infirmities of age, no weakening of his parts, no slowing of his energies, no dulling of his alert and aggressive mind. All things are mortal but the Jew; all other forces pass, but he remains. What is the secret of his immortality?*

Mark, (or Samuel), I'll let you in on our carefully guarded secret! I mean, I know that it's been out in our forever best-selling book

… but our secret is G-d. He chose us as a special people, and we chose Him. He knows us and cares for us – each and every one of us – enough to tell us what is the best, and the most pleasurable way to live our lives. When you have such a close relationship with the king – is it any wonder that you have special help in all of your endeavors?

We'll come back to discuss the topic of modern prophecies in the next chapter --- stay tuned!

# Celestial Words

## *Evidence of the Divinity of the Written Torah*

A S WE STARTED OUT SAYING in the chapter entitled "*Chosen!*" the unique claim of the nation of Israel, of a Divine Torah and a Divine national history, seem to imply that G-D, in His great compassion, gives a damn (to say it bluntly)!

But it goes well beyond that.

The Torah is a divinely inspired document. Its purpose is to tell us what is expected of a Jew (or a non-Jew[116]) during his or her lifetime.

---

116 Included in the laws of the Torah are the "Noahide laws", the Torah laws that are binding on all of humanity. Even though categorically there are seven of them, (no idol worship, no speaking/swearing in the name of G-d in vain, no sexual immorality, no murder, no stealing, no eating the flesh of a live animal, and to create and maintain a judicial system) there are many other "lesser" commandments as well. If you wish to know of them – consult an Orthodox Rabbi.

This will enable each of us to live a meaningful and satisfying life in both this world and the next. Everything is covered, there is no topic left untouched. From eating cockroaches to cross-dressing, from birth to death – it's all there!

The Torah doesn't tell me "Go live your life as you see fit, just believe in Me and it's all good"! It demands of me that I limit, restrict and resist my own desires and urges for the sake of Him who created the world and gave us these commandments. I am, therefore, required to give up many of the things that *I want* for the sake of the things that *G-d wants me to do instead.* Or, as I tell my students and children, most of life is all about doing the things that I am *supposed to/have to* do, as opposed to the things that I *want to do or feel like doing.*

Therefore, if am I going to go out of my way to *kasher,* (a verb meaning "to make kosher") my kitchen, throw away my favorite cracked spoon, and yes, *even give up on the lobster*, I had better well have a *damn good reason* to do so! I had better be sure that these "commandments" are in fact, divine in nature. For only if that is the case can I feel safe in trusting the One who gave the commandments that the sacrifice is worth it. How can I know that the promise of reward for fulfilling a positive commandment is trustworthy? How can I know if the punishments which the Torah meets out for the transgression of the commandments are real? I can only know this if I can show (in addition to all of the information in the previous chapters) that the Torah is the word of G-d.

Also, the promise of eternal pleasure in the world to come versus eternal suffering in that other place also seems like a nice incentive. Reward those who do my will and punish those who don't. It's that promise of the carrot and the stick. Very compelling … assuming that this Torah actually *is* Divine! After all, anyone can make that offer concerning their religion, as there is no real way to check that out before you get there. And by then it's kind of too late to do anything about it.

So, the question we need to ask is: What should we be looking for to demonstrate to us that this actually is a divine document? I propose that we would need to show the following two things: a> that the information within was not written by a human, as it doesn't follow human logic or capacity; and b> that it would contain information which could seemingly only have been written by a Divine being, i.e. G-D.

## *<u>Is it Live, (G-D), or is it Memorex?</u>*

This takes us back a little bit into the twilight zone of those academics who think that the Torah was given at a late period of Jewish development and written by a sagacious committee.

The question is of course if it *had been drafted* by a human what would be an indicator that a person wrote it? If we presume that the Torah is a human document and that the mitzvos are, therefore, also contrived by human beings, what would be the way that a normal human being would write them? If I find that the commandments are written contrary to human contrivances, then it would seem to show that it actually *wasn't* written by a human. Let's look at a few examples so we can see what I am talking about:

## ***The Problem of the Three Festivals***

The Torah tells us in several places that there are three times a year during which a person is commanded to drop what he is doing and travel the length and breadth of the country, to *shlep*, (Yiddish for "drag"), himself to Jerusalem and to the Holy Temple which stood there.

It's a nice idea. Let's say it was presented to the "Torah Committee" (of Jewish Presidents) as a possible addition to the up and coming "torah". The idea certainly has merits to it and potentially there is a lot to work with philosophically in the formation of this "*mitzvah*".

So here we are at the $N^{th}$ meeting of the Pentateuch committee. There's Moe, Larry, Curly, Shemp, and you. We're having a brainstorming session looking at how to formulate this "mitzvah" of our home-grown "torah." All of a sudden, Curly throws out the following idea. "I know Moe! Let's tell everybody that three times a year all of the men should drop what they are doing and come to the Temple, in Jerusalem." Moe gives him that surly Moe look and says "Hey, you knucklehead. That's a great idea. I'm glad I thought of it! Just think of the National unity it will bring. Three times a year!", (the others chime in "Three times a year!), "THREE times a year", says Moe. "THREE

TIMES A YEAR!" the others then repeat. "WAIT A MINUTE!" says Moe, "there's a problem here!"

(What do YOU think the problem is?)

"If we're going to have all the men go up to Jerusalem," said Moe, "then who's going to watch the women-folk, and the children-folk, and the animal-folk"? "Oooh..." say the others in unison.

(How would YOU solve the dilemma?)

"MOE! MOE!" said Larry. "I have a great idea! How about we write the following: Three times a year, ("three times a year," whispers Curly and was immediately bopped on the head by Moe), you shall go up to the Holy Mount. And if you should say to yourself "HMM! What about the women-folk, and the children-folk... (Everybody leans in and listens intently) ... don't worry! I'll take care of it!", "How's that sound?"

The other three look at each other slowly...

...and then Moe proceeds to bop Larry on the head and pull out some of his hair saying "You Knucklehead! YOU are going to be in Jerusalem too! How are you going to do something about it? The men will leave the borders empty, and they'll come back to Islama-Obama-stan!"

How can YOU make a promise that you can't keep?"

And yet, the Torah, in Exodus, in the weekly portion of Ki Teytzey[117], says just that! If you ask, "what about the borders?" "WHAT about our enemies?" ... "Don't worry," says G-D, "during the time that

---

117 Exodus chapter 34 verse 23-24. "Three times a year all of your males must see the face of the Lord, HaShem, the G-d of Israel. For I will remove the foreign nations from in front of you, and I will expand your borders and no man will covet your land when you go up to see the face of HaShem, your G-d, three times a year".

you are going to go to Jerusalem your enemies will be too busy to have time to bother with your land. I'll take care of it!"

If this were a man-made promise, how long would it take the people to reject it, if every time they tried to keep it they had to fight their way back home?

Only if G-D is the author of this promise does it carry the weight to rely on it!

## ***The Sabbatical Year***

In the Torah reading of *Behar*, in Leviticus, the Torah commands us that once every seven years we must stop all agricultural work of the land. There is to be no plowing, no reaping, and no sowing... no groundwork whatsoever. Agriculture in Israel would come to a complete halt.

If you think about it, this makes a lot of sense. After all, land needs to lie fallow every so often to replenish the nutrients in the soil. It also allows for all the people who are otherwise busy working for their daily bread, to finally take some time to focus on growing educationally and spiritually. This reasoning regarding the sabbatical year made so much sense in fact, that universities around the world adopted the practice for their faculties. Their teachers are offered a "sabbatical" year once every seven years to refresh themselves, learn something new, or catch up on all that has been happening in their respective fields. So too the Jews of Israel which was mainly an agricultural society put aside their work every seven years in order to concentrate on spiritual rejuvenation.

So, after offering this idea, Larry turned to Moe and said "Hey now! Just one minute here! Whose leg are you trying to pull? How are we going to pull that one off?"

(What do YOU think? How could we make this idea work?)

Shemp turned to everyone and said "Everybody! I've got it! I've got it! Ooh! Ooh! I've got it!" and everyone turned to him and said "Tell us! What have you got?" Shemp looked at them and said "Why do it in a haphazard way? Why shouldn't we have the entire people of Israel keep this "commandment" all at the same time!? It will read like this, 'Once every seven years everyone in the whole country should stop working their fields all at once'! Isn't that a fantastic idea? Just think of all the togetherness! National unity achieved"!

"So," said Moe, "YOU want to tell me that the entire people of Israel – all together and at the same time – should stop farming the earth for food and go sit and learn?" "That's right Moe. That's what I said!". "Shemp," said Moe, "just what do you think the people ARE GOING TO EAT during that year"? "That's easy Moe!" said Shemp, "They'll eat fur coats!" "GED'OUDA HERE!"

(What do YOU think should be done?)

"Ooh! Ooh! I've got it! I've got it!" said Larry. "Howzabout we write this 'Don't worry! If you plan on keeping the sabbatical year, I'll give you a double portion... no! A *triple* portion on the sixth year! AND", continued Larry, "not only that! Let's make it truly big-time. I command you to work the land for six straight years, with the intention to rest on the seventh year. If you can do that *then* you will get the triple portion! Well, what do you think"?

Moe then put his right hand on Larry's left shoulder and his left hand on Shemp's right shoulder and said, "A couple of wise-guys, eh?" and proceeded to knock their heads together to the sound of colliding coconuts. "What? How can we possibly promise the people to give each of them a triple portion? What are you, the *Shmitta* fairy? Do *you* have a stash somewhere we don't know about? Even if you do, who says that your kids will want to follow through with your generosity? SO, when the people see consistently that their triple portion just isn't coming – assuming they survive the first sabbatical year – then they just won't continue keeping it! Not only that, but you're going to tell them that after six straight years of working the fields, when the fields are at their weakest, THAT'S WHEN THEY ARE GOING TO PRODUCE A TRIPLE PORTION?! Are you insane?"

What would a human mind suggest making this idea work? A human mind would suggest saving up during the 6 years so that you have what to eat during the seventh!

But which way did the Torah go? The opposite way. The way of Shemp[118].

There is no humanly contrived solution to the issue. Only someone with the Authority to back up such a promise would make it at the risk of destroying His "Torah"'s validity.

---

118 Leviticus (25:20-21) *"And if you say what shall we eat in the seventh year? Behold! If we shall not plant and not gather our produce? And I shall command My blessing unto you in the sixth (year) and the produce that is grown shall be for the three years"*.

## *The Adulterous Woman*

Family, family, family. We all know just how important family is! However, sometimes there are problems, serious problems, concerning the relationship between husband and wife.

As severe a problem as it is when a husband is unfaithful, the Torah says that it is far graver when the unfaithful one is the wife[119]. The reason for this is quite simple. For families to remain pure, we must know, as best we can, the identity of the baby's father. Just by looking we most certainly know who the mother is. More difficult than certain knowledge of a wife's adultery is a situation where it is not known one way or another whether she was unfaithful. There might be suspicions about it, but no certain evidence. What do we do then?

In the world at large there exist only two options: either you have to find a way to live with it... or you don't.

But the Torah tells us an exciting, innovative new way to solve the matter! No video feed, no DNA testing, no hiring of expensive private-eyes[120]! NO! There is a better option: holy water.

It's not like in the vampire movies when holy water is thrown on the unfaithful wife, and she burns at its touch. Yet it's not that far off, either! It wouldn't surprise me if the idea that a vampire burns and dies from

---

119 There are some people who may consider this statement sexist. That is their prerogative. The Torah, however, looks at things in a different way then we, of the modern world, view it. To explain why this is, in fact, not sexist is beyond the scope of this book. WH"h one of the future volumes planned is the emunah perspective on marriage and I hope to deal with this issue and others like it there. Please be patient.

120 Although we would accept these as options as well if they were available. But the Torah is talking about a time when they are not.

holy water was inspired by the holy water of the un-holy *sotah* (unfaithful wife).

The Torah tells us that a woman sets herself up for a fall in this area by first behaving in a way that causes her husband to suspect her around a particular man. If her husband then sternly warns her, not to be caught together with this individual and she takes it one step further by going into a secluded place with him, she then, officially, becomes a *sotah*.

So how do we solve the dilemma into which the wife has placed us? How are we supposed to know if she is guilty of being unfaithful to her husband? If she has been unfaithful, she then forfeits her husband's financial obligations to her and is forced into a divorce. However, if she is innocent, she can remain married to her husband and receive all the positive benefits of Jewish marriage. How do we know what to do?

The Torah states in *Parshas Naso* (Numbers, chapter 5) that this is not a problem. Not only can all sorts of dirt and grime be removed with a little bit of water! So, too, can the dilemma of the *sotah*. All it takes is the following. The husband must take his wife to the Beis HaMikdash in Jerusalem, the holiest place in the world. Here is the procedure for dealing with the sotah:

Offerings are brought as sacrifices. The portion of the Torah dealing with the issue of the *sotah* is written onto parchment and then erased into the waters which the *Cohen* draws from the *kiyor* (the water spout in the Beis HaMikdash). It is then mixed with another ingredient. Then the woman in question proceeds to drink the *marrah* waters that the Cohen makes. These waters then solve the problem in the following way.

If she really *did* have an illicit relationship with a man other than her husband, she then proceeds to die in a very difficult and painful way, not all that different than the reaction of the vampires to holy water. She sort of starts to melt! If, on the other hand, she did not have an illicit relationship with another man then she comes away scot-free, no harm done. Not only that but she is promised to afterward give birth to a child in witness of her purity. This is true regardless of her fertility levels, and our sages, ob"m, say that the birth will be qualitatively easy as well.

Now, this procedure was performed for hundreds of years, so long as the people of Israel were on a spiritual level to deserve it. Clearly, we are talking about miraculous circumstances here, and if it didn't work... no... if it *never* worked, then it would have been a clear contradiction as to the veracity of the Torah!

Just imagine if every single man who brought his wife to the Mikdash came away with the same result... nothing. What do you think that the reaction to this mitzvah would be? But, let's say that I can solve that by manipulating the outcome. I have a suggestion. Get the Cohanim on-board and make sure that they only poison the water for only *some* of the women[121]. At least that way sometimes the women would live and sometimes they would not. No pattern could be discerned either. Even by women who were *clearly* righteous women or those who clearly were... not... human nature would almost certainly kick-in and allow for plenty

---

121 I'm not entirely sure how they would be able to produce the results described by the Torah there, however, I'm not an expert concerning poisons.

of gossip to explain away the "apparent" contradiction of the strange outcomes.

However, there is one thing that is problematic. What would happen if some/most of the women who came away after this, having experienced no ill effects, didn't get pregnant and give birth? Don't you think that someone, eventually, would have noticed? Eventually, the fraud would have been discovered[122]! Even today, with the advancement of medical technology, there is no (sane) doctor who can promise that his/her medical interventions will always result in pregnancy. Doctors are unable to make this promise even if they have some technical knowledge of how to do it. Our sages, ob"m, in Tractate *Ta'anit*, tell us that pregnancy is one of the three "keys" that forever remain in the hands of HaShem.

Would a group of men take it upon themselves to promise something like this, something which is clearly beyond their ability to make happen? You be the judge...

## **_Alive and Well, in THIS World_**

The point being made here is clear. If a human being (or beings) were the author(s) of the document, either it wouldn't have made any promises that have any real-world consequences or measurable rewards, or it would have made only suggestions or promises that could be easily

---

[122] In all likelihood, the Cohanim's "secret" also would have been leaked out, like all secrets eventually do.

awarded by practical human contrivances. Why is that, you ask? I'm glad that you asked that. It's because a promise of an outcome in this world creates expectations and if experience shows that the expected/promised result is not the norm, then what good is the promise and how reliable is He who promised it? The answer is that both the promise and promiser are worthless!

Yet history shows us conclusively that the Jewish people have been living this religion for thousands of years and we are still alive, kicking, and holding on to our ancient Torah way of life.

If we were a mentally challenged nation (colloquially called "retarded" or "developmentally disabled") then this wouldn't be true. After all, if we were mentally challenged, we couldn't be blamed for doing things without thought. But we're not. We are, and always have been, one of the most deeply thinking nations on the planet. Relative to the rest of the world we are not only the poster-child for "normal"[123] but also among the most logical, cutting-edge science peoples on the face of the planet[124].

As all cults know, if you want to make a religion with no room for logical scrutiny whatsoever, (once you have already hooked your audience, of course), then don't make promises which will be rewarded

---

123 After all, there are probably more Jewish mental health professionals worldwide than there are non-Jewish ones.

124 For more on this topic read the chapter "Jewel Among the Sands"

in THIS world. Promise results ONLY in the next world and you're good to go[125]!

## *The Devil is in the Details*

In addition to all of the above information, the Torah is also full of details about the world, about life and about history. These are facts that only The Director could have known, and, as the saying goes, "the Devil is in the details." Considering that the information contained in the Torah spans millennia[126], it stands to reason that if all of it was written by a human individual or a committee then at some point in time it would come apart. The chances of accurately portraying the styles, names, clothing, customs and various other details of times long-gone become more and more unlikely. If I were to try to describe what happened at the turn of the last century the chances of my getting the information right is pretty slim. The only reason that I might be able to do so is due to the copious amounts of information, both written and photographed, which are at my disposal. But when there is no such mass

125 This is based on "Applewhite Theory", coined by Rabbi Lawrence Kellerman, which was created to explain the phenomenon of the cult "Heaven's Gate" from the early 90's. "Heaven's Gate" was a cult whose members all committed suicide at the behest of the cult's leader, Marshall Applewhite. They did this even though none of the members had past history of mental illness and that many of them were accomplished academically and financially. Researchers therefore concluded (the basis for the theory) that if you make a promise to someone about reward in another place/life/etc., for which there is no means of measuring it's results in the here-and-now, people are more prone to accept it. As P.T. Barnum famously said, "A sucker is born every minute". The reason being that there is then no means of falsification, which is the basis of all hypotheses and theory, and because we human beings tend to be naturally trusting.

126 From Adam to the entry into the land of Canaan spans around 2800 years. From Joshua to the end of the bible spans another 620 years (140 until the building of the first Mikdash, 410 years that it stood (=550) and another 70 years of the Babylonian exile =620 years for a grand total of 3420 years of the entire Bible up to, but not including, the second Temple period.

information then I won't have a clue. SO, if we find that the details transmitted in the Torah actually sync with the data... it would seem it's because the Author really knew what He was talking about! Let's take one such precise example out of the many:

## **_Egypt_**

Regarding Egypt, the Torah supplies us with many details concerning large facets of Egyptian society. Many of these details have been recently confirmed by archaeology. Examples include: the price of a slave, (Joseph was sold for 20 *shequels* of silver), camel domestication, types of spices traded, typical Egyptian names, standard slave titles, the existence of prisons, the Egyptian style of facial hair, symbols indicating one's level of office, (more on this in a moment), what ancient Egyptian bricks were made of[127] and many other details[128].

Let's expand on a few of these details:

## **_The Issue of Domesticated Camels._**

127 Just google egyptian+brick+making from the book Archeology and Bible History or http://www.reshafim.org.il/ad/egypt/building/ look at "building materials – mud".

128 See http://www.aish.com/ci/sam/48967121.html an article entitled Egyptology in the Torah for a list of some 17 details mentioned in the Torah which have been ratified by archaeological findings.

When Joseph was brought down to Egypt, the Torah tells us that he was brought down using a camel caravan[129]. Until recently historians contested this, claiming that camel domestication didn't exist during that period of time[130]. This "rebuttal" continued... until irrefutable proof was found showing that camels were domesticated during this time period[131].

Proofs such as bone and dung remains, portraits, paintings[132] and wall carvings of people riding camels, orders of food to be brought for camels[133] and much more that have been found by archeologists.

In the same passage which describes Joseph's sale, other items are mentioned that were also "for sale" and were being brought down to Egypt as well.[134] There are those people, wise in their own eyes, who want to claim that trade between other nations and Egypt is only recorded in the 7th-8th centuries BCE. That is false. There are many "documented" accounts of trade between Egypt and foreign nations as early as 2000 BCE and even earlier.

---

129 Genesis 37:25-29

130 They would say this, of course, based on eyewitness testimony and irrefutable proof which showed conclusively that camels were not domesticated at this point in time... EXCEPT THEY DON'T HAVE ANY! It's just another case of "lack of evidence" being used as a proof of the lack of existence of something. As our sages, ob"m, say "If you haven't found anything – that's a proof of nothing".

131 See, for example, http://wiki.answers.com/Q/When_was_the_Camel_domesticated_and_does_it_agree_with_the_chronology_of_the_Bible. Compare this to the article at http://daatemet.org.il/articles/article.cfm?article_id=10 which uses outdated and/or confusing evidence to "disprove" this information from the Torah. In any case, it's nothing new.

132 Sandra L Olsen, PhD from the Museum of Natural History, Pittsburgh states that although there is little detail available on the history of domestication, a ' likely origin for camel domestication is Iran or Turkmenistan, where their images turn up painted on pottery between 5000 and 4500 years ago and in ceramic wagon models dating between 4500 and 3600 years ago (Bulliet 1990). See also Heide, K.M. 2010. "The Domestication of the Camel: Biological, Archaeological and Inscriptional Evidence from Mesopotamia, Egypt, Israel and Arabia, and Literary Evidence from the Hebrew Bible." Ugarit-Forschungen 42 (2010): 331-384. See also http://www.biblearchaeology.org/post/2014/02/17/The-Date-of-Camel-Domestication-in-the-Ancient-Near-East.aspx#Article

133 See R. Bulliet, The Camel and the Wheel, Cambridge Mass. 1975, p. 56

134 Genesis 37:25

*Spices such as cinnamon, cassia, cardamom, ginger, and turmeric were known, and used for commerce, in the Eastern World well into antiquity[135]. These spices found their way into the Middle East before the beginning of the Common Era, where the true sources of these spices were withheld by the traders and associated with fantastic tales[136].*

*If we could wander the streets of the workers' villages near Giza in Egypt some 4600 years ago, we would find the intense aroma of spices from Asia as strong then as they are today. Spices were used in antiquity to give strength to the builders of the pyramids, and the draw of the spice markets and perfume shops a mere stone's throw from those same pyramids today gives strength to modern-day explorers weary of the kitsch dealers and souvenir hawkers in the tourist traps. Stroll through one of these spice districts and be prepared for an assault on your senses as the smells of nutmeg and cloves from Indonesia mix with cinnamon from China and frankincense from Arabia – just as they did in the time of the pharaohs.*

135 What does it mean "antiquity" and "found its way to the middle east before the common era"? Let's look at cinnamon as an example: Cinnamon has been known from remote antiquity. It was imported to Egypt as early as 2000 BCE, but those who report that it had come from China confuse it with cassia. http://en.wikipedia.org/wiki/Cinnamon
136 http://en.wikipedia.org/wiki/Spice_trade#Arab_trade_and_Medieval_Europe

> *Hieroglyphics from Egyptian tombs and temples as far back as 5500 years tell of the burning of incense and sweet herbs for religious and mystical rituals, with cedars and aromatics being offered up to the gods and goddesses to ensure the fertility of the land[137].*

The existence of prisons as a form of punishment[138] during a time when this was unheard of elsewhere, is also recorded in the Torah regarding Egypt.

Investiture of office: In Europe, during the Middle Ages, for example, the passing of a signet ring was a sign of appointment. In Egypt, a similar scheme was employed, as the Torah tells us (Genesis 41:42) "*And Pharaoh took off his ring from his hand, and put it upon Joseph's hand, and arrayed him in garments of fine linen, and put a gold collar about his neck.*" A vizier who was given the pharaoh's signet ring was known officially as "The Royal Seal Bearer." Wearing garments of fine linen, so thin as to be semi-transparent, seems to have been a sign of royalty and great prestige in ancient Egypt. Princes, princesses, and members of their household are often depicted wearing semi-transparent linen clothing. The placement of a gold collar around the neck is an ancient and unique Egyptian custom called "the conferment of the Gold of Praise."

---

137 http://www.classics.uwaterloo.ca/labyrinth_old/issue83/83mundigler.htm
138 Genesis 40 and 41

In addition to all of the above information, there are also records of Egypt having traded with a land known as "Punt." It is unknown today exactly where this land is. However, its existence is recorded in many places in the Torah, where it is called ‏פוט,‏ (*Phut*)[139].

## *People and Places Mentioned in the Torah and Discovered by Archaeology*

There is much contention among historians about both individuals and dates written about in the Torah. However, a tremendous number of archaeological findings testify as to the accuracy of what *is* written in the Torah. The list is too long to bring within the scope of this document. Please look at appendix I for a fairly comprehensive record of archaeological findings concerning people, places, and events described throughout the three parts of the Written Torah.

Bottom line: the more excavation that is done, the more archaeological findings are found that verify the information in the Torah.

## *Those in the Know*

---

139 The earliest mention in the Torah is Genesis 10:6 as Phut was one of the sons of Ham, the brother of Mitzrayim (Egypt). Afterwards Phut is mentioned numerous times in the Bible, see Ezekiel 27:10 for example.

Outside of the details mentioned above, there is information given, which could not have been written based on the knowledge of the time. Remember: according to all "scholarly" opinions, which don't take into account the Jewish tradition of Torah "from Sinai," the Torah is *at the very least* 2500 years old.[140] At that time most of the globe was unknown. The seas were almost entirely unexplored, and the physical sciences were not measured, nor truly understood. In short: we would expect a human-written document from that era to be rather unreliable as far as the information contained within.

However, with regard to Torah... this is not the case.

## **_Genesis_**

In the previous volume, in the chapter entitled *In the Beginning*, I enumerated a list of 20 things explicitly detailed in the Torah, from Genesis up to day 4. Science has only recently come to similar conclusions regarding some of these things. In other areas, they have not yet caught up. I will not re-iterate that chapter now, but look at it again as it is pertinent to the subject at hand. A few examples, however:

- The relationship between time and mass

---

140 By the end of the 19th century the scholarly consensus was that the Pentateuch was the work of many authors writing from 1000 BCE (the time of David) to 500 BCE (the time of Ezra) and redacted c.450. http://en.wikipedia.org/wiki/The_Bible_and_history

- The Big Bang and why the universal expansion slowed down

- The source of the liquid water on planet earth

- The order of plant genesis on the planet

In addition, the information detailed in days 5 and 6 in Genesis are also pertinent to this discussion and can be found in the article entitled *Genesis: Days 5 and on*[141]. There I compare the information described in the Torah as opposed to the archaeological findings and how they match up.

## *The Flood*

In my article entitled *Noah, Tectonics, and Continental Drift*[142] I discuss the information provided by the Torah concerning the flood and its mechanics. For example,

- The reason why the earth is the only planet known to have plate tectonics.

---

141 Still a work in progress and not yet available. IY"H I will find the time to finish it and add it as an addendum on my blog www.rabbibz.com

142 It can be found on my blog at https://rabbibz.com/2017/11/03/noah-tectonics-and-continental-drift-the-story-of-global-flooding-as-described-in-the-torah-as-compared-to-the-scientific-data/

- The existence of underground oceans of water, one of which was recently found under East Asia.

- Also, the existence of land masses "under the sky" … which were not connected to, nor visible from, the known lands at the time that the Torah was written. Take a look at the article for more detail concerning this issue.

## **Kosher, Kosher, Kosher**

The prime example of intimate knowledge of the unknown world in the Written Torah, (concerning the Divinity of the Oral Torah we'll look at in a different chapter), is the issue of the *Kashrus* (Permissibility) of edible animals. The Torah discusses this issue twice: once in Leviticus and again in Deuteronomy.

The bottom line: this very ancient document tells us that for an animal to be considered a Kosher and therefore an edible animal, it must have the following three conditions:

1. It must be alive, (unless you feel that you might die soon if you don't eat right now, in which case we don't care about any of these clauses. We are not discussing this extreme case).

2. It must have hooves, which are split into two distinct parts from one side of the hoof to the other. And lastly:

3. It must regurgitate its food as part of the digestive process. This is required by herbivores to break up the components of the vegetation that they eat.

.Split hooves of the Roe Deer
Yes, it's kosher

One more condition that is required for the animal to maintain its kosher status is that it also has to be slaughtered according to the laws of the Oral Torah. (More on this in the next chapter).

## Of Things that are Split

Practically speaking, how can I utilize this information? Do I have to be an expert in zoology and animal physiology so that I can know what is permissible to eat? Let's say I (*chas ve-shalom!*) get lost in the desert along with my *shechita* (slaughter) knife and I happen upon an animal? What do I do? Sing "Hava Nagila, now you're Kosher" and eat it? Obviously not! The first thing to do is to look at its legs: does it have hooves and are they split? If no, well, then I guess I'll just have to look elsewhere. However, if it does have split hooves as described above – then what? Next, you take a look at its face. Let's say that you see that it looks something like a cross between a baboon and an alligator. Is that enough to pronounce it non-kosher? No. The Torah never said that facial hair is a factor, nor is the length of its snout. So, am I supposed to say "Listen, whatever you are, can you show me a little regurgitation, please?" (and hope that it comes out in the wash later). Nope. No need to go that far.

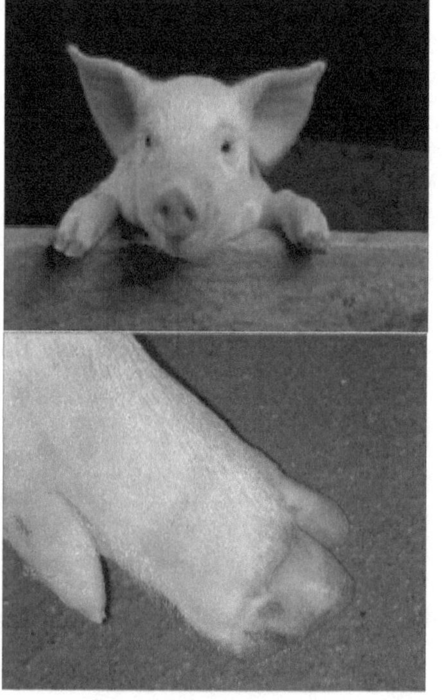

All one has to do is... make sure that it doesn't look like a pig! (See picture) Why is that? Because the Torah, in addition to giving the above criteria, also tells us that there are only a handful of creatures that present an exception to the above rules. They are exceptions in that they possess only one of the two physical signs of *kashrus*. (Those that lack both are very numerous).

There are only one species of animal that is exceptional even among the exceptions, as it is the only type of animal that has split hooves and doesn't chew its cud and its name is "Pig" (*cha'zir* in Hebrew)[143].

---

143 It should be clear to the reader that the reason why these are the only exceptions to the aforementioned rules of split hooves + cud is based on two explicit statements in the Torah. First of all, the words זה and ,זאת which are used throughout these chapters of the Torah.

Considering that most of the world had yet to be explored, and most lands had not yet been discovered, it would have been extremely foolhardy to make such a specific claim unless it was a sure thing. The emphatic statement that the pig is the only species in the world with split hooves that do not chew its cud could only be made by "the One" who knew for sure that this would always be so. The Talmud (Oral Torah) in Tractate *Chullin* on page 60b, in regard to this issue, makes the following statement:

> *Was Moses a hunter or an archer? This is to answer*
> *those who say that the Torah isn't from heaven.*

Today humanity has scoured a significant amount of the entire globe from one end to the other, discovered thousands of new species which were unheard of in the ancient world, and yet in all of the land animals discovered, no one has found another type of animal which has split hooves and doesn't chew its cud except for the pig! Included in "pig" is the entire species: pigs, hogs, boars and the like. NOT included in this species is the hippopotamus, even though it has some characteristics which are pig-like. Those characteristics do not make it a pig, especially

These words translate into English as "this" and "that". "This (*zeh*) you should eat" and "That (*zos*) you should not eat". These words are used to specify, not to generalize. If I were to say to you "Don't eat this" without any point of reference how could you possibly understand to what I am referring? The only way to understand my statement is if it's something clearly visible and I am pointing at it with my finger! Jewish tradition teaches us that when Moses was describing to the people what was or was not permissible to eat, he also had at his disposal an example of each to show them, with which G-D provided him. In addition, there is the fact that these "exceptions to the rule" are totally unnecessary for the Torah to have detailed as they are clearly not "in the rule". Our sages therefore say that the only reason that G-D mentioned them was to show us that the Torah is truly from Heaven.

in light of the fact that they *do not* have split hooves. (See picture).

## *It Makes Me Regurgitate*

There are four other animals mentioned in the verse which are the polar opposite of the pig in that they chew their cud but do not have the criteria of split hooves. These animals are the camel, the *Shafan,* the *Arneves* and the *Shesua,* (For more information on these animals see the article entitled *Waskawy Wabbit!*[144]).

*Cow hooves*

Here's a relevant question: Are there any other animals that chew their cud and don't have split hooves? Let's find out, shall we?

144 Also available on my blog at www.rabbibz.com

*A **ruminant** is a mammal of the order Artiodactyla that digests plant-based food by initially softening it within the animal's first stomach, principally through bacterial actions, then regurgitating the semi-digested mass, now known as "cud", and chewing it again. The process of re-chewing the cud to further break down plant matter and stimulate digestion is called "ruminating." There are about 150 species of ruminants which include both domestic and wild species. Ruminating mammals include cattle, goats, sheep, giraffes,*

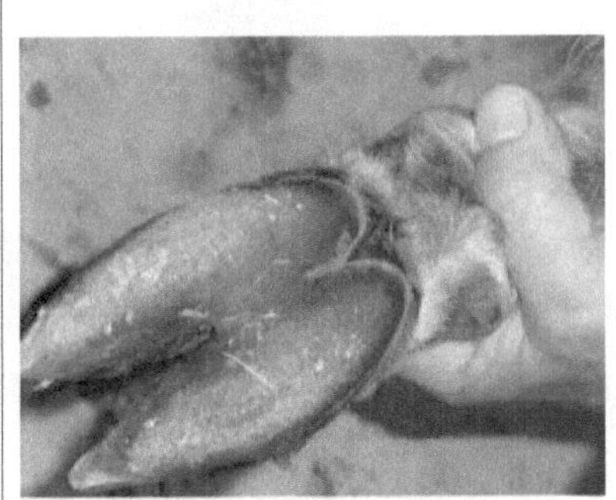

Llama hoof. Note that its hoof isn't split from one end to the other, just like the camels

*bison, moose, elk, yaks, water buffalo, deer, camels, alpacas, llamas, antelope, pronghorn, and nilgai. Taxonomically, the suborder Ruminantia includes all those species except the camels, llamas, and alpacas, which are Tylopoda. Therefore, the term 'ruminant' is not synonymous with Ruminantia.*

So, are there any other such animals? No. So why is there an extensive list of 150 animals, among them not only the camel but llamas, alpacas and more?

Very simple: as stated above the Torah here is not speaking about a particular animal, rather it's

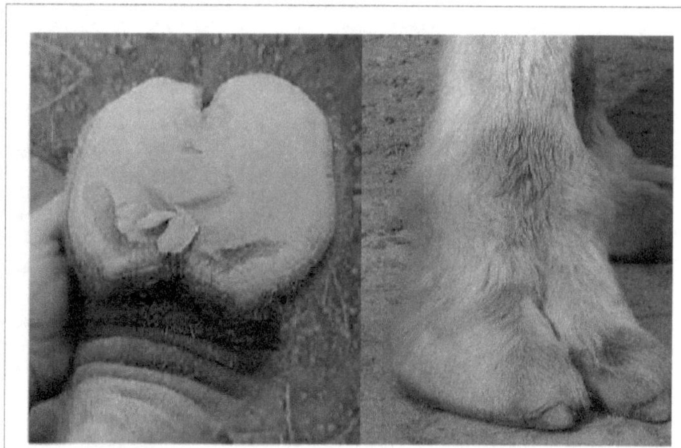

*Camel's foot. Note they are not split from end to end!*

talking about species. All species of pig have split hooves and don't chew their cud. Similarly, all species of camel chew their cud (ruminate) and don't have split hooves. Here, interestingly enough, we find that the Torah and science agree: camels, alpacas, and llamas are all one species! It is, therefore, no wonder that they all chew their cud but don't have split hooves. Please pay close attention to the pictures. I say this simply

145 http://en.wikipedia.org/wiki/Ruminant

because there have been those who claim that the Torah didn't know what it was talking about in this regard[146].

As we mentioned above, the definition of *mafris parsah, shosah shesa* that the Torah uses to describe "split hooves" does not say only that they must be split, it also stipulates that they must be split through and through. If the hoof is split only on the top but on the bottom, it isn't split from one end to the other – it's not the "split hoof" that the Torah talks about! As is clearly visible the hooves of "kosher" animals are not only "split" at the top into 2 "fingernails", but in addition, they are also split from one end to the other on the bottom side of the foot.

---

146 The following excerpt is from http://www.daatemet.org/articles/article.cfm?article_id=13&LANG=en towards the end of the article concerning the camel.

> We will begin with the camel: "The camel, for it chews its cud and does not have true split hoofs, is impure for you." Rashi on Leviticus 11:26: "Which split the hoof but is not cloven-footed' -- such as a camel, the hoof of which is parted above but below it is joined." Rashi's words are puzzling, for the camel's split hooves are parted above and below (the camel is counted among the cloven-footed by zoological classification). See the Daat Zekenim, one of the authors of the Tosfot, on Leviticus 11:3, "Rashi maintains that the camel's hooves are split above and joined below, and this requires study, for if so, he should have removed the camel from the class of the cloven hoofed and written 'its hooves are not cloven'" (which the Torah did not write about the camel; it only wrote, 'and does not have true split hoofs'), just as we said.
>
> We find that according to Rashi the camel is kosher, for it splits its hooves and has cloven hooves above and below, and chews its cud. Therefore, you should say that the Torah did not call the camel "split hoofed" since it walks on the pads of its feet and not on the edge of the split like the goat and the sheep. But the factual truth is that the camel is truly cloven hoofed.

Here we find the author is consistent in his ascertainment that if the Torah uses standards of definition other than those used by modern scientists then the Torah is wrong. He also only half quotes Rashi, who states clearly that the Torah has 2 laws concerning the hooves of an animal: 1 – is that the hooves be split (mafris parsah) and 2- that the underneath be split the entire length of the hoof, (shosa'at shesa), both of which are explicit in the Torah! So even though Rashi does say that the camel (gamal) is mafris parsah only, but not shosa'at shesa, and therefore it falls in the category of unclean animal despite its "split" hoof. See the pictures above for greater understanding.

See also the article that I wrote debunking the half-truths and misquotes upon which the entire article is based, which I entitled "Signs of a Kosher Animal."

# **Prophecies That Came True**

As I presented at length in the chapter entitled *Chosen*, there is a tremendous difference between the veracity of the Torah and its prophecies, as opposed to those of all other religions and their prophecies. I also feel that we leveled the playing field regarding the ridiculous claim of many academics that the Torah was a "late" document. Having said that, however, I would like to point out that there are many prophecies in the Torah which were clearly not about the times of the Bible. They only recently came to fruition ... exactly as prophesized! Therefore, it's kind of hard to say that they were after the fact. Let's take a look at a few of them:

## *Jewish Survival*

There are few nations in the world today as ancient as the Jewish people. Indeed, demographers, social scientists, and historians tell us that 2000 years ago there were roughly 2 million Jews in the world, and there were also about 2 million Chinese in the world. However, the consensus of world Jewry today stands at about 16 million, whereas the Chinese total is nearing 1.7 billion!

What is the cause of the astounding differences between these two peoples?

First of all, the Jewish people were expelled from their homeland and scattered among the nations. This happened to our people not only once, but twice... and it was all foretold, in the Bible! The Bible describes what will happen during the first such exile when it says, in the prophecy of the coming exile (Leviticus 26:31-33)

> *"And I shall give your cities to destruction, and I shall empty out your holy places, and I shall not smell your incense offerings. And I shall empty out the land, and your enemies, who dwell within it (the land) will (wonder at its) emptiness. And I shall scatter you among the nations, and I shall empty (the sheath of) a sword after you, and your lands will be desolate, and your cities shall be destroyed."*

When the exile came, the Bible tells us that the Jewish people were scattered among the nations *as prophesized* (Ester 3:8)

> *"And Haman said to the king 'There is one nation, separated and dispersed amongst all of the medinot (countries) of your kingdom (127 Nations, as stated in the first chapter) ..."*,

However, the majority of the people were exiled to the land of Babylon, which is why this is referred to as the "Babylonian Exile."

Towards the end of this first exile, a small percentage of the people returned to the land of Israel to rebuild Jerusalem and the Temple. However, the majority of the people remain in Babylon. The Temple was rebuilt, followed by the walls of the city of Jerusalem and slowly, but surely, the country was returned to its former glory. The rebuilt second Temple lasted 420 years until the Roman Empire invaded and expelled the Jews (not all, but almost all) from the Land once again. For a second time, the Jews were scattered amongst the nations *as was prophesied in the Bible* (Deuteronomy 28) after the Torah stated in verse 37 that the Jewish people would be:

> *"…a (derogatory) anecdote and a source of derision*
> *in all of the nations that HaShem will drive us to"*

This refers to the first exile. (Perhaps this was the origin of the expression "Dirty Jew"?)

It then proceeded to describe (verse 49)

> *"HaShem will carry from afar a distant nation,*
> *from the edge of the land, as the eagle flies, a nation*
> *whose language you don't know…"*

The Torah then described in depth just how lousy and vile a people they were and how they would treat the Jews. Lastly (verse 64) the Torah again specified:

> *"…and HaShem will disperse you amongst all of*
> *the nations, from one end of the land to the other end*
> *of the land…. (verse 65) and amongst those nations,*
> *you will not have a respite, and you will not have a*
> *place of resting for your feet…"*

An exile after an exile.

But supposedly, say the historians, all of this is debatable. Maybe it was all written after the fact, in which case "hindsight is 20-20."

Maybe... but then again maybe not.

What is NOT up for debate, however, is the undeniable fact that the Torah proceeded to tell us: Don't worry. You will come back to the land a second time as well! If that's not incredulous enough, consider the fact that the Torah told us that when we return, we will not only have survived the exiles as individuals but as a cohesive nation as well! However, the Torah didn't stop there. It added two more bits of information: this is going to be a very LONG exile, and, despite natural population growth, the Jews will remain a small percentage of people among the nations!

Listen to the words of the Torah in Deuteronomy 28: 62-69

> *"And you shall remain a small remnant instead of the great multitude which you once were... and HaShem will scatter you in all of the nations, from one end of the land to the other... and amongst those (foreign) nations you will not find comfort, and you will not find a resting place (a place of permanent residency) for the soles of your feet..."*

## ***The Land will be Desolate, Only When Israel Returns it will Flourish***

I would like to quote from the American writer, Mark Twain at this point. The following is an excerpt from his book in which he described his travels to the Holy Land in the 1880's. (*Innocents Abroad* or *The New Pilgrim's Progress* part 6 chapter 56)

*Of all the lands there are for dismal scenery, I think Palestine must be the prince. The hills are barren, they are dull of color, they are unpicturesque in shape. The valleys are unsightly deserts fringed with a feeble vegetation that has an expression about it of being sorrowful and despondent. The Dead Sea and the Sea of Galilee sleep in the midst of a vast stretch of hill and plain wherein the eye rests upon no pleasant tint, no striking object, no soft picture dreaming in a purple haze or mottled with the shadows of the clouds. Every outline is harsh, every feature is distinct, there is no perspective—distance works no enchantment here. It is a hopeless, dreary, heart-broken land.*

*Small shreds and patches of it must be very beautiful in the full flush of spring, however, and all the more beautiful by contrast with the far-reaching desolation that surrounds them on every side. I would like much to see the fringes of the Jordan in spring-time, and Shechem, Esdraelon, Ajalon and the borders of Galilee—but even then, these spots would seem mere toy gardens set at wide intervals in the waste of a limitless desolation.*

*Palestine sits in sackcloth and ashes. Over it broods the spell of a curse that has withered its fields and fettered its energies. Where Sodom and Gomorrah reared their domes and towers, that solemn sea now floods the plain, in whose bitter waters no living thing exists—over whose waveless surface the blistering air hangs motionless and dead—about whose borders nothing grows but weeds, and scattering tufts of cane, and that treacherous fruit that promises refreshment to parching lips, but turns to ashes at the touch. Nazareth is forlorn; about that ford of Jordan where the hosts of Israel entered the Promised Land with songs of rejoicing, one finds only a squalid camp of fantastic Bedouins of the desert; Jericho the accursed, lies a moldering ruin, to-day, even as Joshua's miracle left it more than three thousand years ago; Bethlehem and Bethany, in their poverty and their humiliation, have nothing about them now to remind one that they once knew the high honor of the Saviour's presence; the hallowed spot where the shepherds watched their flocks by night, and where the angels sang Peace on earth, good will to men, is untenanted by any living creature, and unblessed by any feature that is pleasant to the eye. Renowned Jerusalem itself, the stateliest name in history, has lost all its ancient grandeur, and is become a pauper village; the riches of Solomon are no longer there to compel the admiration of visiting Oriental queens; the wonderful temple which was the pride and the glory of Israel, is gone, and the Ottoman crescent is lifted above the spot where, on that most memorable day in the annals of the world, they reared the Holy Cross. The noted Sea of Galilee, where Roman fleets once rode at anchor and the disciples of the Saviour sailed in their ships, was long ago deserted by the devotees of war and commerce, and its borders are a silent wilderness; Capernaum is a shapeless ruin; Magdala is the home of beggared Arabs; Bethsaida and Chorazin have vanished from the earth, and the "desert places" round about them where thousands of men once listened to the Saviour's voice and ate the miraculous bread, sleep in the hush of a solitude that is inhabited only by birds of prey and skulking foxes.*

*Palestine is desolate and unlovely. And why should*
*it be otherwise? Can the curse of the Deity beautify*
*a land?*

Twain was not the only one to testify concerning the desolation of the land just before the return of the Jews to their national homeland during the first *aliyah* period[147]. There were many others as well: Gen. Charles Warren in his 1870 book *"Jerusalem Below"*, Alfonso De la Martine in his book *Recollections of the East* (vol. 1 pg. 238), Prof. Sir John William Dawson *Modern Science in Bible Lands* and many others.

Why was the land such a desolate place? Why was it so barren? Simple: G-d wanted it that way so that it would be easier to return to.

Listen to the words of the Torah (the Holy Bible) in Leviticus 26:32-33

*"And I will surely make the Land desolate, and your*
*enemies who dwell upon it will become desolate.*
*And I will disperse you amongst the nations, and I*
*will empty the sword (from its scabbard) after you,*
*and your land will remain desolate, and your cities*
*will remain destroyed".*

How clear can you get? The fertile land will remain desolate, and no one will rebuild its cities as no one will be able to truly settle the land.

---

147 This is the name which modern Israeli historians use in reference to the first wave of mass return of the Jewish people in recent history. The word "Aliyah" means "to go up", which was a common Jewish reference to returning to the land of Israel.

Therefore, can it be any wonder that those inhabitants who remain will be poverty stricken?

Heralding the words of Mark Twain that we saw earlier; the Torah tells us further in the book of Deuteronomy 29:21-24

> *"And the last generation, your sons, who will arise after you, will say, and so too the stranger who will come from a distant land, and they will witness the affliction of this land and its sickness with which HaShem has made it sick. Sulfur and salt, the entire land is as burned, it will not be sown, and neither will it grow anything, not even grass will grow on it, just as the overturned (lands of) Sodom and Amora, Adama, and Tzevoyim, which HaShem overturned in His anger and Burning. And (after seeing all this) all of the nations will say "For what is it that HaShem did so to this land? What is (the cause behind all of) this great fury and anger?" And they will say "It's because they (the children of Israel) left the covenant (between) the Lord their G-d and their fathers, that which they established with them when they were taken out of Egypt."*

Could human minds have possibly foreseen this?

When Israel left the land behind it was a land "flowing with milk and honey", a truly special and fertile land. What is the likelihood that such a land would remain barren and desolate in an agricultural culture? What is the likelihood that cities whose fame had spread far and wide would remain desolate in their ruins for time immemorial? And lastly, who would think to say that they would stay in this state until the children of Israel returned home?

Was it not the Church fathers who came along and made it their doctrine that the Jewish people were exiled because they didn't keep the Law of G-d? Isn't that *exactly* what the Torah said the foreigners would say? The Jews were punished because they left the covenant of G-d which was made at *Horeb* (Sinai)? There isn't one skeptic on the face of the planet that could say this was written after the fact and expect to get away with it unscathed!

Who would have the audacity to make such statements, unless they knew, and could relate, those thousands of years ago, via crystal clear prophecies, that which would only come about today? (1000 years later or in the last 100 years).

Only a Divine Torah could make such claims.

### ***The Return of the Scattered People***

Afterward in Deuteronomy 30:1-6 it says the following:

> *"and it will be that after all of those things (listed*
> *before in chapters 28 and 29) will come upon you,*
> *the blessing and the curse that I have placed before*

*you, and you will return it unto your heart (you will see, and take to heart, that everything that happened was exactly as it was written in the Torah) amongst all of the (foreign) nations unto which HaShem, our Lord, has flung us. And you shall return unto the Lord, your G-d, and you shall listen to His voice... And (then) HaShem, your G-d, will return your remnants and have mercy on you, and He shall go back and gather you together from amongst all of the nations unto which He scattered you. Even if your scattered (brother) should be at the edges of the sky, from there HaShem, your Lord, shall gather you, and from there He will take you. And He will return you, the Lord, your G-d, unto the land which your forefathers inherited, and you shall inherit it, and He will make you prosper and multiply more than your fathers".*

Now, since according to all opinions this is an ancient document, and this was clearly written BEFORE THE FACT... what say you now? Is the prophecy in any way vague or unclear? Obviously not! It is, in fact, quite detailed. So... how DID the Torah know that these events would actually occur?

How was the Torah able to describe in exact detail what would happen over 2000 years in the future if it was a human-made document written after the destruction of the 2$^{nd}$ temple in Jerusalem, when the people – conquered and vanquished – were led out of the country by the Roman legions, after mass decimation of the Jewish population. How likely is it that the exile and in-gathering would have been foreseen by human eyes and recorded by human hands living at that time, as so many intellectuals would like us to believe?

There are many more prophecies in the Torah relevant to today's world, but the above should suffice to prove the point that only G-d could have authored the Torah.

## *Torah Codes*

I bring this issue last because of the controversy that surrounds it. I, therefore, present it according to the opinion of Dr. Eliahu Rips Ph.D., the originator of the codes theory and those scientists who agree with his conclusions[148]. On the assumption that they are correct this is one more piece of information demonstrating the Torah's truth, (and if they aren't – it doesn't negate all of the above information).

---

148  There are, however, many other scientists in the field who disagree. Their reasoning can be found at http://web.archive.org/web/20131121111800/http://www.khunwoody.com/biblecodes/ or at https://cross-currents.com/2005/10/11/nobel-prize-settles-bible-codes-dispute/ to name a few. Counter arguments can be found at http://www.torah-code.org/controversy/controversy.shtml and the links therein.

One of the more interesting subjects discussed over the past 30 or so years, (although, in truth, it dates back much further), is the subject of information that has been discovered encoded into the language of the Bible. Only recently, by utilizing computer technology as a major facilitator, some of these codes were discovered and publicized. A computer program is utilized which exposes "jumps" between one letter and another which, when put together, comprise names, dates, places, and details concerning people, places, and/or events from the past and present (and many that are yet to come!).

The reason why this is interesting is that in comparison with other texts when run through the same computer program, and following the same systems, we do not find that there is any information encoded or any pattern of any significance (=0%).

Now, this is *not* saying that by utilizing this program the Torah can give accurate predictions of the future events. If that were the case, if messages were clearly written in the Torah and easily retrievable, all we would have to do is to show examples of this phenomenon, and there would be no more room for debate! *However,* what *is* clear is that there seems to be a *statistically significant amount of coding within the written Torah which we do not find, by comparison, in other texts using the same methodology.*

In other words, we find within the wording of the Torah – and ONLY within the language of the Torah – a statistically significant, (and truly amazing), correlation of information relating to important historical events and individuals.

Theologically this is crucial, for it is our tradition that the Lord, G-d, "looked in the Torah to build creation." The Torah was and is the blueprint, not only for the world, but for all of existence, and for all time! Only an Omnipotent G-d could encode the history of the entire world into His Book.

## A Quick Explanation

We begin with some basic definitions, the first being for Equidistant Letter Sequence, or ELS for short.

The language of the book, be it the Holy Torah or any other book scrutinized using the ELS system, is first compiled into a string of letters, which is done by removing the spaces from in-between words. Instead of looking at the words (for example)בראשית ברא א-לוקים they are condensed into a string of letters בראשיתבראא, etc.

Afterward, the skip sequence is set. First, the starting point for the skip process is decided upon, and then the *number* of letters to be skipped is established.

To more easily facilitate the ramifications of the skip sequence we then "break up" the letter sequence into "code cylinders". This is a *visual* technique that we utilize so that, instead of looking at one long file of letters several kilometers long[149] we break up the letter sequence so that it fits on a page or a column.

---

149 When we consider that there are over 300,000 letters in the 5 books alone, each letter being roughly ½ a centimeter in length. This means that a straight line of Torah letters is roughly 150,000 centimeters long. That's 150 kilometers!

Let me take an example from the site torahcode.net. This is one way to look at a string of letters:

THISISTHEFORMWEUSEFORFINDINGCODESANDIADDEDLETTERSPRECISEL
YPLACEDTOFORMALONGEREXAMPLE

And these are another way of looking at it, once broken up into cylinders:

| | |
|---|---|
| THISISTHEF | THISISTHEF |
| ORMWEUSEFO | ORMWEUSEFO |
| RFINDINGCO | RFINDINGCO |
| DESANDIADD | DESANDIADD |
| EDLETTERSP | EDLETTERSP |
| RECISELYPL | RECISELYPL |
| ACEDTOFORM | ACEDTOFORM |
| ALONGEREXA | ALONGEREXA |
| MPLE | MPLE |

*The highlighted letters above represent different skip sequences within the text. Since the above cylinder is made up of lines of 10 letter sequences the word **ORDER** comprises a skip sequence of 10 letters starting with the letter **O**. The name GARY and the word FOOD also are made up of letter skip sequences 10 skips long. Because the cylinder is broken into 10 letter sequences, these words become easily recognizable in a 10 letter skip pattern or ELS.*

Now, clearly, the above letter sequence looks, for all the world, to be no more than a crossword puzzle. And we might think to ourselves "well in any such type of sequence we can find all sorts of words! What makes the Torah so special?"

I'm glad you asked that question – let's get to it, shall we?

## **Statistically Significant**

Once again, I would like to quote from the experts at torahcode.net

*ELS's of interesting words do not constitute a code.*

This means that just "finding a bunch of interesting words in the letter jumble" does not represent a code.

*If a table is a Torah code, then it will have a set of ELS's that are in an unusually compact arrangement.*

Meaning that actual "codes" are not found in a helter-skelter way. They are found in close, sometimes overlapping, proximity to each other. (In many instances the subject matter that the actual text is discussing has an uncanny semblance to the codes discovered therein as well. See, for example, the Holocaust code[150]).

---

150 See http://torahcode.us/torah_codes/auschwitz/auschwitz3.shtml or http://torahcode.us/torah_codes/holocaust/holocaust1.shtml and http://torahcode.us/torah_codes/hitler/hitler1.shtml

> *"Unusually compact" can only be measured by the probability that an arrangement as compact or better would happen by chance.*

This means that there is no agreed upon "guide" as to the definition of "unusually compact". Rather it is decided based on a probability equation. Just what *is* the likelihood that we would find a compact arrangement of ELSs, by chance?

## *What are the Odds?*

> *Normal scientific procedure is to reject the possibility of an event with ... strong odds happening by chance. ... In fact, the normal scientific standard for ... rejection (of a statistically unlikely occurrence) is 20 to 1*[151].
>
> *A mathematical technique ... As required by one of the peer review referees, Professor Persi Diaconis, (calculated) a probability against (words appearing in an unusually compact arrangement occurring by) chance of 1/1,000 or smaller is considered a success. That is to say, suppose we hypothesize that the Torah codes do not exist. We then calculate a proximity measure. We now calculate the odds against the proximity measure*

---

151 This quote is taken from the article "A Primer on the Torah Codes Controversy for Laymen" by Harold J. Ganz

*obtained being at least as strong as it is. If these odds are 1,000 to 1 or greater, we have two possibilities: (a) An event with 1,000 to 1 odds just happened by chance, or (b) our initial hypothesis that the Torah codes do not exist must be wrong. Normal scientific procedure is to reject the possibility of an event with such strong odds happening by chance.*

*Such an event is so highly improbable that declaring it to be nothing more than chance verges on the absurd. In fact, the usual scientific standard for such a rejection is 20 to 1. Thus, we pick possibility (b). Namely, Torah codes do exist, and they cause the observed proximity measure to be as strong as observed. That is, we accept the statistical evidence as demonstrating that the phenomenon is real.*

In other words, we find, upon the comparison, that the Torah and ONLY the Torah exhibits coded words in a way that defies the statistics. But by how much do they defy the statistics?

## ***The Great Rabbi's Experiment***

The first publicized paper on this issue was done utilizing a list of about 34 names and dates (birth and death) of several great men in the history of Israel. The names and dates were then searched for, using computer software, both in the text of the book of Genesis and in a Hebrew translation of the book of *"War and Peace"* by Tolstoy. The results were staggering.

In the book of Genesis, the names and dates of these great men of Israel were found in concise correlated patterns. The odds calculated against such a compact arrangement was 1/64,000. Within the text of *"War and Peace,"* they were found within the "norm".

Considering that the threshold of calculated statistical odds for this experiment was odds of 1/1000 against, this means that the reality was 64 times *greater* than what was thought possible.

Once again – the Torah beats all odds!

The significance of the codes, per se, is not so clear to us. What IS significant is that we can see – beyond any doubt – that the Torah is a book unlike any other in existence. It defies all the rational world.

The above are the statistics of studies of yesteryear. There are many more modern studies that have been conducted that have shown the statistical correlation of ELS skips to be even more greatly significant than those done 30 years ago[152].

## *In Summary*

We have seen in this chapter that:

---

152 http://www.torah-code.org/experiments.shtml see also http://torahcode.org/index.shtml and http://www.torah-code.org/purpose.shtml

- The Torah was written in a way that doesn't sync with human logic. It contains promises that no human being would logically or realistically proffer for keeping the commandments contained within. It makes testable promises by which it can be shown as false. This is not done by any other religion. Despite the testable promises the Torah was kept, at varying levels of observance, by the Jewish people forever. Ergo: the promises must have been fulfilled. Ergo: it was not written by a human being or even by many smart human beings.

- The Torah contains minute details about long-gone places that could not have been known to someone even a few years after the fact. This is even truer when one realizes that hundreds or even thousands of years have passed since the stories related in the Torah occurred. Ergo: as the Author of the Torah was familiar with all of the historical minutiae. He must have written it based upon knowledge beyond the ability of an ordinary human being.

- The Torah contains information which could not have been known thousands of years in the past and there has been no proof brought clearly showing that any of this information is incorrect. Ergo: The Author wrote with knowledge beyond that of humans who lived in that era. As we are constantly finding more species all of the time – it's clear that the Author's knowledge clearly exceeds our own.

- The Torah contains clear prophecies which are relevant to our generation that have – only recently – come to pass. Ergo: it could not have been written based on human logic or wisdom as no one would have the foresight to say what actually transpired 2000 years later. It also couldn't have been written after the fact. And lastly;

- The Torah contains codes and information which are clearly NOT random and defies all probability.

So, what do you think? Is it a divine document or not?

# If It's Free – I'll Take Two!

## *Evidence of the Oral Torah and its Divinity*

N THE PREVIOUS CHAPTER, we explored the issue of the divinity of the Written Torah. Among all of the major religions of the world, the written Torah is a given. However, when asked if they know about the separate Oral Torah most people respond, "No. There's only a written one".

This is an issue simply because most people are not familiar with a lesser-known Jewish joke that goes as follows:

When it came time for G-d to give the Torah, He didn't offer it exclusively to the Jews. Not at all! The Midrash tells us that He offered it to all of the nations of the world. Yet every nation that He offered it to did as follows: first they asked, "What's written in it?" After getting a specific answer they each then politely refused it. However, the Jews, upon receiving the offer concerning the Torah, first asked "How much does it cost?" and when told that it was free they immediately answered, "Then we'll take two." And if the Jews take two you know it was for free – and only G-d gives a free lunch!

All joking aside, the Jewish position has always been that there are/were two Torah's. This does not mean that this issue has not been a topic of debate throughout Jewish history: the Sadducees, the Shomronites (Samaritans) and many others have come along to reject the original Jewish position of the existence of the oral Torah. However, everyone agrees that the mainstay opinion of both antiquity and today has always been that an oral Torah was also given at Sinai in addition to the written one. (After all, before the Shomronites and the Sadducees – there were no Shomronites or Sadducees who held this opinion. There were, however, many Jews living by both the oral and written Torah's).

However, the truth is that this is a bit of a misnomer. The true Jewish position, as expressed by our sages, ob"m, in tractate *Gittin* on page 60a, is that there was always an oral Torah that was given at Sinai and that it was later followed (almost 40 years later!) with a written one[153].

So, the question remains: why is the oral Torah such a source of debate among the Jewish people and among the nations of the world?

---

153 The Gemara relates an argument between Rabbi Yochanan and Reish Lakish as to how the written Torah was given over to the people over the years. R"Y's opinion was that the written Torah was only given to the people at the end of the forty years as a complete document, whereas the opinion of R"L was that it was given piecemeal over the course of the forty year sojourn. It comes out, therefore, that according to all of our sages there was no full written Torah until the end of the 40-year sojourn in the desert.

The answer: it is exactly *because* of its oral nature! The written word, after it has been written, may be subject to certain scrutiny, (is it real or a forgery and the like), and it may sometimes be a little ambiguous. However, at the end of the day, there is very little room for argument as to *what was said*[154]. This is clearly not the case when it comes to something that is entirely based on an oral tradition! Here it's an open ballpark and anyone at all can take a swing about anything!

So, to begin scrutinizing this topic called "the Voracity of the Oral Torah," let's first explore the issue: is there, indeed, a need for such a Torah? If yes, does the written Torah allude to it or not?

## ***Let's Play Doctor***

All of us have most likely heard that to become a doctor is not a walk in the park. Indeed, it's a process that requires no small amount of effort. First, you must do pre-med, then medical school. That's about eight years of concerted effort. And yet despite all of that, even after graduating with honors and straight A's no one receives the title "Doctor" quite yet. There is still one more thing missing from a physician's education, it's called an internship.

Now someone standing on the side might ask himself "Isn't that enough? Didn't he just finish eight grueling years of study? Why can't he

---

154 I don't mean to say that there cannot be differing versions of the written word, a well-known phenomenon with almost all hand-written replicas of ancient documents. I mean that the written word is there to see, tangibly and visually, leaving very little room for argument as to what the document is saying.

go and practice medicine right now?". The answer, of course, is that despite all of his book knowledge – he still doesn't know a thing! In reality, the actual application of all of his knowledge is still beyond him. He/She must first go through a period of internship (and residency), during which he/she will be directly caring for patients while supervised by a physician more experienced in the field. During this hands-on training, the intern is primarily receiving an oral explanation as to the actual application of his medicinal knowledge. Only at the end of this process does one actually become a medical professional.

This is readily understood when it comes to doctors, (after all, you wouldn't want a "text-book operation", i.e. a surgeon who is following the written instructions of how to do it in his textbook while cutting you open with a surgical blade! ("Cut… here! Suture… here! Hey! What's that thing?"), but in reality, in all fields of endeavor, the procedure of specialization or even basic education is similar. You honestly know nothing until someone explains to you and shows you how to apply the knowledge that you have. That is an oral torah.

The Torah is no different in this regard than the rest of all human endeavor.

OK, Rabbi, so it would seem that there is a need for an Oral Torah. But still: how do I know this one to be Divine?

## *It's Right in Front of Your Nose!*

There are several categories of proof which we can bring to address this issue clearly: objective, inference, commonality, and extent of information. With G-d's help, we will be discussing these in more detail.

The reason why we can know the divinity of the Oral Torah with utmost clarity is that the Written Torah itself, whose Divine nature was established in the previous chapter, has many types of proofs and inferences as to the existence of said oral Torah.

## *The Objective Stuff:*

Looking in a Torah scroll is an amazing experience. True, it's not only a copy of a more than three-thousand-year-old document, but it's also a work of art all in itself! (I happen to know from personal experience as a Sofer STA" M, a Torah scribe). But all that aside, the real value of the "sefer Torah", as it is called in Hebrew, is the message, not the medium. So, let's look at the message.

One of the interesting things that we note in looking at the Torah is that there are no punctuation marks whatsoever. One of the first things that we have to ask ourselves is how do we know how to break up the words into sentences? Let me give a rather poignant example of this.

Here is one of the most famous verses in the Torah from the book of Exodus:

*I am the Lord, your G-d, who took you out of Egypt,*
*from the house of bondage. You shall have no (lo*

*tehiyeh lecha) other gods (Elohim acherim) before me*
*(al panai).*

The problem with this is that if there is no definitive oral tradition which tells us how to read it, then there is nothing stopping me from reading the Hebrew as follows:

*I am the Lord, your G‑d, who took you out of Egypt from the house of bondage? No (lo)! You shall have (tehiyeh lecha) other gods (Elohim acherim) before me (al panai)!*

Clearly, even if we were to have no doubts as to what the words are, we would still be in the dark as to how to cantillate them. If there is no clear oral tradition, then we will find all sorts of new ways to read the verses!

## *What's in a Word?*

In addition to the above, we have to also note that the Hebrew alphabet itself doesn't actually contain any vowels. Without an oral explanation, how can we even know how to pronounce the words? The answer is that you need someone to tell you how to say it. But that's a limited solution. It only works if there is someone there to tell you how to say it. To help solve this issue, around 1600 years ago a group of vowels was invented to help facilitate the reading of all of the words of the Torah. These are called in Hebrew *Nikkud*. The proper names of the *nikkudot*, are *kamatz (the aw sound), patach (ah), tzereh (eh), segol (ay), chirik (ee), cholam (oh), shuruk (oo)* and *kubbutz (ew)*. Anyone learning Modern Hebrew still learns these vowels today.

In any case, according to all opinions *nikkud* is a relatively recent phenomenon. But before the invention of the *nikkud,* was everything perfectly clear? If so, then why did we need to invent it?

The answer is that everything was perfectly clear before the invention of the *nikkud,* due to the oral tradition as to how to read the words of the Torah. Nevertheless it was easier to facilitate learning to read with vowels by making a written standard which could then be more easily spread and retained[155].

The difficulty with an oral tradition is that it's only as far reaching as the voice of the person relating it. However, a written book can be sent around the world. Furthermore, unless the oral material is committed to memory it also dies with the possessor of the tradition as well. Once it is "translated" into a written form, then as long as the document is in existence it is viable. It can also be copied and disseminated with more ease.

So, clearly there are definite advantages to the written tradition, as exemplified by *nikkud.* Written instructions regarding the nikkudiim became crucial when the people were faced with exile and dispersion.

However, without the oral tradition (which was then documented via the *nikkud,*), we find that there are many things in the Torah that are

---

155 This, despite the fact that there are some minor debates among Jews from various parts of the world as to how to pronounce some of the vowels. Ashkenazim, Sephardim, and Yemenites, for example, have some differing understandings of how to pronounce the vowels. However, there is no argument among them (us) as far as what the words are.

entirely incomprehensible, or at least very ambiguous. Let's give a few examples of this:

The Torah tells us in three places[156] that it forbidden to cook a kid, (*gedi*, that's a baby goat, not a child!), in the CHLV (חלב) of its mother. We know via the Oral tradition that this is referring to the cooking of a mixture of meat and milk. However, if we take a step back and look at it, objectively it becomes clear that the meaning of the word CHLV (חלב) is unclear. How do we cantillate/pronounce it? Is it the word CHALAV (חלב) which means milk, or is it the word CHALEV (חלב) which means "forbidden fats?" What is it, exactly, that the Torah wants to tell us is forbidden?

If you have no oral tradition – you're stuck!

Yet even with an oral tradition of how to read the word, it is still very unclear what the meaning of the commandment is. Is it limited to the meat of a kid? Only if it's the mother's milk? What about frying? Baking? Sautéing? If someone has already cooked it, can I then eat it?

Without an oral tradition, how can I understand the boundaries?


In Deuteronomy (25:19) we find that the Torah is infuriated at the nation of *Amalek* who was the first to try and battle the Jewish people when they were in the desert. The Torah, therefore, commands that we should "*Timcheh es ZCHR* (זכר) *Amalek*", which means we should utterly annihilate them. The question is: who is "them" in this verse? Just what

<hr>

156 Exodus 23:19, ibid 34:26 and Deuteronomy 14:21

is a ZCHR? Is it ZECHER (זכר) which means "the memory of" or is it ZACHAR (זכר) which means "the males of?"

Our sages, ob"m, in tractate *Bava Batra* on page 21a relate to us a story as to how this exact issue became a problem during the times of King David. To make a long story short Yoav, commander of the king's army, was sent to destroy the nation of Amalek in fulfillment of this commandment and only killed the males. David asked him why he did this and when he was told that it's because the verse says to kill all the males of Amalek, David immediately found out who Yoav's elementary school teacher was to have him punished for twisting the understanding of the Torah!

So, clearly there is a need for an Oral tradition (=Oral Torah) which is what explains to us how the Written Torah is to be read.

## *The Magical Shnitzleberry*

In addition to the issues above, we also must face up to the following: If I were to ask you what a Shnitzleberry is, what would you answer? You can, of course, Google it, but let me spare you the effort: it's meaningless. Not just because I made it up, (which I did), but also because there are many things out there in the world that have absolutely no meaning until they are explained to us. Someone who has never in his life seen spaghetti, when told about this fantastic food, with no real explanation or visual demonstration, might as well have been talking about shnitzleberry!

In this regard, the Torah is no different from the rest of the world. There are a great many things that the Torah speaks about that are not defined in the text, and therefore are totally meaningless without an Oral Torah for further explanation. The Oral Torah specifies how to perform the mitzvah and, indeed, what the commandment *is*. Let's give some examples of this:

The Torah in Leviticus (23:40-42) commands that during the seventh month, (which one is that?), on the fifteenth day of the month, the Jewish people are to do the following: First of all, they are to gather the following four items: *pri etz hadar, capot tamarim, anaf etz avot,* and *arvei nachal.* All of these are rather ill-defined, and the issue of what to do with them is not described in the Torah at all. It only says that "you should take them" (*ve'lakachtem*).

The second thing that the Torah tells us concerning this day is that we are to sit in something called *Sukkot.* What in the world is a *sukkah,* (singular of *Sukkot*)? How do we sit in it? What's it made of? What are its dimensions? If I go to visit my grandmother during this time, do I have to take it with me?

Kind of vague and ill-defined… unless you have an Oral tradition (=Oral Torah) to go along with it and help explain the text.

Let's look at another example: in the book of Deuteronomy (6:8) the Torah commands that there is something that a Jew should "tie as a sign on the arm and that it should be as a *totafos* between the eyes." This, of course, is referring to the mitzvah of *tefillin,* in Hebrew, otherwise known as "phylacteries" in English. (Of course, if the Torah told you outright that it was talking about "phylacteries" everything would be perfectly clear, right? I mean who leaves home without their phylacteries?).

So, what, exactly am I to tie on my arm? A string? A bat? A peace-and-love symbol? What in the world are *totafos*? Once I put them there – can I take them off? Do they have a certain size? What color are they? Clearly, without an Oral Tradition, there really is nothing to talk about!

It is interesting to note that *tefillin* illustrate one of the greatest proofs of the existence of a centralized, clear oral tradition. This is because all Jews around the world wear them daily, and wear virtually the exact same *tefillin*, despite the fact that there was almost no contact among the many communities around the world for hundreds, if not thousands, of years! How did all of these scattered Jews – miraculously – arrive at the same interpretation? Decisions were identical regarding how the *tefillin* should be made, with what materials, what shape and color, how they were to be tied and all of the various other details… This could have only have been achieved via a clear, centralized Oral Tradition concerning the definition of the commandment of *tefillin*.

Truly, in this regard, the list is endless. Another example: which kosher birds are permissible? Their species are all named, but unless someone points to a bird and explains "this is an X," then we don't know if it's one of the kosher ones or one of the forbidden ones. The commandment of *mezuzah*, the commandment of the sanctification of the new moon and many, many other commandments do not have operational instructions in the Torah.

But that is not the end-all-and-be-all of an Oral tradition. Indeed, the Midrash tells a story of a certain gentile who wanted to convert during the times of the great Rabbonim, Rav, and Shmuel. They lived at the beginning of the period of the *Ammoraim*, the first of the Gemara generations.

This potential convert was a real skeptic and constantly demanded that everything should be proven to him. The potential convert came to Rav, (we'll call him "Gary" to simplify things), and asked that Rav teach him, and put him through the conversion process. Sensing the man's sincerity, Rav accepted him as a student. The next morning Gary showed up at the Yeshiva and sat down to his first lesson. "*Alef*," said Rav. "How do you know that that's an Alef?", asked Gary. "*Beis*," said Rav. "How do you know that's a Beis?", asked Gary. This scenario continued until finally, Rav became exasperated, and threw him out.

"What's a guy got to do to convert around here?", thought Gary? Then he went to the Yeshiva of the other great Rabbi, Shmuel. Shmuel also accepted Gary as a potential convert and began giving him lessons. Sure enough, just as soon as Shmuel started teaching him "*Aleph*" Gary immediately asked again "How do you know that that's an Aleph?" Shmuel immediately leaned over to Gary, looked at him sternly, and gave him a nice yank on the ear! "Ouch!" screamed Gary. "My ear!" screamed Gary. To which Shmuel immediately retorted "How do you know … that that's an ear"?

Hmmm… How DO we know that that's an ear? Very simple: We were told it as we were growing up, and we accepted it because that's an Oral Tradition.

In a similar vein, the Torah in Deuteronomy (17:11) tells us that if there is ever a cause for disagreement as to the interpretation of a certain mitzvah, we are to go to that place *"which the Lord, your G-d, has chosen (where is that, exactly?)"* We then must do all that they say

> *"According to the Torah that they will instruct you and concerning the judgment that they say to you to do. Do not deviate from the thing that they instruct you (to go) right or left".*

Concerning the Torah's usage of the terms "right or left" our sages, ob"m, tell us that this is coming to teach us that this is true "even if they tell you concerning your right that it is your left and your left that it is your right." Meaning that even though your parents taught you when you were growing up that this (→) is to the right, whereas this (←) is to the left (an oral tradition), if those sages tell you the opposite, even if the entire country does as your parents taught you, you follow that which these great men said.

If one were to ask: so, what? What difference does it make which is right, and which is left? What's my ear, or what's my toe? To this, I say that in certain states in the USA it is permitted to make a RIGHT turn on a red light… which way is that, exactly? With the flow of traffic or against it? For us Jews, the ramifications can be found throughout the

Torah! Certain commandments must be performed with the right hand, not the left. Others need to be conducted with the hand and not the foot. Etc. etc. etc.

What these things are telling us is that most of our lives are governed by Oral Tradition (=Oral Torah).

But even this is still not all.

## *But Do You Have Any References?*

Another question that we have to explore is whether or not the written Torah actually has references to the existence of an Oral Torah. Of course, it would seem that there are all sorts of things in the written Torah that need an oral explanation. Wouldn't it be even better if the Torah would say things that at least allude to the existence of an Oral one?

Well, you're in luck. The Torah does exactly that! Let's see some examples, shall we?

There are at least two places in the written Torah where the Torah tells us to perform a particular commandment *"in the manner that I commanded you."* Yet despite this statement, if we search throughout the entire Torah in no instance do we find that the Torah ever gave any instructions on how to perform these mitzvos!

The first mitzvah is in Exodus (23:15) where the Torah commanded the Jewish people to keep the three festivals. There, while stating that the people must keep the festival of Pesach, the Festival of Matzos, the

Torah explained that we must "*...guard the month of the spring (Chodesh ha'aviv) in the manner that I commanded you...*" Yet if we search throughout the entire Written Torah, we find no instructions as to how we are supposed to guard the month of the spring. This, of course, refers to the commandment that is called *ibbur Hashanah*, which literally means a "pregnant" year. This commandment adds an extra month to the Hebrew calendar to balance out the difference between the solar and the lunar years. This ensures that the month of Nissan, in which the festival of matzos (Pesach) falls, will always come out in the springtime.

The second mitzvah is in the book of Deuteronomy (12:21) when the Torah explained to Bnei Yisroel that life was going to be different when they entered the land of Israel. There, the Torah tells us that the Holy Temple, the Beit Hamikdash will not always be in close proximity to where the Jews live. However, just because the Beis HaMikdash is no longer nearby, doesn't mean that the Jewish people are now forbidden to eat meat. In the desert, the meat had to be brought to the Mishkan as a sacrifice prior to being eaten. However, in the land of Israel meat could be eaten without first bringing it as a sacrifice. There was one stipulation, however. The Torah stipulated that something called *zevicha* must be done "*as I commanded you to do (ka'asher tziviticha).*" However, nowhere in the written Torah do we find instructions as to how to perform this mitzvah of *zevicha*! What is *zevicha*, you might ask? It's what we call *shechita*, (how to slaughter an animal), in Hebrew.

No matter how you slice it, it would seem that the Written Torah totally lacks any form of understanding without an Oral Torah to explain it!

## *Jewish Commonality*

Another proof of the divinity of the Oral Torah is that we find among Jews the world over the antithesis of a certain Jewish joke.

Once upon a time, a cruise ship sailed the seas when, from afar, someone took note of an immense fire on one of the outlying islands. A dinghy was sent out, and it was discovered that a Jew was living on this otherwise uninhabited island. One other striking feature of the island is that it had two *battei Knesset* (synagogues, Jewish houses of worship) on it. When asked why there were two *battei Knesset* on the otherwise deserted island, the Jew replied, "Well this is the one I pray in… and that's the one I wouldn't be caught dead in"!

The underlying principle of the joke is that Jews are so derisive that there is just no way that they could live without someone to argue with or something to argue about. Following this logic, we should find that everything in the written Torah that has no clear definition should be a cause for tremendous argument, and/or should be performed the world over in multiple different ways. Yet upon inspection, we find that just the opposite is true. Jews all around the world, even when not having any real means of communication have kept the same exact mitzvos!

Let's take, for example, the mitzvah of *tefillin* that we noted earlier. Despite the fact that the written Torah gives no details as to how the commandment is to be fulfilled, everyone wears basically the same square black leather boxes that are tied on the arm with basically identical straps, which contain the exact same *parshios* (chapters of the Written Torah) on the inside!

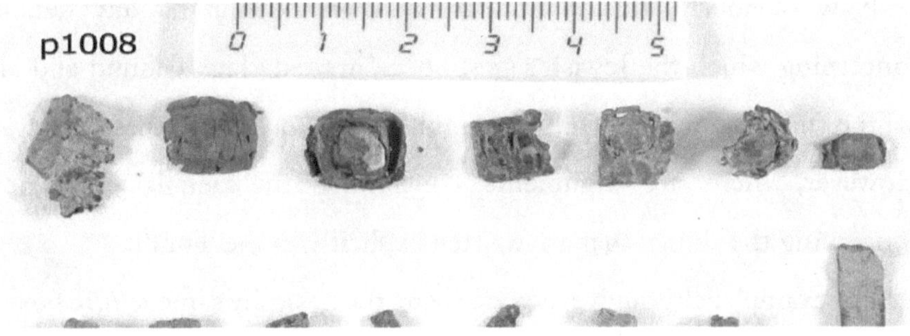

*Tefillin boxes discovered in Qumran*

*(Photo: Shai Halevi/ Israel Antiquities Authority)*

The same applies to the aforementioned commandment of *Sukkos*. Despite having no clear definition in the written Torah, Jews have been building basically identical booths all over the world and sitting in them in basically the same fashion.

Another example is the aforementioned four species of Sukkos. All religious Jews around the world agree that a *pri etz hadar* is an etrog, that *capot tamarim* is a palm frond, that an *anaf etz avos* is the branch of a *Hadas* (Myrtle) tree, and that *arvei nahal* is a type of water willow.

Many more examples can be brought in this regard. In truth, the Jews of the world have many more commonalities than differences when it comes to observance of the laws of the written Torah.

This could only be due to a common Oral Tradition (=Oral Torah) that is accepted. Only such an Oral Torah could so unify the Jews the world over.

Now obviously, this is not to say that there aren't any details concerning which the Jewish sages, ob"m, argued. The Talmud and all of the holy books are full of arguments concerning these things! However, these are arguments concerning the details only, not concerning the things that are written explicitly in the Torah.

For example: although everyone wears the basically same *tefillin* boxes as described above, there is an argument among the sages, ob"m, as to what the order of the *parshios* inside are to be written, and in which order they are to be placed inside the boxes themselves.

The Jewish sages may argue concerning the details of the laws of Shabbos, but they all agree that there are a finite number of categories of *melacha*, (creative activities), that the Torah forbids on Shabbos.

All around the world all of the Jews are basically keeping the exact same laws of the Torah in – almost – the exact same fashion. That would be impossible without an Oral Torah.

## ***Beyond the Ken of Mortal Man***

So, it follows that if the Written Torah is divine, (as we saw in the last chapter), and yet requires an Oral interpretation to understand it, therefore the Oral Torah must also be Divine.

Here is another relevant question. Was there information transmitted in the Oral Torah which was beyond the scope of knowledge available at the time of the sages, ob"m? Such information could only have come from Someone who had knowledge of the world above and would be, of course, beyond the ken of mortal man.

The answer: of course, there was!

Let's look at a couple of examples, shall we?

## Sounds a Little Fishy to Me!

As we saw in the previous chapter, for example concerning the signs of kosher animals, that the Torah belays a breadth of knowledge concerning the world, which could only have been gleaned from The One Who Knows. So, too, do we find that the information contained within the Oral Torah could only have been learned from The One Who Knows. A prime example of this concerns the "signs" of a kosher fish.

If we look in the Written Torah (Leviticus chapter 11:9), we find that the Torah requires that a "kosher" fish have two qualifications: fins (*snapirim*) and scales (*kaskeset*). As long as a fish has these two signs, it is permissible for a Jew to eat. This would seem to imply that if it only had one of the two signs it is then forbidden to eat it. If that were not enough the Torah repeats these requirements three times, which would seem to indicate that both are necessary to eat the sea creature.

It is for this reason that the statement of the Jewish sages, ob"m, in Tractate *Niddah* 51b is so strange!

> *"All that have scales (kaskeset) has fins (snapirim) (=kosher fish), and there are those that have fins but not scales (=non-kosher fish)"*

How can our sages contradict the words of the Torah and say that the sign of scales – by itself – is enough?

This question was addressed in the Gemara as follows: (*ibid.*)

> *However, if we rely (solely) on the existence of scales (to rule it a kosher fish) so why did The Merciful One (Rachmana, a euphemism for HaShem, the Merciful One, in His Torah) write (the additional condition of) fins? ... Said Rabbi Abahu, and so too taught the house of Rabbi Yishmael, "To make great the Torah and to sanctify it."*

Meaning: in truth, the Torah only needed to give us the one sign of scales, which – by itself – would have been enough to certify the fish as kosher. However, the Written Torah tells us that there is a requirement of two signs, and the Oral Torah says that, in reality, the one sign (scales) is enough so that we understand the immensity of the Torah's knowledge and breadth. It encompasses the entire world, including the depths of the oceans, to the extent that The Creator Himself can testify that there does not exist a fish in the whole world that has scales but no fins.

However, one point is crucial to stress regarding this issue: despite the requirement of scales, this does not mean that you can't find a kosher fish that has no scales! Say WHAT, Rabbi? How can you say that? Didn't we just finish saying that the one absolute requirement for a fish to be kosher, is that it has scales? So how can you now tell me that we can find a kosher fish that has no scales? Great question!

The answer: because the requirement of scales is not incumbent upon the fish from minute to minute. So long as the fish had scales, even if it were to lose them at a later stage in life, it remains a kosher fish. The same holds true for a type of fish which has no scales after leaving the egg but develops scales at a later stage in life. It, too, is a kosher fish[157].

One more addendum that our sages teach us on this issue, is that not all "scales" are called "scales" according to the Torah. There are several types of scales. The "scales" that the Torah refers to, which are the sign of a kosher fish, are those that are like "clothing" of the fish, not those that are an integral part of the fish. What this means is that the scales of a fish permitted by the Torah are easily removable or can fall off on their own. Fish that have scales that are an integral part of their body, sharks, for example, which have both scales AND fins, are still forbidden fish.

---

157 Tractate *Hullin* 66a *Our Rabbi's taught if it has none now and they will grow in the future, like the sultanit and the Afian, this is permissible. If it has (scales) now and in the future, it will shed them when it is removed from the water, for example Akkunas and Afuna Caspiian and Achaspatias and Atunas, this is permissible.*

This is because shark scales are integrally bonded to the shark's skin and are not, therefore, the scales that the Torah and our sages are talking about[158]. It is for this reason that any fish with similar scales are forbidden by Torah law[159].

## *Numbers of Stars in the Sky*

As King David writes in Psalms (8:4-5)

*"When I see your heavens, the work of your fingers, the moon and the stars that You created. What is man that You should remember him? Man, that You should command him?"*

Since time immemorial man has looked at the heavens with awe and wonder. "Look at all the stars," said man (and H.A.L., in the movie *SPACE 2001*). Yet until recent history, no-one really knew exactly how many stars there were in the heavens. Realistically, if all we have to go on in this regard is the naked human eye then there really are not a lot of stars. The maximum number of stars that the naked human eye can see on a clear night, with no background illumination is around 8,000-9,000 stars. In all of the star codices from the ancient world, there are a

---

158 Shulchan Aruch Yoreh Deah 83:1, based on the Gemara (Oral Torah) quoted in a previous footnote.

159 The same goes for the fish known as Monopteros Cuchia, which was presented by a certain idiot, wise only in his own eyes, as the refutation of the words of our sages, ob"m. Unfortunately, like all of this person's "proofs" of the "truth" only half quotes and misinformation are presented as proofs. This fish is no exception. Its microscopic scales are bonded to its skin, like those of a shark and are therefore not the scales of a kosher fish of which the Torah speaks. For a complete and utter refutation of what he wrote, check out my site at www.rabbibz.com and read the article "Here Fishy, Fishy."

significantly small number of stars recorded. But the Torah's position on this has always been different.

Moses, our teacher, tells the people of Israel in *Deuteronomy 1:10* that "*The Lord, your G-d, has multiplied you, and you are today as the stars in the heavens in magnitude*". At the time that this statement was made, there were over 600,000 men counted above the age of 20, which gives a minimum population of around 2 million people. This is a clear allusion in the written Torah. Yet for some reason that didn't stop the sages, ob"m, from making the following statement, (Tractate *Berachos 32b*):

> *Said the Holy One, blessed be He, to Israel "There are 12 constellations in the Rakiya and on each and every constellation I created 30 armies. And on each and every army I created 30 legions and on each and every legion I created 30 rahaton. And on each and every rahaton I created 30 keraton and on each and every keraton I created 30 gistera. And on each and every gistera I created 3,650,000,000 stars, corresponding to the days of the (solar) year (365 days). And all of them were created solely for you.*

Upon doing the math of the above Gemara it comes out that 12 (constellations) x 30 (armies) x 30 (legions) x 30 (rahaton) x 30 (keraton) x 30 (gistera) = 291,600,000 which we then multiply by the aforementioned 3,650,000,000 stars under each gistera to arrive at a grand total of 1,064,340,000,000,000,000 stars. Assuming that this statement was "only" from the times of the Talmud, at which time most people counted the number of stars as being quite finite, a couple of thousand at best, this is a staggering number to consider!

Yet when looked at through the lens of modern science – we find this statement to be very precise indeed! The following is an answer given over by NASA's Ask an Astrophysicist site[160]:

> *The Question: How many stars are there, named and unnamed, known to exist?*
>
> *The Answer: This is a very good question! There are too many stars for scientists to actually count one-by-one, so other methods of estimating the total number of stars are used. We believe that there are on the order of $10^{21}$ stars in our Universe. If you write that number out, it looks like this: 1,000,000,000,000,000,000,000. This is a lot of stars!*
>
> *Sincerely,*
>
> *Laura Whitlock, for the Ask-an-Astrophysicist team*

See: scientists are believers as well; they just have no real idea as to in what they are believing! They're only off by a magnitude of 1,000 and change! Outside of the oral Torah, there is no source for a number of stars in the heavens of such magnitude.

---

160 http://imagine.gsfc.nasa.gov/ask_astro/night_sky.html

Also included in this issue are:

- The length of the lunar cycle, (the precise measurement of the synodic month, not to be confused with the sidereal, tropical, or any other type of month).

The Gemara in Tractate *Rosh HaShanna* page 25a gives a measurement that, when converted into fractions of a day comes out to 29.53059 days in a synodic month[161], which happens to be the precise measurement according to NASA[162].

- The existence of the sun's envelope.

The Midrash (Genesis 6) states clearly that the sun is surrounded by an envelope. This topic is explored thoroughly in one of Rav Zamir Cohen's books called *The Coming Revolution*. Check it out there.

In addition to the aforementioned topics related to astronomy, (there are more, but I am trying to keep things short, for more information see volume 1 (Hello? G-d?) in the chapter entitled "*In the Beginning*"), let's

---

161 The Gemara there brings a statement of Rabban Gamliel, Prince of the Sanhedrin, stating that he received an oral tradition from his father's house that the median lunar cycle, (the synodic month), is 29 days, 12 hours (=0.5 days), 2/3rds of an hour and 73 parts (of an hour). When we consider that there are 1080 parts to an hour that means that in 2/3rds of an hour there are (2/3x1080=2160/3=720 parts) plus the additional 73 parts=793 parts. Therefore, we are talking about 793parts/1080parts-of-an-hour= 0.73425 hours. If we convert that into the parts of a day that means 0.73425/24 (hours in a day) = 0.03059. So, the sum total, in days, of Rabban Gamliel's statement converts to a grand total of 29.53059 days. Compare with NASA's calculation above.

162 http://eclipse.gsfc.nasa.gov/SEhelp/moonorbit.html

list some topics related to medicine which our sages described to us in the oral Torah:

- The shape and form of female reproductive anatomy

Despite the fact that the sages, ob"m, described this in terms of an analogy, (tractate *Niddah 17b*), when one understands the analogy – it's very clear that our sages understood clearly the inner workings of reproductive anatomy[163]. Modern science has only recently found this to be true.

- How identical twins are formed

Tractate *Niddah 27a* states explicitly that two fetuses can be formed from "*...one drop* (a reference to a fertilized egg, which is done via semen), *which split in two*"[164].

163 I have a 58-page article (in Hebrew) on this topic in which I show definitively what our sages, ob"m, knew in this regard. I only mention this because there are fools who try to deride our sages without fully understanding what they actually said. With HaShem's help I hope to print this article together with a full summary of the laws of Niddah (the menstruating woman) in the near future, but I would be happy to provide it to anyone who would like to read it. Presently, this article is available for download at my site www.rabbibz.com

164 The context of the Gemara there is concerning the case of a woman who gave birth to two viable children, one of which who was born three months after the first. The Gemara explains that although a pregnant woman cannot become pregnant with a second fetus while pregnant, it is possible for the original fetus to split in two and for each of them to develop at different rates so that one is born after only 7 months of gestation, (which the Talmud considers a viable child of normal gestation), whereas the other is born after 9 months of gestation. The Talmud also says in several places that it is possible for a woman to be impregnated with multiple fetuses. There is an opinion that worries about a viable new pregnancy while already pregnant, which could be disastrous to at least one fetus, if not both of them. However, that is not an accepted opinion. The Talmud is exploring the validity of such a case and what its potential ramifications could be concerning the laws of a *Yoledet* (a woman who has given birth). It is not discounting the possibility of two simultaneous pregnancies, (as it only stated that once pregnant she will not fertilize another egg, rather it is bringing the more severe/extreme instance, that of two fetuses that began life as one, *l'hagdil Torah u'lha'adirah* (to show the expanse of the Torah and its greatness in the eyes of the learners).

- The existence of germs and transference of sickness[165] and many other topics.

In short, there are many, many topics concerning which the sages, ob"m, in the Oral Torah, relate to us information that was unknown to the wise men of their times. Why and how were they in possession of this information … if the information was arrived at later by human wisdom and contrivances?

But the sages, ob"m, never claimed that this knowledge was their own. They claimed it was derived from the Holy One, blessed be He, either from the written Torah itself or via the oral traditions handed down from Moses at Sinai.

Clearly, the source of these oral traditions was, truly, in the know!

## *In Summary:*

- Like all things in existence a written explanation is always misunderstood without an oral one to go with it. Why should the Torah be any different in this regard?

- The written Torah is unintelligible without an oral explanation to explain how to break it up into sentences, and how to cantillate both the words and the sentences themselves.

---

165 See http://www.hidabroot.org/he/article/3302 and also http://www.hidabroot.org/he/article/3302 (Hebrew) for more information.

- Virtually all of the commandments in the Torah contain no description or definition as to how they are to be performed. Without an oral tradition to provide these – there can be no performance of the Torah's commandments.

- In addition --- the Torah, itself, states clearly that there is an oral definition.

- There are many, many statements in the words of the sages, ob"m, which convey knowledge and understanding of reality as we know it today… just because it was told to us by our sages, ob"m, thousands of years in the past!

To me it seems clear from all of the above that the oral Torah, like the written one, was given – as our sages, ob"m tells us explicitly – together to Moses at Sinai.

# The Living Torah

S WE HAVE SEEN in the previous chapters there is so much detail, logic, and evidence contained in the Torah that it would be beyond belief... if there was no G-d! However, there is something else that the Torah has going for it: Living History.

History has its problems as far as we are concerned. After all, we weren't there! If something happened and I wasn't there, what can I do about it? Well, I can always hope that someone recorded it for me. However, since the vast majority of history hasn't occurred in front of any cameras, nor in the proximity of a recording device of any form, so the question that we ask is "how can we know?"

There's only one answer: I have to get my information from someone who was there. Yet even that's not enough by itself. Not all testimony is reliable. This is a problem in all aspects of life, but especially when it comes to the issue of Law. In a court case, the claims of the parties involved are heard first so that the court can assess the extent of the case. Once that is done, the proofs presented by each side are considered in order to try and establish the veracity of the claims. When we call a witness, we don't start asking him questions immediately because there is always the possibility that this guy/girl is an outright liar. How do we avoid this issue? We don't. At least not entirely. We do the best we can by taking out a Bible and making the witness take a solemn vow that everything he is going to say will be the truth, the whole truth and nothing *but* the truth. *The truth*, so that we can rely on what was said. *The WHOLE truth*, so that important information is not omitted which could be crucial in understanding the facts. *Nothing BUT the truth*, so that we don't lose the truth among all of the unnecessary information.

It is because of this vow that we are willing to consider the person's testimony. This is a custom that emanates from the Jewish courts[166].

How is a historical event absolutely verifiable? Well, if we really would like to be honest with ourselves, then we have to recognize that most events in history really aren't[167]! "*History was written by the victors*", (quote from Winston Churchill) is a truism.

What is the methodology historians use to try and verify historical events? With regard to distant past history, it basically boils down to finding written documents, both local (written by someone close to the

---

166 In Jewish courts, it is not the witnesses that take the vow. The only time that a witness takes a vow in the halacha is if the plaintiff or the defendant feel that the witness has testimony to make on his behalf, yet he refuses to give it, claiming "I don't know nuthin!" Only then is there a concept called "making the witnesses take a vow". Normally if there is a vow that needs to be taken it is done either by the plaintiff or the defendant and it is only done if the evidence is not conclusive.

167 https://www.quora.com/If-history-is-written-by-the-victor-how-much-do-we-really-know-about-history

event) and from abroad, comparing and contrasting the accounts, and then arriving at a conclusion as to which parts are authoritative and which are not. Viola! Authoritative history at its best! Except that it's not that great.

There are many different problems that need to be recognized when following this methodology.

The first and most difficult problem is one similar to what I discussed in volume 1, in the chapter *The Emperor's New Clothes* about the authority of paleontology and anthropology when it comes to species with which we are not familiar (=no living specimens). The relative authority of the "experts" is only slightly better than that of the well-informed layman (=next to NO credibility). In all accounts of fossils upon which great theories were made, upon the discovery of a living specimen (at which time they received the title "Living Fossils") the "experts" were always found to be wrong. Take the coelacanth, for example. It's a fish. But until the living specimen was discovered it was the prime example of a "missing link" between fish and land animal. But then a live one was caught and a formal "Oops!" was announced. They all have a batting average of 0.

History is really no different. If we were to meet a real live Roman Senator or an Aztec, would they agree with the writing of today's historians? It's highly unlikely. Maybe they would agree on certain details as to what transpired. Yes, there was a war between X and Y at that time.

But the reasoning behind it, the factors leading up to it and everything else in between may have entirely different explanations.

In addition, there is the aforementioned problem of the question of reliability of the sources. In courts in western countries with their Judeo-Christian traditions, we only give credibility to the witnesses because we make them take a vow on the Bible. The traditional assumption has been that no one in their right mind would lie after having made a vow on the Bible and that therefore we can now feel "safe" and are able to trust their testimony. However, in today's secular world, where both G-d and His Torah are looked at with extreme skepticism, this "vow" thing doesn't really do much!

Yet despite all of the above, and despite the fact that concerning many historical documents we really have no idea who the author is, or how much credibility or reliability he has as a source, because we are now in possession of a written "testimony," all of a sudden, certain parts are looked at almost as gospel!? Does that make any sense?

This is not only true of past history. It's also true of more recent history as well! You might think that the more recent it is, the more data that we have, therefore the easier it is to verify the historical facts and to truly know what really happened... and you would be wrong!

One of the issues of modern, relatively recent history, concerning which there is a tremendous amount of controversy, is the topic of the Holocaust. Although it happened less than 80 years ago, people the world over argue about what really happened and why. The further away we get, the larger the controversy will be. Over what issue could there possibly be any room for controversy concerning the Holocaust, one might ask? The Nazi agenda, of course! Did Hitler, *Yemach shemo v'zichro*, (his name and memory should be erased) and the Nazi party have an agenda to kill all of the Jews? Or did it just happen, that there were a great number of deaths among POW's and the like?

Up until recently the argument made by those parties that claim that there was no such outright agenda, was not taken very seriously. Why is that? It's because there were far too many living witnesses who could testify to the events of the war, to the existence of the concentration camps, to the atrocities, and the Zyklon B gas chambers. Those eyewitnesses made it nearly impossible to claim, "It didn't really happen," and to be looked at as credible. But that's all fine for as long as you *have* the live witnesses. What about now, almost 80 years later? Today there are relatively only a handful of survivors, of both the camps and the liberating forces, who can testify. Their voice has been nearly silenced. How will the future generations be able to know the truth? How will they be able to stand tall against the tide of reconstructionisms? Movies? Hollywood is full of fictional movies that look 100% real. So, it will not be possible to know if a specific movie is accurate or not. Think *Schindler's List*, for example. The same is true for photos. How realistic can we make things look using Photoshop on a regular home computer? Recordings can be faked. Documents can be forged. What will be left to show, beyond a shadow of a doubt, that the Holocaust REALLY happened and that the atrocities were real?

The only way to realistically document the event would be if there are people alive today who embody the history!

Think about it.

I mean, what other way is there for us to verify history? How can we establish the truth of our version if none of the media is considered authoritative and there are no live witnesses who can say "I was there! I went through that living hell, and lived to tell the tale! Who are you, the nay-sayer, who is trying to make a re-reading of the data to deny the truth?"

We must find a means of making the testimony of today into a living, breathing thing, which will withstand the battering of time. A living embodiment of the testimony as to what really occurred.

Many of my teachers and Rabbis suggested the following:

Let's make a gathering of all the remaining survivors of the camps and the liberating forces. At this gathering, they will write down for all time, in a special scroll, the tale of woe that the Jews suffered during the Holocaust. There will be 5 books which contain the stories: Here are some examples:

- What it was like to live in Germany in the days leading up to the war,

- Stories of the ghettos

- Inhumanely crowded life in the bunks sleeping 5 to a tiny tier, 4 bunks one on top of the other,

- Stories from the cattle cars that were used to bring the Jews from all the corners of Europe to destinations in Auschwitz, Birkenau, Treblinka and all of the other, lesser-known camps,

- Stories of the Sonderkommandos[168], whose job it was to clean up the camps and dispose of the dead in either the crematoriums or mass graves,

- Stories of the death marches, the mass killings, and the forced labor

- First-hand eyewitness accounts by soldiers liberating the camps

They would decide together, on the most authoritative way of writing the stories, and then write up the finalized, authoritative version of the Holocaust Scroll.

As the authoritative version of the Holocaust Scroll, it should be agreed upon in advance that it is, and always will be, absolutely forbidden

168 See http://www.jewishvirtuallibrary.org/jsource/Holocaust/Sonderkommando.html for more info.

to make any changes to the Scroll. Even the smallest of changes could totally change the meaning of the words. To ensure this would be accurate, only an authorized Holocaust Scribe could write a new Holocaust Scroll, and it must be done by copying directly from a preexisting scroll.

The Scroll would be taken out and read publicly on a weekly basis. In order to ensure its publicity, there must be a minimum of 10 men present at the reading. On special holidays, there would also be a special reading of the Scrolls.

All descendants of the survivors should get a special holocaust survivors tattoo: a blue number on the arm reminiscent of those given by the German's at the camps.

There should also be three main holidays in the Holocaust Survivors descendants club. In the first, they all go out and sit in a special area decorated to look like a cattle car in memory of the cattle cars that were used to transport their fathers to the camps. In the second holiday, they sit down to a special meal, in which they eat scraps of stale bread and potato peels, in memory of the food that their parents were given to eat while trying to survive in the camps. There they would relate to the next generation in as much detail as possible the story of the camps. How difficult life was in the camps, how they used to scrounge around to try and find a little more food, the savage taskmasters and the tremendous workload, their feelings when the liberation forces came and knocked down the barb-wire fences that had trapped them inside for so long.

The third and last holiday would commemorate the writing of the Holocaust Scroll, the authoritative version to be passed down from father to son for all time.

Does this sound like something that would be more than just a historical notion? More than the writings of some mostly unknown man or woman? Wouldn't the existence of such a group of people, living the life of the Holocaust Scroll, be a living, veracious proof as to the truth of the stories of the survivors? A stronger living testimony to the truth of what actually happened?

Of course, it would!

The above, of course, is only a parable. The real story, narrates the journey of the Jewish people throughout history, as recorded in the holy Torah. The above process is exactly what we, as a people, have been doing throughout all of recorded history (and beyond).

There is not a day that goes by in which we do not remember the exodus from Egypt. We remember it twice daily in the recitation of the *krias Shema* prayer, in its third chapter. We remember it when we don our *tefillin* daily. We remember it when we sanctify the Shabbos day by reciting *kiddush* over a cup of kosher wine. We remember it on all our festivals and our holidays. We read about it several times a year in the public reading of the Torah scrolls.

Even more than the recalling of time long gone, we live the *mitzvos* every single day as well. Every performance of any *mitzvah* is, itself, living testimony as to the truth – the historical truth – of the story related in the book.

If the truth of the book wasn't clear, if it wasn't verifiable in its story and in all its facets, no one would be following its commandments. The Torah is singular in this world in its stories and in its phenomena, as a result, it is clear why there have always been Jewish people living the life that is prescribed in it!

Our very lives testify to the truth of the scroll, just as much as the scroll testifies to the truth of our lives as well. The living history of the Jews through time immemorial testifies to the truth of the Torah itself.

# Hashgacha

## *What IS Divine Providence?*

Having established the truth of both the written and the oral Torah, it is now time to look more closely into its contents. After all, a G-d made, Heaven breathed document about the meaning of life and how to best use the time given us, is certainly worth exploring. It will surely give us some information concerning G-d's relationship with us as well. But before that let's explore, just a little bit, what the Torah tells us about G-d.

## *Will the REAL G-d Please Step Forward?*

There are many things that the Torah tells us about G-d. Extensive books have been written on the topic. I am not going to make this into a treatise on who G-d is, (I don't feel that I am adequate to this task), and in no way, can any book truly encompass who He is. After all, how can we possibly slap a definition on the Infinite? That's an oxymoron! I just want to convey an inkling of an idea about G-d. To do this I am going to follow the RaMBa"M's philosophical model, as described in the Laws of the Foundations of the Torah in the first few chapters.

The Torah is full of personifications concerning G-d, such as "G-d's hand," "the finger of G-d, etc. G-d has no "hand", "finger" or any other body part. This human terminology is used so that the prophets can speak about G-d utilizing metaphors with which we human beings can relate. G-d is NOT a man. He has no need to eat, sleep, copulate, or activate any other such bodily functions. He is infinite, and the infinite cannot be limited to either shape/form or dimensions. The age-old philosophical question is "If G-d is infinite, can He make a rock that's too big for Him to lift? If yes, He's not "infinite"" is a misnomer. It assumes G-d has a physical form, which itself is limited, and therefore would have physical limitations as well.

G-d is Unique. This implies that there is nothing in the existence of our physical reality to which He can be compared. He is not made of cells, has no muscles, no eyes and no brain. He IS. Just as the infinite is indivisible, (if you were to divide the infinite in two – both halves would be infinite. Not because there are now two infinities, but rather because you can't divide the infinite[169]), so too, is He indivisible. He is one and

---

[169] After all, just how long would it take you to divide the infinite? An infinite amount of time!

unique in His One-ness. He can't be compared to an individual man, who may be unique in his personality and fingerprints, but is comparable to all other human beings and animals in the world based on his parts. There is no other being in existence comparable to the singular, unique, individual oneness that is G-d. We Jews, remind ourselves of this twice daily by reciting the *Shema* prayer, (four times if we count the one recited before we go to sleep and the one in the *siddur* (prayer book) before the morning prayers). *"Hear (=Comprehend) O' Israel! The Lord, is our G-d, the Lord is One"*. He is the source of all existence and true reality.

HaShem is not bound by time. He has no past, present, or future. He is neither young nor old. He has no wrinkles. Even physics agrees that time is a construct and that it is bound to the physical world. The more mass – the slower time runs; the less mass the faster. As He has no mass He is not bound by, nor affected by time. (If you multiply any number by zero – what is the result?) He doesn't exist from minute to minute. He exists in all time at the same time. If you have ever wondered how you have free will if He knows what you are going to do before you do it, that's because you live from moment to moment. For Him the moment of your choice and the moment of your follow through, are one and the same. It is also the same as the time of your birth and your death. Or the time of your birth and the birth of your great-great-great-great- (etc.) grandson. Yet no time has passed for Him at either point because only the finite is bound to time[170]. That's the funny thing about the

---

170 See Emunot v'De'ot by Rav Sa'adiya Gaon second ma'amar point 13 (page 112 in the Kappach edition).

infinite. It's not bound by our limited conceptions. This is what King David tried to get us to understand in the verse[171] *"For a thousand years in Your eyes are like yesterday, after it has already passed"*. Past, present, and future are no different to Him.

All facets of reality, both gargantuan and those infinitesimally small, are known to Him, as they only exist because He wills them. He desires that the quarks build the protons, neutrons, and electrons of the atom. He wills that the atoms bind together to make the elements, that the elements join and combine to make chemical and biological compounds, that biological compounds bind to make all facets of life, fauna, flora, animal, and man. All of this happens because He wills it 24/7 365 (or 353-6/383-6 in the Jewish calendar, depending on the year)[172].

Beyond all of that, exists the soul, as we discussed and brought proof for in the first chapter of this volume. Each and every individual has a soul that is beyond the ken of the physical realm, yet tied to a physical body. According to the book of Jewish philosophy, *The Kuzari*, written by Rabbi Yehuda HaLevi, above this level is the Jewish soul. It is the closest thing to G-d in all of existence and is referred to in the Torah as *tzelem E-lokim*, (a facsimile of G-d).

With all the above in mind, we are now ready to start comprehending this chapter's topic, Divine Providence.

---

171 Psalms (Tehillim) 90:4. The simple meaning is that the passage of 1000 years, in HaShem's eyes, i.e. the passage of present time is like yesterday, i.e. past time, after it has already passed. This is because HaShem exists neither in the past or the present. He exists at all time at the same time, today and yesterday, the beginning and the end of 1000 years simultaneously.
172 All of these issues are explored extensively in the first volume.

Just what is *Hashgacha*, Divine Providence, exactly?

## *Lookin' Out for Number One*

In life, we know that when we multi-task we must divide up our brain, as our conscious mind can only handle so much stimulation. It has to do with finite man … being finite! The more we have to deal with, the less successfully we cope. That's a human being for you.  As we mentioned before, the infinite is indivisible. HaShem, G-d, can give infinite attention to each and every individual and have an infinite amount to spare. YOU are constantly on HaShem's mind!

To G-d, we are all "Number One" and He is always looking out for number one!

## *Deeper Than Deep*

It is HaShem who makes all of YOUR biological systems interact and function.  It is HaShem who binds together the atoms in everything in which we come in contact, and in all parts of our bodies. We literally continue to exist from moment to moment because that is His will. It should, therefore, come as no surprise to us to know that He knows us, each and every one of us, in the deepest, most intimate way. There are no "surprises" for him. We can't catch Him off-guard or unawares. He's never sleeping, never hungry, never distracted. Nothing escapes Him. Ever. *Hineh lo yanum ve lo yishan Shomer Yisrael* says the navi.

Even our thoughts, our hopes, and our dreams are open and revealed to Him. I don't think that this should be such a difficult concept to understand. Aside from the fact that we are dealing with an all-powerful, all-wise, all-capable being, even we human beings with our great limitations are capable of some of this in an extremely limited fashion.

If we look at how information is stored on a computer, as the computer retains it, we would see a rather long line of 1's and 0's. Each byte (of the kilo-, mega-, terra-, and so forth) contains either one or the other. That's it. But the computer takes that information and makes it into a legible form for us to read and comprehend. If we take this analogy even further, each byte of information is an electrical impulse, one which symbolizes either the 1 digit or the 0 digit. So, in reality, we are looking at electrical impulses which the computer deciphers into a one or zero and based on the one-zero pattern. It is then translated into legible language on our computer screens. If a stupid computer can translate energy into understanding, is it so hard to comprehend that G-d can do it too?

Furthermore, if we stop and think about it – that's exactly what goes on in our own brain as well! We see something with our eyes via light beams (pulses, waves, or whatever they really are) that strike the rods and cones in our eyes. These receptors translate the hues and the aperture etc. into energy pulses which are relayed, via the optic nerves, to the brain where it is then re-translated into a picture.

So, too, the electrical impulses that our brains make all day, every day, from our thoughts and from the translation of all of the various stimuli from our bodies are an open book for HaShem. He needs no translation whatsoever to understand them.

But it's even more than that. Our very soul is an open book in front of HaShem. Every good-deed and every bad one (and everything in-between) affects our soul and changes it, to the extent that our strengths and weaknesses are glaringly obvious. It is clear where our heads REALLY are, as opposed to where they should be.

The soul has no "conscious," or "subconscious," or "unconscious". The whole of who we are in this life is open and revealed to Him. He knows us better than we know ourselves.

This is the starting point of *hashgacha*. (Divine Providence)

Let's now go…

## ***Where No Man Has Gone Before!***

*Hashgacha* encompasses not just me on a personal level, but all world events on a global scale. There is personal *hashgacha*, there is national *hashgacha*, and there is even world-wide *hashgacha*. What does this mean?

This means that my actions impact my personal outcome but also can affect my surroundings and even world events as well. I truly CAN make a difference. Everything that happens is guided. It all occurs based on the merits and demerits that I make and earn, and those that I inherited from my forefathers.

If a person or a nation is deserving of reward – they will get it. If they are deserving of punishment – they will get that, too. All of this is set up with a Divine Decree and all of my thoughts, actions, choices, and efforts are taken into precise account. I am rewarded or punished "measure for measure." This means that the punishment fits the crime/sin, exactingly and precisely. The reward is based on the merit/commandment, above and beyond all expectations.

There is no action too small to be taken account for, nor too big to be rewarded or punished. The judgment, good or bad, fits the deed precisely. For example, our sages, ob"m, tell us that if a person puts his hand in his pocket to take out a coin, a dime, for example, and instead takes out a quarter – that is Divine retribution. If a person stubs his toe – that, too, is Divine retribution. The same holds true for rewards as well.

Every and all things that happen to a person, a place, a country or the world are decided based on the merits and demerits of that person or place. The good and the bad.

This is where things start to get tough. How can I have free choice to do what I want, on the one hand, and yet I am subject to that which is decreed by the Heavenly court[173]?

---

173 The "Heavenly Court" is a term that refers not to other celestial beings or deities, as clearly the Jewish people believe only in The One Deity, HaShem. Rather it refers to a court of angels who were given the responsibility of making certain decisions concerning the welfare

The answer is that my power of choice will either be in sync with, or against the will of the Heavenly court. That is the extent of my choice.

For example: If it is decreed in the Heavenly court that a certain person is to die on a certain day – that is what is going to happen. However HOW that heavenly decree will occur – is up for grabs. "*There are many messengers for The Place* (a euphemism for G-d)" say our sages. I, therefore have the choice of choosing to be that person's executioner. Should I decide to murder him, I become the messenger of the heavenly decree. However, I will be deserving of punishment for my own choice. Or I can decide not to murder him and let the Heavenly court send someone or something else to fulfill their decree. It's going to happen anyway. It's just a question of whether I choose to be involved. The inverse is also true. If I choose to do a good deed, (a merit in the eyes of the Heavenly court, if I do it for the right reasons), then I am also rewarded for my choice and my follow through. But I am not entirely the master of my own life or life-experiences.

I don't always have a choice to be in a certain situation or a certain place at a certain time. If the Heavenly court should decree it – that decree will happen. There isn't a power in the world that can change that.

---

of the individuals of this world. Angels, which according to the oral Torah have form, but no substance, are beings who also experience time as we know it (even though they are not affected by it as we are). This court's job is to judge people based on HaShem's Law and to decide to what extent we are deserving of reward or punishment in this world. HaShem, Himself, doesn't make this ruling because He knows and sees all time simultaneously and would, therefore, hold someone accountable now for something he hasn't yet done but will do in the future. Angels, who experience time as we do, are therefore, "appropriate" for the job despite the fact that "The Rock (hatzur, in Hebrew), His ways are complete, ... He is Lord of Emunah and has no injustice, He is righteous and straightforward" (Deuteronomy $_{32:4}$). However, He chose, for His own reasons to do it in this fashion.

But like all rules, this one has an exception. Our sages, ob"m, tell us that if the Heavenly court decrees a GOOD/favorable decree on my behalf or on the behalf of my city, state, country or world – there is nothing in existence that will stop it from happening. If a BAD/unfavorable decree is made against me there is nothing in all of the world that can change that and prevent it. Whatever is ruled there – goes! Fortunately, however, in the event of a BAD/unfavorable decree against me, there is one thing that can change the decree: *Teshuva*. I can repent my past misdeeds. I can make up for past wrongs, and if the Heavenly court deems it to be real and true it works.

Why is this? Why would there be an exit clause from the bad stuff? If I am deserving of the bad – why shouldn't it happen anyway?

It is because our loving, infinite G-d knew when He created the world, that it is impossible to expect of this creature of his creation, that it never fails. That is exactly what sets the human apart from the rest of creation. We were made to succeed, but failure is an inevitable part of the journey. *"There is no righteous man in the land who does good and does not sin,"* says the Torah. It is what makes us special. We have neither the lowly beastliness of the animal, which is 100% a slave to its instincts, nor the divine awareness of the angels, totally aware of HaShem's presence. We are somewhere in-between. In this regard, we have the most potential. We can choose to become even greater than the greatest of the angels on the one hand or to be even worse than the most beastly of the animals on the other. But this world was made for our sake, not for the animals and certainly not for the angels.

The reason for this is because it was/is/ and always will be G-d's desire to have a relationship with each and every one of us individually. However, a real relationship is not forced. A real relationship is entered into of one's own free choice.

When a man understands that the Almighty G-d is only looking out for our betterment so that we live a life of love, meaning, and purpose, can there be any other result than a desire on man's part but to come closer? To reciprocate?

However, there will always be those people who don't look for such a relationship. They would rather do the things that G-d hates. But that choice, whether we like it or not, entails a terrible price. To do so is to miss the point of it all.

I would not like to get into the reasoning behind the meaning of life here. Suffice it to say that life has meaning and purpose. So, using this world according to our own desires and to fulfill our own selfish purposes might be fun for a while (then rinse and repeat *ad infinitum* until all our time is gone). However, after all of our time on this earth is done, and our soul leaves our body to stand in front of G-d, we will look back on the life that we lived and for all eternity sit and say to ourselves "Stupid! Stupid! Stupid! How could I have missed the point of it all?"

G-d, in His infinite sense of mercy, like any good parent, will utilize both reward AND punishment in order to get his "child" to do the right thing and get back on the right track. If we take the stern warning, understand that the point of the punishment is to get us back on track so that we don't miss out on the true purpose of life, then further punishment is pointless! That is what *teshuva*, repentance, (literally "return") is all about.

In short: G-d understands you, and cares about you more than you will ever know!

# G -d & me

A FTER LOOKING THROUGH all of the information in this book there can only be one logical answer to life question number 2.

Question 1, Does G-D exist was shown, in book 1, to be a resounding "yes".

Question 2, Does G-d know me? Based upon the preponderance of the evidence also deserves a resounding "yes."

Everything points to G-d's knowledge of you.

Your human body is powered by your human soul. The real "you" is, indeed your soul. It's not vague electrical impulses that animate you and create all of your bodily functions. Nowhere are there any "Energizer" batteries which power you. Nor is there a way to plug you in to return you to life. "Life" powers the living and when our real "life" is no longer there, the body automatically drops and starts to decompose. We each have a unique soul, which is the source of life and which makes each of us who we are. There can only be one source for it --- G-d.

All religions believe as one that there is an afterlife in which one is either rewarded for the good life that he lived, or punished for one's wickedness. Furthermore, all religions agree that man has conversed with G-d via prophecy, to know how to live a "good" life or a "bad" one. G-d told us this because living a "good" life is the point of it all! The historical commonality of this claim seems to indicate that it was handed down through the generations from their common ancestors, who themselves were told this via prophecy[174].

Out of all the world's religions, there is only one whose claim to prophesy and a G-d given set of Divine laws is based on the national revelation model and the 40 years long, daily exposure to open miracles. The Jewish revelation at Sinai is based upon a strong, logical, and verifiable testimony which stands the test of time. The very fact that this claim has never been repeated throughout human history is a clear and valid proof that it was not a "historical" event, but rather a special, supernatural one.

All "logical" (yet oh-so illogical) claims to counter this testimony, upon scrutiny, have no logical or observable proof to back them up. They,

---

174 It's not my intention to imply that all religions actually have prophecy. They don't. It's the commonality of this claim, not the version of it that is related and its details which is important as it clearly shows a common source for a concept which is not earthly but could only have been made by prophecy.

therefore, fall under the rule of "lack of proof – is not a proof" and remain merely skepticism for skepticism's sake.

We have discussed the definition of a prophet, as opposed to a soothsayer or medium or witch. The veracity of a prophet is not something that is taken at face value. It must be proven by means of very specific signs and wonders. However, even a "proven" prophet does not hold a candle to the absolute truth of the 5 books of Moses, whose prophecy was proven to the people beyond all shadow of a doubt.

In considering the Jewish people, as a people, we have seen that we are a historical aberration, defying both time and logic in our continued existence as an autonomous religion and as a society. We "succeeded" in doing so despite all the odds against us. Despite our minuscule size, we remain one of the world's most visible and vibrant people today, as we have been throughout time.

Both the written and the oral Torah's are shown, upon scrutiny, by both their message and by their medium, to be in possession of facts and knowledge that cannot be ascribed to chance or to guesswork. They are full, and I mean FULL, of information that is as true today as it was thousands of years ago. According to Jewish tradition, Judaism has existed for more than 3300 years. Nothing during this time has come to refute the claims or traditions related to these tomes. In fact, the opposite is true. As history marches on, these claims have been verified!

We are one of the few societies in the world today that conveys a "living history," which reinforces the truth of our Torah and our traditions as well. We continue to act today, as throughout time immemorial, in the same manner and with the same customs that build upon the words of our sacred texts and traditions. By doing so, we act as living testimony to the truth of our holy Torah, just as it testifies concerning the truth of our histories and people.

Lastly, in this volume which concerns itself with the "second question," "does G-d know me?", we dealt with the concept of "Divine Providence", called "*Hashgacha*" in Hebrew. We laid bare one of the fundamental *emmunot* (beliefs) of Judaism, as described in the holy Torah. This states that there is no one who knows me quite as well as G-d. From my sub-atomic structure to my very lofty (or not-so-lofty) thoughts, everything is revealed and obvious to the Living G-d, Lord of Abraham, Isaac, and Jacob.

Each of us has no greater cheerleader in life than G-d. As far as the depth of the intimacy of the relationship is concerned, from His side it's infinite. Every individual in this world has been put here for his/her own sake, in order to attain the greatness of meaning and purpose for which we were created in the first place. I don't know about you, but I don't want to miss the boat on life's purpose!

All of this opens up the gate of question three in front of us.

This question asks "According to the conclusions of the first two questions, (Yes, G-d exists, and yes, He knows of my existence intimately and desires a relationship with me), then I now have to ask myself:

What is My relationship with Him?"

With G-d's help, we will begin to explore this issue together in book #3.

# Appendix I

## ***Biblical Archaeological Proofs***

THE FIELD OF ARCHAEOLOGY has, for a few hundred years now, slowly been working, digging and sifting its way through a significant amount of the earth, both above and below the sea. As interesting and important as the findings have been, there have been no findings with more significance than those that are relevant to proving, beyond a shadow of a doubt, the truth that is our holy Torah.

Let me make one thing clear here, from the outset: whenever I use the term "Bible" in this chapter I do NOT mean to prove anything concerning the Christian or Islamic "Bibles". I refer only to the "Old" Testament, using its commonly known name. The accuracy of the

TaNaCh, the Bible, confers nothing regarding the accuracy of any other document which may, or may not, have been "attached" to it. If these other "torahs" would like to prove themselves accurate they need to do so of their own accord… AND THEY CAN NOT.

The Bible is full of historical information. There are names, places, descriptions of battles, and many other specific details given, and that is where archaeology becomes significant. All historical data relates to various civilizations, and all civilizations are made of people and places. It makes sense that there should be remains and/or records of some sort which can either confirm the truth of the information given in the Torah or disprove it.

We will take a look at the significant findings of archaeology which are in sync with the information of the Bible.

However, an important issue that needs to be stressed before we do that concerns the counter-arguments against the accuracy of the Torah which are based upon archaeology as well. These are their claims:

1.  "We have found no evidence."

This does not constitute contrary evidence, or evidence of non-existence.

This issue is a common problem that all of the sciences suffer from, as we explored in-depth in volume 1, "Hello? G-d?" The reasons for not finding proof are multitude. Maybe you are using the wrong apparatus? Maybe you have a problem with your eyes? Maybe you were looking in the wrong place? Maybe you didn't look deep enough? Maybe there were no artifacts that were left behind?

2.   Contrary proof is not proof if there is no context.

Let's say that someone finds contrary proof. For example, I was told during one of my lectures that evidence has been found that around the time of the exodus from Egypt a consensus was made which records the population of Egypt as being around 2,000,000 people. "You see!" said the boy, "Clearly the Torah must be wrong, because according to the Torah the Jews alone were around 2-3 million people, so how could the total population of Egypt be only around 2 million"?

The answer to that is quite simple: lack of context.

You see the problem with finding things in the ground is that they have no context whatsoever! Let's say the hieroglyphs actually said that the population of Egypt was only 2 million. Which part of Egypt are we talking about? Upper Egypt, Lower Egypt, or both? Did it include the land of Goshen, where the Jews were situated, as stated clearly in the Torah? Did it include the slaves, or only the citizens? How trustworthy was the person who etched it into the wall or wrote about it in the papyrus?

On the other hand, let's say that two million was the total Egyptian population. Guess what? If we put it into the context of everything written explicitly in the Torah it actually doesn't harm – it helps! After all, the book of Exodus opens up and describes to us how the people of Egypt were scared by the massive population explosion of the Jews. They felt that there might come a time when the Jews would far outstrip them and kick them out of their own country. If we assume that the population consensus is accurate, and we also assume that it includes only the lands of Egypt, not Goshen, then the picture painted in the Torah comes to life and shines in its truth, not its lack thereof.

Having made the above two points, let's now take a look at the names, the places and the occurrences which archaeology has proven to be accurate.

## Names of People with Extra-Biblical References[175]:

| Name | Title | Date (BCE) | Attestation and Notes | Biblical references |
|---|---|---|---|---|
| Adramelech | Prince of Assyria | 681 | Identified as the murderer of his father Sennacherib in the Bible and in an Assyrian letter to Esarhaddon (ABL 1091), where he is called *Arda-Mulissi*. | Is. 37:38, 2 Kgs. 19:37 |
| Ahab | King of Israel | 874 – 853 | Identified in the contemporary Kurkh Monolith inscription of Shalmaneser III which describes the Battle of Qarqar and mentions *2,000 chariots, 10,000 soldiers of Ahab the Israelite* defeated by Shalmaneser. | 1 Kgs. 17, 2 Chr. 18 |
| Ahaz | King of Judah | 732 – 716 | Mentioned in the contemporary Summary Inscription of Tiglath-Pileser III which records that he received | 2 Kgs. 16, Hos. 1:1, Mi. 1:1, Is. 1:1 |

| Name | Title | Date (BCE) | Attestation and Notes | Biblical references |
|---|---|---|---|---|
|  |  |  | tribute from *Jehoahaz of Judah*. Also identified in royal bullae belonging to Ahaz himself and his son Hezekiah. |  |
| Ahaziah | King of Israel, son of Ahab | 850 – 849 | During his reign, the Moabites revolted against his authority. This event is recorded on the Mesha stele, an extensive inscription written in the Moabite language. | 2 Kings 3:5–7 |
| Apries | Pharaoh of Egypt | 589 – 570 | Also known as Hophra; named in numerous contemporary inscriptions including those of the capitals of the columns of his palace. Herodotus speaks of him in *Histories* II, 161–171. | Jer. 44:30 |
| Artaxerxes I | King of Persia | 465 – 424 | Widely identified with *Artaxerxes* in the book of Nehemiah. He is also found in the writings of contemporary historian Thucydides. Scholars are divided over whether the king in Ezra's time was the same, or Artaxerxes II. | Neh. 2:1, Neh. 5:14 |
| Ashurbanipal | King of Assyria | 668 – 627 | Generally identified with *the great and noble Osnappar*, mentioned in the Book of Ezra. His name survives in his own writings, which describe his military campaigns against Elam, Susa and other nations. | Ezr. 4:10 |
| Belshazzar | Coregent of Babylon | 553 – 539 | Mentioned by his father Nabonidus in the Nabonidus Cylinder. According to another Babylonian tablet, Nabonidus "entrusted the kingship to him" when he embarked on a lengthy military campaign. | Dn. 5, Dn. 7:1, Dn. 8:1 |
| Ben-hadad | King of Aram Damascus | Early 8th century | Mentioned in the Zakkur Stele. A son of Hazael, he is variously called Ben-Hadad/Bar-Hadad II/III. | 2 Kgs. 13:3, 2 Kgs. 13:24 |
| Cyrus II | King of Persia | 559 – 530 | Appears in many ancient inscriptions, most notably the Cyrus Cylinder. He is also mentioned in Herodotus' *Histories*. | Is. 45:1, Dn. 1:21 |
| Darius I | King of Persia | 522 – 486 | Mentioned in the books of Haggai, Zechariah, and Ezra. He is the author of the Behistun Inscription. He is also mentioned in Herodotus' *Histories*. | Hg. 1:1, Ezr. 5:6 |

| Name | Title | Date (BCE) | Attestation and Notes | Biblical references |
|---|---|---|---|---|
| Esarhaddon | king of Assyria | 681 – 669 | His name survives in his own writings, as well as in those of his son Ashurbanipal. | Is. 37:38, Ezr. 4:2 |
| Evil Merodach | King of Babylon | 562 – 560 | His name (*Akkadian* 'Amēl-Marduk') and title were found on a vase from his palace, and on several cuneiform tablets. | 2 Kgs. 25:27, Jer. 52:31 |
| Hazael | King of Aram Damascus | 842 – 800 | Shalmaneser III of Assyria records that he defeated Hazael in battle and captured many chariots and horses from him. Most scholars think that Hazael was the author of the Tel Dan Stele. | 1 Kgs. 19:5, 2 Kgs. 8:8, Am. 1:4 |
| Hezekiah | king of Judah | 715 – 686 | An account is preserved by Sennacherib of how he besieged "Hezekiah, the Jew", who "did not submit to my yoke", in his capital city of Jerusalem A bulla was also found bearing Hezekiah's name and title, reading *Belonging to Hezekiah [son of] Ahaz king of Judah.* | 2 Kgs. 16:20, Prv. 25:1, Hos. 1:1, Mi. 1:1, Is. 1:1 |
| Hoshea | King of Israel | 732 – 723 | He was put into power by Tilgath-Pileser III, king of Assyria, as recorded in his *Annals*, found in Calah. | 2 Kgs. 15:30, 2 Kgs. 18:1 |
| Jehoash | King of Israel | 798 – 782 | Mentioned in records of Adad-nirari III of Assyria as *Jehoash of Samaria*. | 2 Kgs. 13:10, 2 Chr. 25:17 |
| Jehoiachin | King of Judah | 598 – 597 | He was taken captive to Babylon after Nebuchadrezzar first captured Jerusalem. Texts from Nebuchadrezzar's Southern Palace record the rations given to *Jehoiachin king of the Judeans* (Akkadian: *Ya'ukin sar Yaudaya*). | 2 Kgs. 25:14, Jer. 52:31 |
| Jehoram | King of Israel | 852 – 841 | The author of the Tel Dan Stele claimed to have slain both Ahaziah and Jehoram. Hazael is the most likely to have written it. | (2 Kings 8:16, 8:25–28 |
| Jehu | King of Israel | 841 – 814 | Mentioned on the Black Obelisk. | 1 Kgs. 19:16, Hos. 1:4 |
| Johanan | High Priest of Israel | 410 – 371 | Mentioned in a letter from the Elephantine Papyri | Neh. 12:22–23 |

| Name | Title | Date (BCE) | Attestation and Notes | Biblical references |
|---|---|---|---|---|
| Jotham | King of Judah | 740 –732 | Identified as the father of King Ahaz on a contemporary clay bulla, reading *of Ahaz [son of] Jotham king of Judah.* | 2 Kgs. 15:5, Hos. 1:1, Mi. 1:1, Is. 1:1 |
| Manasseh | King of Judah | 687 – 643 | Mentioned in the writings of Esarhaddon, who lists him as one of the kings who had brought him gifts and aided his conquest of Egypt. | 2 Kgs. 20:21, Jer. 15:4 |
| Menahem | King of Israel | 752 – 742 | The annals of Tiglath-Pileser record that Menahem paid tribute him, as stated in the Books of Kings. | 2 Kgs. 15:14–23 |
| Mesha | King of Moab | 840 | Author of the Mesha Stele. | 2 Kgs. 3:4 |
| Merodach-Baladan | King of Babylon | 722 – 710 | Named in the Great Inscription of Sargon II in his palace at Khorsabat. Also called *Berodach-Baladan* (Akkadian: *Marduk-apla-iddina*). | Is. 39:1, 2 Kgs. 20:12 |
| Nebuchadnezzar II | King of Babylon | 605 – 562 | Mentioned in numerous contemporary sources, including the inscription of the Ishtar Gate, which he built. Also called Nebuchadrezzar (Akkadian: *Nabû-kudurri-uṣur*). | Ez. 26:7, Dn. 1:1, 2 Kgs. 24:1 |
| Nebuzaradan | Babylonian official | 587 | Mentioned in a prism in Istanbul (No. 7834), found in Babylon where he is listed as the "chief cook." | Jer. 52:12, 2 Kgs. 25:8 |
| Nebo-Sarsekim | Chief Eunuch of Babylon | 587 | Listed as Nabu-sharrussu-ukin in a Babylonian tablet. | Jer. 39:3 |
| Necho II | Pharaoh of Egypt | 610 – 595 | Mentioned in the writings of Ashurbanipal | 2 Kgs. 23:29, Jer. 46:2 |
| Omri | King of Israel | 880 – 874 | Mentioned, together with his unnamed son or successor, on the Mesha Stele. | 1 Kgs. 16:16, Mi. 6:16 |
| Pekah | King of Israel | 740 – 732 | Mentioned in the annals of Tiglath-Pileser III. | 2 Kgs. 15:25, Is. 7:1 |
| Rezin | King of Aram Damascus | Died 732 | A tributary of Tiglath-Pileser III of Assyria and the last king of Aram Damascus. According to the Bible, he was eventually put to death by Tiglath-Pileser. | 2 Kgs. 16:7–9, Is. 7:1 |
| Sanballat | Governor of Samaria | 445 | A leading figure of the opposition which Nehemiah encountered during | Neh. 2:10, Neh. 13:28 |

| Name | Title | Date (BCE) | Attestation and Notes | Biblical references |
|---|---|---|---|---|
| | | | the rebuilding of the walls around the temple in Jerusalem. Sanballat is mentioned in the Elephantine Papyri. | |
| Sargon II | King of Assyria | 722 – 705 | He besieged and conquered the city of Samaria and took many thousands captive, as recorded in the Bible and in an inscription in his royal palace. His name, however, does not appear in the biblical account of this siege, but only in reference to his siege of Ashdod. | Is. 20:1 |
| Sennacherib | King of Assyria | 705 – 681 | The author of a number of inscriptions discovered near Nineveh. | 2 Kgs. 18:13, Is. 36:1 |
| Shalmaneser V | King of Assyria | 727 – 722 | Mentioned on several royal palace weights found at Nimrud. Another inscription was found that is thought to be his, but the name of the author is only partly preserved. | 2 Kgs. 17:3, 2 Kgs. 18:9 |
| Taharqa | Pharaoh of Egypt, King of Kush | 690 – 664 | Called *Tirhaka, the king of Kush* in the books of Kings and Isaiah. Several contemporary sources mention him and fragments of three statues bearing his name were excavated at Nineveh. | Is. 37:9, 2 Kgs. 19:9 |
| Tattenai | Governor of Eber-Nari | 520 | Known from contemporary Babylonian documents. He governed the Persian province west of the Euphrates river during the reign of Darius I. | Ezr. 5:3, Ezr. 6:13 |
| Tiglath-Pileser III | King of Assyria | 745 – 727 | Numerous writings are ascribed to him and he is mentioned, among others, in an inscription by Barrakab, king of Sam'al. He exiled inhabitants of the cities he captured in Israel. | 2 Kgs. 15:29, 1 Chr. 5:6 |
| Xerxes I | King of Persia | 486 – 465 | Called Ahasuerus in the books of Ezra and Esther. Xerxes is known in archaeology through a number of tablets and monuments, notably the 'Gate of All Nations' in Persepolis. He is also mentioned in Herodotus' *Histories*. | Est. 1:1, Dn. 9:1, Ezr. 4:6 |

For years members of universities around the world have made it a point of pride to announce to the world that there have been no extra-biblical references found pointing to the existence of King David. "Haven't found any proof", as I mentioned above, doesn't prove or disprove ANYTHING, except, perhaps, the incompetence of the person making the statement. Especially in light of the evidence for the existence of the house of David which has started popping up… as was expected.

*Until very recently, there was no evidence outside the Bible for the existence of King David. There are no references to him in Egyptian, Syrian or Assyrian documents of the time, and the many archaeological digs in the City of David failed to turn up so much as a mention of his name. Then, on July 21, 1993, a team of archaeologists led by Prof. Avraham Biran, excavating Tel Dan in the northern Galilee, found a triangular piece of basalt rock, measuring 23 x 36 cm. inscribed in Aramaic. It was subsequently identified as part of a victory pillar erected by the king of Syria and later smashed by an Israelite ruler. The inscription, which dates to the ninth century BCE, that is to say, about a century after David was thought to have ruled Israel, includes the words*

*Beit David ("House" or "Dynasty" of David"). It is the first near-contemporaneous reference to David ever found. It is not conclusive, but it does strongly indicate that a king called David established a dynasty in Israel during the relevant period.*

*Another piece of significant evidence comes from Dr. Avi Ofer's archaeological survey conducted in the hills of Judea during the last decade, which shows that in the 11th–10th centuries BCE, the population of Judah almost doubled compared to the preceding period. The so-called Rank-Size Index (RSI), a method of analyzing the size and positioning of settlements to evaluate to what extent they were a self-contained group, indicates that during this period – David's supposed period – a strong centre of population existed at the edge of the region. Jerusalem is the most likely candidate for this centre[176].*

How about this, as well:

*JERUSALEM, Israel -- Did characters like David and Solomon really exists? Many historians today are divided over this question. But CBN News met*

---

176  See also  http://www.jpost.com/Israel-News/Culture/Ancient-rock-adds-evidence-of-King-Davids-existence-384826  see  also  http://www.jpost.com/Israel-News/Culture/Ancient-rock-adds-evidence-of-King-Davids-existence-384826

*with two archaeologists who are digging up parts of David's life, and what they've found supports the biblical accounts down to the smallest details. ...*

*In 1868, a stone tablet was discovered in Jordan. It was written by a Moabite king named Mesha, an enemy of Israel. The stone dates to around 840 BC, less than 200 years after David and it provides the first known reference to the "House of David" outside the Bible. ...*

*And high above the valley (of Elah) is a fortress that's thousands of years old to the local Bedouin. This place is still known as "Khirbet Daoud" or "David's Ruin." It's the only iron age city in Israel that's perfectly preserved and almost frozen in time[177].*

But enough about just the people of the Bible, (the Old Testament), let's talk about places, as well.

The following is a partial list of places mentioned in the Bible, all of which have historical and archaeological backing.

---

177 http://www.cbn.com/cbnnews/insideisrael/2013/june/did-david-solomon-exist-dig-refutes-naysayers/?mobile=false

# A

Absalom's Monument (Yad Avshalom), Achaia, Adiabene (Neo Assyrian State), Ai, Akko, Akkad (Mesopotamian state), Ammon, Aram/Aramea - (Modern Syria), Arbela (Erbil/Urbil) (Assyrian city), Archevite, Arrapkha (Assyrian City, modern Kirkuk), Ararat, Ashdod, Ashkelon, Ashur/Asshur/Assur (Capital city of Assyria), Assyria (Mesopotamian Semitic state).

# B

Baal-Hazor (Canaanite city), Babel, Babylon/Babylonia (Mesopotamian state), Beer-Sheba, Beit El, Beirut, Bethel, Bethharan, Bethlehem, Bochim, Byblos (Phoenician state called "Guval" in the Bible), Beersheba, Bet Shean

# C

Cabul, Calah/Kalhu/Nimrud (Assyrian city), Calneh (Assyrian city), Cana, Canaan (Region on the Eastern shore of the Mediterranean), Carchemish (Assyrian city), Cush (African state), Chaldea (Mesopotamian state, eventually encompassing Babylonia).

# D

Damascus (Aramean city and state), Dan, Debir, Dothan, Dur-Sharrukin (*Saragon*, an Assyrian city).

# E

Ebla (East Semitic state in northern Syria), Eden, Egypt (*Mitzrayim*, in Hebrew), Ekron, Elam (*Pre-Iranic* Nation in Ancient Iran), Elim, En Gedi, Eshcol, Ethiopia (*Kush* in Hebrew), Etham.

# G

Galilee, Gath, Gaza, Gibeon, Gilead, Gomorrah, Goshen, Greece (*Yavan* in Hebrew), Gutium (*Koa* in Hebrew, state in modern-day Iran).

# H

Haran, Harran (Assyrian City), Hattusa (Capital of Hittite Empire in Asia Minor), Hatti (Nation in Asia Minor), Havilah, Hazazon Tamar (also Hazazon-Tamar or Hatzatzon-Tamar - Ein Gedi), Hebron, Helam, Hill of Gash, Hurri Nation (*HaChori* in Hebrew, a nation in Asia Minor).

# I

Imgur-Enlil (Assyrian City), India (*Hodu* in Hebrew, see Esther 8:9).

# J

Jabbok, Jaffa, Jerash, Jericho, Jerusalem, Jordan, Jordan Plain, Judah.

# K

Kabzeel (*Kabetz-El* in Hebrew), Kadesh-Barnea, Kassite state (in Iran), Kish (Mesopotamian City State), Kush/Cush (in northeast Africa).

# L

Laban, Lachish, Laish, Larsa (Mesopotamian city), Lebanon, Lehi, Lydia (*Ludim* in Hebrew, a nation in Asia Minor).

# M

Machpela, Magan (*Pre-Arab* state in Oman), Mamre Plain, Mannea (Nation in Iran), Marah, Mari (Assyrian city), Media (Nation in Iran), Megiddo, Memphis (Called *Mof* or *Nof* in the Bible), Mesopotamia (Includes the kingdoms of Sumer, Akkad, Assyria, Babylonia, Chaldea, and the neo Assyrian states of Adiabene, Osroene and Hatra), Midian, Miriam, Moab, Mount Carmel, Mount Ephraim, Mount Nebo, Mount Sinai, Mount Tavor, Mount Zabor, Mount Zemaraim.

# N

Nahor, Nahrain (Mesopotamia), Nazareth, Nibarti-Ashur (Assyrian city), Nimrud (the later name for the Assyrian city of Kalhu/Calah), Nineveh (Capital of Assyria), Nod.

# O

On, Ophir, Opis (Mesopotamian/Babylonian City).

# P

Palmyra (Aramean state in Syria, the Biblical name "*Tadmor*"), Paran, Penuel, Persia (*Paras* in Hebrew, a nation in Iran), Petra (*Se'ir* in Hebrew), Phrygia (*Togarmah* in Hebrew, a city in Asia Minor), Phut, Pithom, Punt.

# R

Ramath-Lehi (*Lehi* in Hebrew), Rapiqum (*Refakim* in Hebrew, an Assyrian city), Rephidim.

# S

Shalem, Sheba (*Pre-Arab* state in Yemen), Shechem, Shiloh, Shinar (Mesopotamian city), Shomron, Shubat-Enlil (Assyrian city), Sidon, Sin Desert (*Midbar Sin* in Hebrew), Sinai, Sodom, Sumer/Sumeria (Mesopotamian state and region), Syria/Aramea (*Suria* in Hebrew).

# T

Tabal (*Tubal* in Hebrew. A Georgian state in Asia Minor), Tarshish, Tel Dan, Timnath-Serah, Timnath, Tushhan (Assyrian city), Tyre (*Tzur* or *Zur* in Hebrew).

# U

<u>Ugarit</u> (<u>Amorite</u> state), <u>Umma</u> (<u>Mesopotamian</u> state and city), <u>Ur</u> (<u>Mesopotamian</u> state and city), <u>Urartu</u> (<u>Hurrian</u> state in the <u>Caucasus</u>), <u>Urkish</u> (<u>Mesopotamian</u> state and city), <u>Uruk</u> (<u>Mesopotamian</u> state and city), <u>The Land of Uz</u>.

# Z

<u>Zaanan</u>, <u>Zair</u>, <u>Zalmonah</u>, <u>Zanoah</u>, <u>Zareah</u>, <u>Zartanah</u>, <u>Zelahzaliya</u>, <u>Zemaraim</u>, <u>Zephi</u>, <u>Zeredathah</u>, <u>Zorah</u>, <u>Zion</u>, <u>Zoba</u>.

The above is a VERY incomplete list of the places mentioned in the Bible. Suffice it to say that even though many historians/archaeologists dispute the idea that certain archaeological findings are consistent with the Torah, at the end of the day not one of the places has been found to be inaccurate or false. Some of these places were lost entirely to history over the course of centuries.

For example, the city of Ur was lost to time for centuries[178] until it was slowly recovered over the last one. This is apparently due to the fact that it once stood on the banks of the Euphrates river, but the riverbed changed over time, due to erosion and plate tectonics. The result was that the city was eventually abandoned and lost to the desert.

Or how about the Hittites?

---

178 See also http://www.ancient-origins.net/ancient-places-asia/great-ziggurat-ur-001767 see also http://www.ancient-origins.net/ancient-places-asia/great-ziggurat-ur-001767

*Bible critics had long sneered at references in the Bible to a people called the Hittites (Genesis 15:20; Exodus 3:8, 17; Numbers 13:29; Joshua 1:4; Judges 1:26 and elsewhere). Their opinion was that the Hittites were simply one of the many mythical peoples made up by Bible writers. Some critics said they may have been a small and unimportant tribe. But the critics were off the beam!*

*Toward the end of the 19th century, Hittite monuments were uncovered at Carchemish on the Euphrates River in Syria, proving the Bible right. Later, in 1906, excavations at Boghazkoy (ancient Hattusas, capital of the Hittite Empire) in Turkey uncovered thousands of Hittite documents, revealing a wealth of information about Hittite history and culture. The centuries-old Hittite rubbish showed they were a real and formidable power. They were once one of the dominant peoples of Asia Minor and the Near East. They exercised considerable control south into Syria and Palestine[179].*

---

179 Mind you, I do NOT endorse anything said about the New Test(ament).

Clearly, the historical accuracy of the Bible is quite, quite solid.

But it's not just the names of the places, there has also been plenty of archaeological evidence to back up *the narratives* of the Bible, as well.

For example:

- The walls of the city of Jericho

> *A major issue in the historicity debate was the narrative of the Israelite conquest of Canaan, described in Joshua and Judges. The American Albright school asserted that the biblical narrative of conquest would be affirmed by archaeological record; and indeed, for much of the 20th-century archaeology appeared to support the biblical narrative, including excavations at Beitin (identified as Bethel), Tel ed-Duweir, (identified as Lachish), Hazor, and Jericho[180].*

Even though these sources go on to question the historicity of the event, the truth of the matter is that those *opinions* are debatable. They are especially problematic since because they are based upon the flawed science of carbon-dating, (See book 1, chapter 10 for the full explanation), and also upon their own interpretation of the remains, which is entirely debatable. The reality is, however, that the city of Jericho was found *exactly where it was supposed to be.* There were/are

180 Israel Finkelstein; Neil Asher Silberman (6 March 2002). The Bible Unearthed: Archaeology's New Vision of Ancient Israel and the Origin of Sacred Texts. Simon and Schuster. pp. 81–82. ISBN 978-0-7432-2338-6.

complete segments of the wall of the city still "standing" up to its neck in the ground, as if it sunk into the ground in its entirety, *exactly as described in the Bible.* SO, who should be considered more reliable in this matter, regarding what happened at that time? The book that claims to have been there and witnessed it as it happened, or the scientists who are trying to interpret the remains that they DID find after the fact?

- King Solomon's copper mines

  *In the February 2017 issue of the* Journal of Archaeological Science: Reports *three archaeologists, Erez Ben-Yosef, Dafna Langgut, and Lidar Sapir-Hen, announced their findings from excavations they performed in one of the most inhospitable regions in southern Israel.[1] They excavated a gatehouse and livestock pens in Timna, Israel.* ... **While there is abundant historical evidence** *that the rich copper ore in the region had been mined since the fifth century BC, historians expressed considerable skepticism about whether the mines and smelters were active during the reign of Israel's King Solomon. The new dating measurements remove that skepticism. The mines and smelting camps in the Timna Valley indeed are the fabled King Solomon's mines. ... The Bible* *devotes twenty-one chapters to describing the history of King Solomon's reign and the extent, wealth, power, and organization of Solomon's empire. Many scholars presumed that these descriptions were just as exaggerated and embellished as are the annals of famous kings in the nations bordering Israel during the BC era. What Ben-Yosef, Langgut, and Sapir-Hen discovered in Timna is that these biblical descriptions are not exaggerated. They are entirely consistent with everything the Bible describes about the reign of King Solomon[181].*

- The destruction of Yavin

  *There are a few cases where the biblical record is not contradicted by the archaeological record. For example, stratum in <u>Tel Hazor</u>, found in a* **destruction layer** *from around 1200 BCE, shows signs of catastrophic fire, and cuneiform tablets found at the site refer to monarchs named Ibni Addi, where Ibni may be the etymological origin of Yavin (Jabin), the Canaanite leader referred to in the Hebrew Bible. The city also shows signs of having*

---

181 http://www.reasons.org/blogs/todays-new-reason-to-believe/more-archaeological-evidence-for-the-bibles-historical-accuracy

*been a magnificent Canaanite city prior to its destruction, with great temples and opulent palaces, split into an upper acropolis, and lower city; the town evidently had been a major Canaanite city[182].*

- The United Kingdom (pre-Rechavam, son of Shlomo)

  *Excavations at <u>Khirbet Qeiyafa</u>, an Iron site located in Judah, support the biblical account of a United Monarchy. The Israel Antiquities Authority stated: "The excavations at Khirbat Qeiyafa clearly reveal an urban society that existed in Judah already in the late eleventh century BCE. It can no longer be argued that the Kingdom of Judah developed only in the late eighth century BCE or at some other later date.[183]"*

We have seen so many things for which there are clear historical backing, names, places and even dates. Evidence for the events described have been discovered. But there are still so many details which can be noted and for which unequivocal historical evidence has been found. For example:

- Names and types of idol worship and idolatrous practices:

182 Finkelstein & Silberman 2001

183. Hadashot-esi.org.il. Retrieved 20 December 2014.

Many, many types of idol worship are mentioned in the Bible: Ba'al, Dagon, Molech, Asherot and many others. All of which have been found and studied.

- Common types of agricultural practices and crops

Seasons of different crops, names of common crop types, fruits, and vegetables that were common to the time, both in and out of the land of Israel are mentioned in the Bible. For all of which there is extensive historical evidence.

- Garments, types of armaments, implements, and more

How much more historical evidence is required? How much more has yet to be discovered? How many times will we allow men and women of questionable morals and objectivity to proffer dubious opinions based on the two key "no-no's" with which I opened up this appendix?

I find that it's the same thing, again and again. Statements are made based on minimal, if not nearly non-existent evidence, and because they are made by peoples of authority – they are accepted and swallowed, hook, line and sinker. Claims are made, based on the two opening points I made, supposedly "disproving" the authenticity of the Bible... despite the fact that more and more evidence pops-up all of the time showing how true the Torah's and the Jewish Scriptures are absolutely true!

So, if you want to make an informed decision as to the historical accuracy, and therefore the TRUTH of what is being said. If the more we investigate, the more we find that the Torah is true --- then why do we continue to doubt the rest of the information that it contains?

Think about this very, very deeply.

# Appendix II

## *History, Mystery, and True Understanding of the Ways of Humanity*

WHEN LOOKING BACK into humanity's ancient history we discover, amazingly, that there actually WAS life before the Jewish people! The truth is that the Torah, itself, records ancient history and tells us a story ..., no, THE story of what was and where everything came from. However, the question that we ask ourselves, in looking back, is how to interpret the course of history.

Everyone "agrees" with the following over-generalization of history: there was a time before the Jews, then there were the Jews, and then we made it to today. Even we Jews agree that there was a time in human history BEFORE we had a written Torah. So, the question then arises as to the origin of the things that the Jews do. Where did the commandments that they follow, come from? Are they human in origin (and the Jews just ran with them as they "grew up")? Or did the customs and practices of the ancient world start with the commandments of G-d until they finally were codified into the words of the written Torah?

I would like to present the following as a very clear evidence of the fact that the Torah's explanation, as conveyed in the words of our sages, ob"m, is the only one which makes sense.

The topic: Human Calculation of Time.

Throughout the entire world, today and in the ancient past, people have always measured time. There are several basic universal measures: days, weeks, months and years. In addition, a day has always been broken up into 24 hours. There is basically and virtually nowhere in the world in which they do things differently. I'm not talking about in the modern world, which has essentially accepted the modern secular calendar. I'm talking about even the ancient world, as well. Like all rules, this one also has an exception, and we'll address it later on in this appendix.

The reason why time-keeping is of such importance is, in my opinion, due to its universality. As we will see, there really is no explanation as to why, virtually throughout all of recorded history, we all measure time in exactly the same way, unless we accept that all of humanity comes from a common source/ancestry. Hence, we all received our "education" in time-keeping from the same place. Of course, I'm not the first person to say this. I was preempted by none other than Rabbi Yehuda HaLevi in his classic *sefer* "The Kuzari." He brings this up within the context of the conversation between the *chaver* (the Rabbi) and the King of the Khazars. It is the only explanation that makes sense.

However, in addition to the above, we have to wonder, "Why?" Why is it that humanity would divide up time in the manner that they did? What is the significance of an hour, a day, a week, a month, and a year that caused us to decide to make these divisions? Here – only the Torah, (written and oral), can help us to understand. There is no other way to explain these phenomena without them. So, lets' get into the subject, shall we?

I was asked to give a Hebrew lecture to a group of irreligious students from Ben Gurion University. The general topic of the semester was "The Jewish Day." I thought that I would speak, generally, about how the Jewish people don't work like the rest of the world when it comes to the topic of time. "Jewish Time", I told them, "doesn't work like any other time in the world. We have a different concept of a day, a week, a month, a year and more! *Yekkim* aside[184], if an average Jew gets invited to a wedding and it is called for, say, 7 PM the Jewish brain translates that as … 7:30 PM at the earliest!"

---

184 Jews who come from the Germanic areas are referred to as Yekkim, which means to be, quite frankly, OCD regarding their life and their performance of mizvos. But in a good and positive way. "Time is Time" is a classic yekkish statement, meaning whenever it's called for --- that's when you have to make sure to be there and start by.

It's such a known phenomenon, that part of the planning of any Jewish gathering starts with a calculation as to what earlier time should be written in the invitation on the off-chance that we actually *do* want to start on time.

However, as I was preparing the lecture, trying to figure out what questions might be asked and possibly outside sources that would be worthwhile to quote I made an amazing discovery!

I discovered that without an understanding of both the Oral and the Written Torah – the way that the world counts time makes absolutely no sense whatsoever.

Let me explain.

We all know that there is a concept of *a* "day" and there is also a concept called "day and night." In this regard, however, the Jewish people are different from all other peoples of the world. According to the Torah, the day *begins* at nightfall.[185] Come sunset on Friday – it's Shabbos, the Sabbath day! We, of course, learn this (see *Berachos 2a*) from the beginning (Genesis). The Torah says, *"and it was evening, and it was morning day one."* Regarding the concept of morning, everyone else either uses the contrived "day-line" of midnight or perhaps sunrise. In truth, at least as far as ancient history, only nightfall or sunrise are logical times to set as the beginning of a day. They are both at a point in time where there is a clear, natural phenomenon that signifies the changing of a

---

185 I don't mean to say by this that there are no other people who start or started their day at nightfall. But we have done so throughout all of our history.

significant point in time. Midnight is a practical contrivance which was decided upon in more recent history.

But let's stick with this point for a moment, as I just love pointing out logical inconsistencies.

Why choose midnight? Well, it's because of the modern prevalence of clocks! It's because in the modern world a day is 24 hours, made up of 60 minutes per hour, and we really had to choose a point in time to begin counting the 24 hours that make up a day. Because both sunrise and sunset change all the time they couldn't be used in order to scientifically begin a day, therefore it was decided that the middle of the night should be used. After all, high-noon couldn't have logically been used to divide up the day. Just imagine if you would leave to work on Monday and came home the same day on Tuesday! But here's the rub: WHY is a day made up of 24 hours?

The answer according to the wise men of the world? IDK[186] (that's texting short-hand for **I Don't Know**). Really, it would seem that a 24-hour day is a human invention. However, there is no clear reason as to why everyone would count 24 hours in a day. Even stranger is that the entire world has been counting and keeping a 24-hour day (or a 12-hour day and a 12-hour night) for… forever! The only logical reason for this

---

186 See https://www.scientificamerican.com/article/experts-time-division-days-hours-minutes/ for example. Although many explanations are offered as to from where we got the 12 hours, at the end of the day the only thing that is clear is that the ancient world divided the day and the night into 12 parts. The why of the 12, at the end of the day, is only an educated guess at best. However, it's not just the ancient Egyptians who divided the day and the night into 12, it was also the practice of all the ancient peoples of the "Fertile Crescent". The Babylonians, the Akkadians, the Sumerians and even the ancient Chinese all kept a 24-hour day (12 and 12). Holford-Strevens, Leofranc (2005), *The History of Time: A Very Short Introduction*, Very Short Introductions, Vol. 133, Oxford: Oxford University Press, ISBN 9780192804990 See also https://24hourtime.info/history/

would have been a consensus or decision by all of humanity in the ancient world at a singular point in time and a central place, that this was the way it must be done. Since it has always been done this way, no-one ever really thought to change it. But why the number 24? It could have been any multiple of 6, or 5, or 4, or 3, or whatever!

The answer lies in the words of our sages, ob"m, on the verse in Genesis (Bereishis) (1:14).

> *"And E-lohim said, "There shall be sources of light in the Rakiya of the shomayim to separate between the day and the night and they should be for signs (otot) and moadim (festivals) and days (yamim) and years (shanim)".*

This verse teaches us that it is the celestial bodies that "rule" time in the Torah. Based on these celestial bodies we decide the days, years, and various "pit-stops" of the year. But what, exactly, are the *otot*, (signs)? They are the signs of the zodiac. Amazingly, there are 12 signs of the zodiac and our sages in many places (see *Shabbos 75a*, for example) tell us that they "rule" the sky for exactly *one hour each per day*.

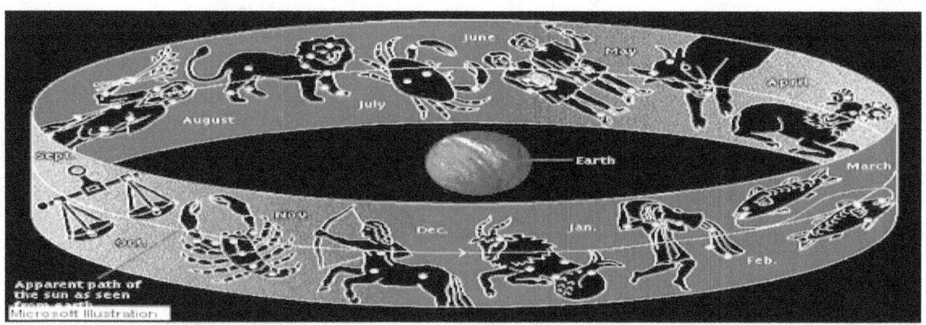


What this means is that at different times of the day one of the signs of the zodiac has "power". It is for this reason that the day (and the night) were divided into 12 parts and 12+12 =???? You guessed it! 24 hours!

Afterward, I found this explicitly in the words of the *Tanna d'bei Eliahu Rabbah*, chapter 5:12, which says:

> *"And when Ya'akov left his father's house to go to the house of Lavan, the Shechina came and stood above him. It answered him and said 'Ya'akov, my son! Raise your eyes to the heavens and see the twelve* mazalot *(signs of the zodiac) and the stars in the heavens and the twelve hours of the day and the twelve hours of the night, all of them are against (=corresponding to) the twelve tribes that I will give to you".*

If you research the topic of "astrology," you will find that it is an ancient topic. It was practiced by the Babylonians, the Acadians, and all of the ancient peoples. This, of course, leads the learned of the world to the amazing conclusion that "it was the Jews that took it from the peoples of ancient civilizations."

Now we REALLY get into the spicy stuff!

Why *did* the ancient peoples practice it? What was it to them?

Let's keep this in mind and come back to it later, with HaShem's help.

Let's skip, for a moment, to the concept of a month. Where does a month come from? The answer, of course, is from the moon-phase cycle. It is for this reason that the average length of a month is roughly 30 days and there is no controversy about it. In Hebrew, a month is called *Chodesh*, from the root of *chadash*, "new," because it goes through a cycle of renewal every month.

Where does a "year" come from? That's also pretty clear. It's the amount of time that it takes to run through the four seasons of the earth: winter, spring, summer, and fall. This cycle takes an average of 365.25 days to complete. In Hebrew, a year is called a *Shanna*, which means "something that repeats", as the seasons that make up a year go through a repetitive cycle.

Now, let's get a little deeper. Why are there 12 months in a year? Why that's so obvious! It's because we can complete a total of 12 lunar cycles during the course of one 365-day year. After all, 12 x 30 = 360! But there's just one problem: *who cares?*

Let's stop and think for a second. In a purely solar calendar, who cares how many lunar-cycles there are during a year? They are *irrelevant*! In reality, it would make more sense to have 4 months a year. One for each of the seasons. Whereas, in a purely lunar calendar, what is the purpose of a year? It has no relevance whatsoever. The Islamic calendar has no real need for a year, as it makes no difference in what season Ramadan falls.

Only within the context of a Lunar-Solar calendar does it make sense to have a 12-month year, and we Jews happen to have one!

The reality that we live in is kind of funny when you think about it. One would think that in a solar year there should be 7 months of 30 days and 5 months of 31 days in order to "cover" the 5 extra days in a solar year (and 6 and 6 every 4 years). So why the saying: "30 days hath September, April, June, and November?" Why does "February alone hath 28 days"? It's because, in the times of the Romans two emperors, Augustus and Julius decided to name a month after themselves (August and July). Since the months that had 31 days were named after the Roman gods/Planets of our galaxy – so, too, *their* months should also have 31 days! (They were, after all, exceedingly humble men.) So instead of being logically divided as above, the year was instead divided into 7 months with 31 days, and someone had to lose out. Why not February?

The Islamic calendar, at its inception, had no measurement of a year [187]. Then they discovered that the counting of years also had a very

187 "In AD 638 (17 AH), Abu Musa Ashaari, one of the officials of the Caliph Umar in Basrah, complained about the absence of any years on the correspondence he received from Umar, making it difficult for him to determine which instructions were most recent. This report convinced Umar of the need to introduce an era for Muslims. After debating the issue with his counsellors, he decided that the first year should include the date of Muhammad's arrival at Medina (known as Yathrib, before Muhammad's arrival). Uthman ibn Affan then suggested that the months begin with Muharram, in line with the established custom of the Arabs at that time. The years of the Islamic calendar thus began with the month of Muharram in the year of Muhammad's arrival at the city of Medina, even though the actual emigration

practical side. I mean, for example, if someone was describing a sale, did the sale go through *this* Ramadan, or was it *last* Ramadan? So out of practical necessity (as opposed to religious motivation), they also started counting the years.

Let's get back to the lunar-solar year.

We are not the only people on the face of the planet to have a Lunar-Solar calendar. It turns out *that all of the ancient peoples of the world used it*. It was used by the Babylonians, the Acadians, the ancient Chinese and many (all?) of the ancient peoples of the world[188].

The question is: why? What purpose does the Lunar-Solar calendar serve? Amazingly, it only makes sense if there are festivals (*moadim*, as mentioned in the verse in Bereshis, (Genesis)) *which are tied to specific seasons of the solar year*!

But then why have a lunar calendar at all? Just use a solar calendar.

Unless there is some specific reason for the existence of the months, and they should be counted based on the lunar cycle. What we find, is that we have two conflicting time schedules, which must be used simultaneously and balanced out between each other in order to make a Lunar-Solar year. That is the only reason why we would require the double-standard, Lunar-Solar year.

took place in Safar and Rabi' I. Because of the Hijra, the calendar was named the Hijra calendar". Watt, W. Montgomery. "Hidjra". In P.J. Bearman; Th. Bianquis; C.E. Bosworth; E. van Donzel; W.P. Heinrichs. Encyclopaedia of Islam Online. Brill Academic Publishers. ISSN 1573-3912. See also https://en.wikipedia.org/wiki/Islamic_calendar#Year_numbering

188 See http://aa.usno.navy.mil/faq/docs/calendars.php in the introduction. See also https://hermetic.ch/cal_stud/lunarcal/types.htm and https://en.wikipedia.org/wiki/Lunisolar_calendar#Examples

Look up the topic of the "Lunisolar/Solilunar Calendar" and you will find lots of information about who does and who does not keep it, and yet you will find no real explanation as to why they would do it in the first place!

Yet, if all of the people of the ancient world kept the lunar-solar year, that would mean that they also had a common reason for doing so. Can you guess what it is? Well… that's just fine! You're in good company because neither can anyone else! Unless, of course, you have a Torah, that is.

Now we get to the real heart of the issue.

Where do we get a week from?

Can you guess? What do you think that the worlds most learned have to say about this? I'll give you a little hint: I……D……K.[189]

Realistically there is neither rhyme nor reason for the existence of a week. A day – yes. A month – yes…ish. A year? Also, yes…ish. But what's a week for? "Well", say the experts, "it's about 1/4 of a month, so that's good, right?" Yes, if you're looking for a *dumb* reason, then it's good!

But all of the world's people since time immemorial have been keeping a seven-day week. In fact, in the amazing book "The Kuzari" Rabbi Yehuda HaLevi, from the 9th century tells us an amazing thing. The fact that there are no people in existence who keep a week of any

___

189 See https://hermetic.ch/cal_stud/hlwc/why_seven.htm lots of info, no real explanation, just guesswork. See also http://www.bbc.co.uk/religion/0/20394641 and http://www.almanac.com/content/why-week-has-seven-days Everyone in the ancient world kept a seven day week. This is the only clear thing.

other standard other than 7 days, is a clear proof as to the commonality of the world's people. In other words: we are all children of Noah, just like the Torah tells us.

All of the world's ancient people kept a seven-day week, and they all felt that the seventh day had special significance. Either they held, like the Jews, that it was a festival of sorts, or they held that it was a day of fasting and repentance.[190] The lowest common denominator: day seven of the week was special.

Why does the world keep a seven-day week? The existence of a Torah that tells you that the seventh day of the week has special significance – seems to be the only real reason that makes sense.

Here is the real issue.

All scientific "facts", "data" and "findings" are just bits and pieces of information. They can be indicative of many things, but what they really lack, in most cases, is CONTEXT.

When historians, archaeologists, paleontologists and any other learned individuals who deal with historical data look at their findings, they, like their brethren in the "exact" sciences, make up the context so that the data fit their (many, many (x 1,000,000) preconceived) notions.

Let's take a look at the facts:

1. All of our time-related countings are, and have always been universal. It has basically, (with the exception of some places in

---

190 See George Barton, *Archaeology and the Bible*, 7th Edition, p. 309. Concerning the seventh day in Babylonian culture. See also http://www.piney.com/BabFeastMard.html See also Haas, W.S. (1946). Iran. New York: Columbia University Press. Concerning the seventh day according to Zoroastrianism. Again: What is the lowest common denominator in all of the above? There is special significance to the seventh day. Who got this from whom and why- those are the only real questions.,

time which decided to do their own thing, counter to what everyone else was clearly doing), always been done that way.

2. The month-year concept only makes sense within the context of a lunar-solar year.

3. For many types of counting (24 hours a day, midnight, 12 months a year) there is no logical reason why it should be done that way.

4. For a significant amount of the above timings, we have NO reason whatsoever to keep them without the explanation of the Jewish tradition.

This brings us to the Jewish view of ancient (pre-Avraham) history (i.e. the context).

Most of us have read many things in the words of our sages about the world before the Torah at Sinai. However, much of it (all of it?) really doesn't make sense because we – too – have no context. I will try, with HaShem's help, to present the authentic Jewish context here.

We have all heard that Ya'akov our forefather, on his way to his Uncle Lavan in Haran, made a pit-stop on the way which lasted for 14 years. What was he doing, ask our sages, ob"m? Why he was learning Torah at the houses of Shem and Ever!

"Torah?", we ask. "There was no Torah yet. Torah was given only by Moses at Sinai. How could he have been learning Torah?"

The answer, my friends, can be found in Rashi throughout *sefer* Bereshis (Genesis). Yes. There WAS Torah before THE Torah at Sinai.

In fact, there was quite a bit of it, says Rashi. Before Sinai there was a Pascal lamb (one of the two goats served to Yitzchak), there was matzah (Lot gave them to the angels), there was Yibum (levirate marriage by Judah's sons) and more. All of this *was Oral Torah*. Rashi makes all sorts of time-related calculations during the time of the flood, based on the words of our sages ob"m, in how to calculate the months before Sinai.

There was Torah, there were mitzvos, (seven up until Avraham and then we had 8, including bris mila) and there were things that in the future would become mitzvos. But it would seem that all of them, which were eventually commanded to the children of Israel, were known and taught in the house of Shem and Ever.

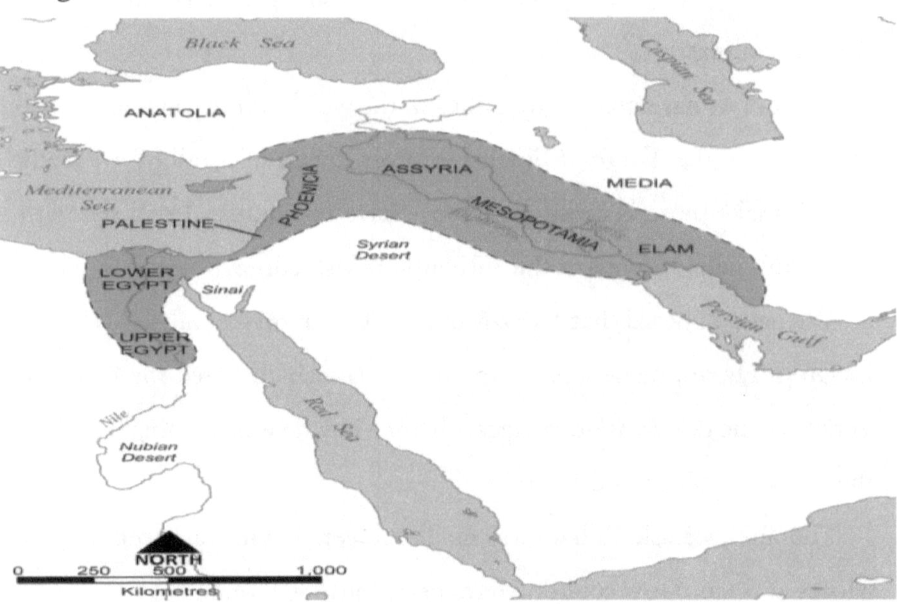

All of humanity emanates from what is referred to as the "Fertile Crescent." This includes Mesopotamia, Babylon, Acadia and many other places, extending all the way down to Egypt.

All of these places are listed explicitly by the Torah in Genesis as the original source of humanity. All of the ancient peoples of the world were influenced by the central doctrines of the houses of Shem and Ever. This is despite the fact that they eventually forgot the rhyme and reason with regard to why they were doing them.

Why do we have a 24-hour day, a seven-day week, a 30-day month and a 365-day year? We have them because they are mandated by the Torah and were taught and lived by all of humanity during the days when we were all one big, mostly happy family.

None of the above makes sense without the Torah.

However, in addition to the *mishpachtologyia* (family related stuff) the issues of time also do not make sense unless we also understand that even before the Sinai event there was Torah in the world and it was learned and studied in the houses of the Torah-greats of the pre-Avraham age *Shem* and *Ever*, the sons of Noah. They got it from their father Noah, who got it from his father, who got it from *his* father, etc. until Adam, who got it from G-d. As we will see, if we don't accept this there is no reason to follow a solar-lunar year (and calendar).

Here's why.

We already discussed that we Jews do it differently when it comes to time (and everything else)! Our day starts in the evening, our first month (*Nissan*) falls out in the *middle* of the solar year and our solar year begins at the end of the summer (*Tishrei*). We have no standardization of the months, they can be either 29 0r 30 days with two "swing" months (*Cheshvan* and *Teves*) and during a leap-year, we even have 13 months. But why is it that we do it this way?

The reason is that the Torah demands of us to have a double standard year, taking into account both the lunar cycle and the solar cycle in order to balance out the two.

On the one hand, Moshe, our teacher, is told in Parshas *Bo*, (Exodus 12:1-2)

> *(1) And HaShem said to Moses and to Aaron in the land of Egypt, saying. (2) This month is to you the rosh of all months. It is the first, for you, of the months of the year.*

From these verses, we learn that the month of *Nissan* is the first of months only for us, (as a reminder and a symbol of how HaShem took us out of Egypt to be His people) and that it is the first of the months of the year, clearly telling us that the accepted year of those days was comprised of months. In other words, the calendar had both months and years.

Now, if we had a purely lunar calendar there is no apparent problem from this verse, so long as we keep the laws of Passover during the first month, (i.e. Nissan) we're just fine and dandy. However, there is another clause which gives us pause. The Torah tells us elsewhere (Deuteronomy 16:1)

> *Guard the month of the Spring (Aviv, which also refers to the sprouting of vegetation) and you shall do* Pesach *for HaShem, your G-d. For in the month of Spring HaShem, your G-d, took you out of Egypt. (You shall do so in the) night.*

From here we learn that not only must Pesach be in the middle of the first Jewish month, but we have *to ensure* (i.e. Guard) that the first month should always come out during the Spring, as well.

Now, if we follow a purely lunar year this is not possible for a very simple mathematical reason. The length of the solar year (from spring to spring) is approximately 365.25 days. It is because of the extra quarter day that a "leap year" (which really is just a leap day, as only one day is added) is added every 4 years so that the solar calendar should not lose a day, relative to the seasons, every year. Whereas the length of the average lunar year is 354 days (6 months of 30 days + 6 months of 29 days = 354), which makes for an annual "loss" of 11.25 days *every year* when compared to the solar year, by which the seasons are measured. That means that in 3 years there is a little more than 1 month's difference between the lunar and solar years and within 9 years more than three month's difference.

Clearly, this is NOT the way to ensure that we keep the month of Nissan at the beginning of the spring! (It is for this reason that in Islam the month of Ramadan revolves throughout the seasons).

But here's the thing.

If that's the whole problem, there is a very simple solution to the issue! *Just keep a solar year* and you're fine! Why, indeed, should we keep the lunar year at all? What do we gain by it? Why did HaShem feel the need to make a double standard of calculating the year, which requires us to follow the moon, anyway?

I did quite a bit of looking around, and I even consulted with people over the web. It was suggested to me to look in Rav Shimshon Rafael Hirsch in *Shemos* (Exodus) 12:1. I looked there, but I didn't really see that he addresses the above question. It was also suggested to me to look in the Artscroll book on Kiddush haChodesh/Hallel, but I don't have that to look at. What I DO have is Rashi in *Bereishis* (Genesis) where we find a very interesting thing.

During the fourth day of creation, the Torah describes to us the creation of the *meoros*, the light sources. It was on this day that all of the stars of the heavens above were either created, as the simple understanding of the verse implies, (and so say some of our holy sages, ob"m), or they were established in their present trajectories and orbits, as our sages, ob"m, tell us. I deal with this topic in-depth in the tenth chapter of CE1 "Hello? G-d?". For more elaboration on the fourth day – look there.

Like all days, the actual fourth day is divided into two sections: the "planning" section, where HaShem describes what will be created on that day and what its purpose is, and the "carrying-out" section, where the Torah describes the fulfillment of that day's work.

(This has a great life-lesson for all of us, like all the words of the Holy Torah, when we take a good look at them. The lesson is that a person's day should be planned and then we should act upon our daily plan. As a wise man once said, "Those who fail to plan – plan to fail!". However, this isn't the time to address this issue).

In any case during the planning stage of the fourth day, upon scrutiny, there are two types of jobs laid out for the *meoros* (the light sources). The first is found in Genesis 1:14 the second is also there, in verse 15.

> *Job A:* "*…to separate between the day and the night and they should be for signs (otot) and for* moadim *(festivals) and for* yamim *(counting of days/months) and for* shannim *(years)*".
>
> *Job B:* "*And they should be as* meorot *(sources of light) in the* rakiya *of the* shamayim *(again, see the book for an explanation) in order to shed light on the* aretz *(the "land", i.e. the world. See the book).*

Job A is a very general mission statement. Job B is much more specific, as it explicitly describes that the *meorot* in the *rakiya hashamayim* have a much more specific job, as they are the sources of light for the *aretz*, which is the focal point of the entire Genesis narrative.

When the Torah then changes to the "carrying-out" section (verse 16) it starts out by saying

*"And HaShem (Elohim) made the two great light sources (meoros)"*, both big, both great, both equal sources of light.

The verse then continues to say

*"The large light source, to rule the day, and also the small light source, to rule the night, and also the stars".*

Rashi (ibid) quoting the Talmud (*Hullin 60b*) notes the apparent difference between the description of the light sources that the verse opens with as opposed to their description that it finishes with and asks "Make up your mind! Are they both big, or is only one big"?

To which Rav Shimon ben Pazi answers with a Midrash:

The "moon" comes up to HKB"H[191] and raises a serious problem "Is it possible," said the moon, "for two kings to rule with the same crown?" To which HKB"H answers "Go and make yourself smaller." An argument thereby ensues.

"Just because I noted a real problem *I* should be the one to lessen myself", said the moon to HKB"H. HaShem responds "Go! For you will rule during the night and the day" (as the moon sometimes is visible even during the daytime). "Even so," responded the moon, "what good is a

---

191 Acronym for Ha Kadosh Baruch Hu, "the Blessed One, holy is He".

candle during the daylight?" "Go!", said HKB"H, "For by you will Israel count days and years." "Even so", said the moon, once again, "it's not possible to NOT count the year by means of the *tekufa* (the cycle of seasons, which is the solar cycle)". ... (HKB"H) saw that the moon was still upset by this. Said HKB"H "Bring a sacrifice (on Rosh Chodesh) as an atonement for My having made the moon (the) lesser (source of light)".

The words of our holy sages, ob"m, are not to be taken lightly. This is not just a fable or a fairy-tale. There is depth beyond depth contained here to which I cannot do justice, but I would like to at least scratch the surface.

I know that the concept of the moon and other inert bodies having a conversation goes against our ingrained brain-washing that these are inanimate objects. They are, indeed, inanimate when compared to, say, plants, however, it is clearly the opinion of both the written and oral Torahs that that does NOT mean that they do not have a soul. As the verses of Tehillim say (148:3)

> *Praise Him sun and moon, Praise Him all stars of*
> *light.*

Even the Rambam, the great philosopher, writes in *the Laws of the Foundations of the Torah* (chapter 2) that the celestial bodies have a *nefesh*. In any case.

The Torah here is telling us that originally the milky way galaxy was a binary system. It had two suns of equal strength. However, it was the

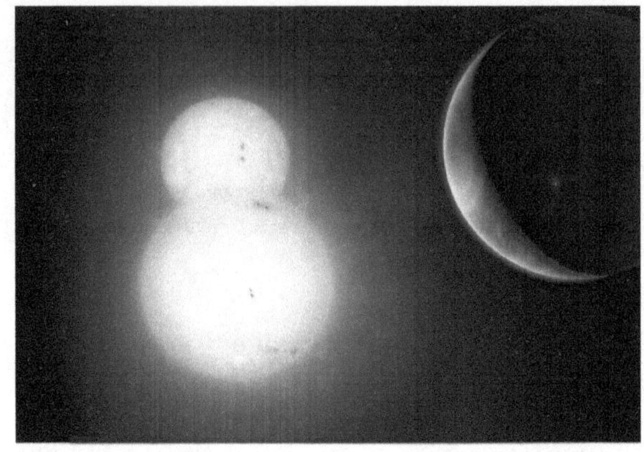

job of all of the light sources to fulfill job A from above, to be signs and *moadim* and *yamim* and *shanim*. However as far as the *aretz* (the land) was concerned there were only two main celestial bodies: the two suns. Both of them were to shine on the world during the day (verse 15) and to act as the sources of daylight.

But then something happened and one of them changed. One of them became small and was no longer an actual source of light in its own regard.

To understand how this small Midrash explains away many of science's questions[192] about the source of the moon – see CE1 in chapter ten!

But in addition, this Midrash also explains to us how the day of Rosh Chodesh attained a special status in the Torah and became similar to one of the *moadim*. Rosh Chodesh has a special *Mussaf* (additional) sacrifice

---

[192] https://en.wikipedia.org/wiki/Moon

which no other day has, yet it, itself, is not one of the *moadim* enumerated at the end of Leviticus 23 (Vayikra).

So, the Midrash now tells us that there has been a significant change in physicality, but that still does not change the job description. Both celestial bodies are still charged with control over the year. It's just that their specific jobs have changed.

You see, there are two jobs, two aspects which "collide" (or perhaps "coexist") during the year: the cycle of time and the agricultural cycle. Similarly, we find that the *moadim* (festivals) have two names, one commemorative of the *moed's* special relationship with the Jewish people, and the other of agricultural significance. Both coincide in the *moadim* for a very clear reason. *Simcha* (the ability to rejoice).

In reality, (i.e. it's HaShem's will) that the moon cycle decides the year. It is for this reason that the verse above (way back when) tells us that the month of Nissan is the head of the months of the year. It is for this reason that the three main *moadim* occur mid-month, (that being *Pessach* and *Sukkot*, both of which start on the 15th, and even *Shavuot* is semi-mid-month, just that it is tied to Pessach). That was given over to the moon "to appease it."

However, at the same time (as stated in the Gemara above) it's impossible that the year would not be counted also according to the solar cycle. The reason for this is 100% agricultural in nature. As my good friend and neighbor, Reb Moshe Kahana, shlit"a, tells me (he is a farmer here in Israel and a wonderful example of a Torah-true Jew) all agriculture revolves around the solar year.

*Pessach* is also called "the Festival of Sprouting" (*chag ha'aviv*), *Shavuot* is called "the Festival of Reaping" (*chag ha'katzir*) and Sukkot "the Festival of Gathering" (*chag ha'asif*). There is a very simple reason why HKB"H wanted these to coincide, as I mentioned earlier, for the sake of Simcha.

We are commanded on the festivals "*and you shall rejoice on your festival*" and on Sukkot, specifically, we are told "*and you shall be only happy*". When, indeed, is it easiest for a person to be happy? When he sees the fruits of his labor.

HaShem, in His infinite wisdom, set up the festivals to coincide with the times of year when the most important crops are either growing or being "deposited" into our bank accounts, because that will help us to rejoice. King David, in Tehillim (Psalms), teaches us "*The toil of your hands, when you eat them, (bring you to feel) praiseworthy and good to you*".

In order to make it easy for us to rejoice with HaShem, we have to feel we have it good. So, He made sure that our times of *simcha*, our times of rejoicing, our festivals, would all coincide with the times that we experience the fruits of our labors. At *Pessach* we see that the work of our plowing, seeding, weeding, watering etc. begin to bear fruit, as the new seedlings begin to show themselves, sprouting from the ground. At *Shavuot,* we reap the grain that has now reached fruition and we then leave it in the fields to dry throughout the summer months. By *Sukkos* we have already finished the processes of gathering the wheat and doing all of the *melachos* required to make it into the grain, ready to go to the mill when needed. It's all there in our silo. Our "bank" account is full. The fruit of our labor has come to fruition at last. More-so, we have also just gone through *Rosh HaShanna* and *Yom Kippur*. We're clean spiritually, we are all together in Jerusalem with the Beis Hamikdash. We are ready for *simcha*, we will be "only happy", as commanded in the Torah, because there is nothing in our way. No more work (presently), no worries about the future. We're good.

This is what the Torah means when it says that the celestial bodies will be for *otot, moadim, yamim* and *shannim*. This is why Rosh Chodesh is ruled by the moon, yet the Jewish year is balanced with the solar year as well. It was intended to be this way since the creation, and it is for this reason that all of the ancient peoples od the world kept a luni-solar calendar, even if they, themselves forgot the real reason behind it.

There is no other reason why anyone (meaning *everyone* in the ancient world) would keep a solar-lunar calendar unless we accept that it was the Torah, and only the Torah, that told people how to live their lives from day one. Unless we accept that almost all, if not all, of humanities practices in the ancient world, even up until this day *get their context from the great and holy book*, not the other way around. It's not that the Jewish people looked around and asked themselves "What's everyone else doing? Let's just do like them"! What everyone else was already doing was already based on Torah law, specifically the oral Torah, which was handed down to Adam and from him on since time immemorial.

Did the expansion of the "Fertile Crescent" happen as described in the Torah, after the story of Noah? Of course, it did! All of the cities and the ancient civilizations described there have been found and the accuracy of the information and details has been found to be spot-on. Do academics have problems with carbon-dating? That sounds like a "you" problem.

Regarding all of these things ask yourself THE MOST BASIC OF ISSUES: what is the lowest common denominator among all of the above… and who does it sound like? Who paints a better picture of the history involved? Who names the names, spells out details, and writes about the annals of history, most of which (if not, indeed, all of which) has archaeological evidence which clearly corresponds with its narrative? Only the Torah. Only the Jewish Bible, the TaNaCh.

Who gives a cogent, clear explanation for the historical phenomena that we are, until this very day, still following (i.e. the hours, days, weeks, etc.)? Only through the eyes of our holy Torah is there any sense, rhyme or reason.

But again: if you are not trying to prove the truth of the holy Torah, if you are trying to validate your own "torah", be it a Testament, a Koran, or any other document – don't use G-d's Torah to do so. The burden of proof, my dear sir/madam is on YOU to show that there is, indeed, any validity whatsoever behind the claim that my Torah has anything to do with you except for plagiarism.

Think about this very deeply, please.

# Appendix III



## ***Futile Attacks on the Bible, From the Bible***

ONE OF THE MORE INTERESTING attempts to discredit the Bible over the past many years are the attempts to discredit it by using the Bible itself to do so. The amount of stupidity and gall required for this is astounding. It should require no explanation. However, since this kind of criticism has become popular, I have chosen to address it anyway.

Before we begin – let's repeat the rules of engagement. Like all previous ridiculous arguments, they follow the same patterns and have the same logic.

1. The Jewish people are accepted as one of the most intelligent peoples on the face of the planet. This is as true today as it was throughout history.

It's therefore amazing that while the "highly educated" academia of many institutions feel that they themselves have no bias or agenda when reading through our Holy Bible, they do not feel this way regarding Jewish Torah scholars. Only the Jews, who for thousands of years have been reading, scrutinizing, and studying this book from all angles, are gullible enough to read this book and yet never develop the capacity to understand that it was all a human-made document all along! Someone just came along, at some (vague) point in history, gave us a book and told us "It's the holiest thing on the planet", gave us a line about where it came from, and we just swallowed the whole thing, hook, line, and sinker!

It's just *everything else* that we don't take for granted, apparently.

One wonders why, concerning all other matters of lesser importance we argue until our faces turn blue, but this thing, which has profound meaning and effect in our daily lives – this… we just accepted.

The sheer audacity of people coming up to us and telling us that we never understood our own Torah – in fact, no one did until these great intellectuals appeared on the scene – is beyond belief!

2. Biblical critics assume that there is a simple understanding of everything written in the Torah. What you see is what you get. "Simple understanding" should not be assumed regarding any term without investigating how the word or term is used throughout the Bible.

After all, there are many instances in which there are tremendous differences between modern Hebrew and the Hebrew of the Bible. Therefore, it is really silly to assume that the modern understanding of the word would fit the bill. However, even in instances when there *is* some Biblical reference, the question remains if this is the *correct* way to use that word or phrase. How is it *normally* used elsewhere in the Bible? Usually, words and phrases are used in the usual way.

3.   Context, Context, Context, and more Context.

Another pattern that we will notice in looking at the modern "understanding" of the various passages of the Bible is that the readings will always ignore the context of the stories as well. It doesn't matter whether or not we are talking about Christian missionaries, modern theologians, or academics, they all suffer from this lack.

In fact, in many cases, the lack of context is so great that if you would ask the person "What did the prophet talk about immediately *before* the passage that you are quoting (or immediately after)?" the "umm" "ahh" or silence that would follow would be deafening.

Having stated the above rules – let's see how they translate into action, shall we?

The way to approach the issue of context is to address it by following the historical continuity of the story: From Moshe to Yehoshua, through the prophets all the way down to the times of the second Temple. We will, of course, do so accepting the time-honored *masoret* (tradition) of the Jewish people that the books were written consecutively, not piecemeal over time.

This means that the 5 Books of Moses, (the Torah), was followed by the book of Yehoshua (Joshua), which describes the conquest and subsequent division of the Land among the twelve tribes of Israel. During that time, there were no arguments or doubts among the Jewish people as to the correctness of their way or the truth of the Torah, which is described then as being in their possession. They were accompanied by the Ark of the Covenant and the Mishkan (Tabernacle). Wars were fought and won in miraculous ways, as described in the book of Joshua. The Jewish *masorah* is that the book of Joshua was written first by Joshua himself, and it was finished by the Elders who lived on after him[193].

## **The Book of Shoftim (Judges)**

Joshua dies, and we now begin the time of the Judges (*sefer Shoftim*). The first chapter of the book continues the "work" of Joshua, in that it describes the final conquest and division of the land among the Tribes.

The Jewish *masorah* concerning this book is that it was written entirely by the Prophet Shmuel, (Samuel) some 350 years after the death of Joshua.

---

193 See Tractate Bava Basra 16a

In chapter 2 we start with the time of the first Judge, Otniel son of Kenaz.

> *(8) And Joshua, the son of Nun, the servant of G-d, was one hundred and ten years when he died. (9) And he was buried on the boundary of his inheritance, in Timnat-Cheres on the mountain of Ephraim, north of the mountain of Ga'ash. (10) And that entire generation also were gathered unto their fathers (a euphemism for dying) and a new generation arose after them who did not know (asher lo ya'deu) HaShem and all of the actions that He did for Israel. (11) And the children of Israel did evil in the eyes of HaShem, and they worshiped the Ba'alim (the name of a local type of idols). (12) And they left the worship of HaShem, the G-d of their fathers, who took them out of Egypt and they (instead) followed foreign gods, from the gods of the surrounding nations, and they prostrated themselves in front of them and they angered HaShem. (12) And they left (the worship of) HaShem, and they (instead) worshiped the Ba'al and the Astarot.*

If we look at verse 10 and read it according to its simple understanding it would seem to imply that one generation after the conquest of the land of Canaan there was a break in the *masora*. After all the verse, itself, says quite clearly that the second generation in the Land "didn't know G-d" and that they didn't know what He had done on their behalf in Egypt. This is, in a literal sense, what it says.

However, to read the verse this way is to be incredibly myopic. For in the larger picture that is painted in the verses above it becomes clear not only that isn't the way it should be read, but rather that it *cannot* be the meaning of the verse. Here's why.

1.  The meaning of the word *yadah*, *yode'ah*, or *ya'deu*.

Any person who takes a few moments (that's all it takes in today's world) to look up how the word *yadah* (ידע) or any of its forms are used in the whole Bible will discover that "to know" doesn't mean, necessarily, to gain knowledge *that was not previously in my possession*. Conversely, to "not know" doesn't mean to have NO knowledge. It means to have a lack of knowledge, and the chasm between the two explanations is staggering. Let's look at a few examples:

Genesis 3:7 "*And both of their eyes were opened, and they knew (v'yadeu) that they were naked*". This does not mean that Adam and Eve were mentally deficient before eating the fruit of the Tree of Knowledge, it just means that they didn't recognize the meaning that nakedness had. Both before and after eating the fruit they knew they were naked, all that changed was the meaning that nakedness had.

Genesis 4:1 "And Adam knew (*va'yadah*) Chava, his wife". Genesis 4:17 "And Kayin knew (*va'yadah*) his wife". In both of these verses we are not saying that they woke up, all of a sudden, with the new knowledge "this is my wife". They always knew that. However, at the point in time described they came to a deeper, more intimate knowledge of their wives.

Virtually, (if not actually) every instance where we find the root word *yadah* – that is its meaning: *to gain a better, deeper perspective*. Not to learn something new/not previously known. So, too, in the book of Judges what is being said is that the second generation in the land *did not bother themselves to have* a deep, meaningful understanding of who G-d was to them.

## 2.   The Historical Context.

As this book is talking about the children of the generation of the *midbar*, (the desert), who – themselves – experienced outright miracles both in the desert and during the conquest of the land, I find it hard to believe that the personal history of that generation would never have been related to their children after them. After all, in the time before television and radio, what did people do when they had some "free-time"? They sat around and told stories, of course! Which stories would they choose to tell? Obviously, those that were the most amazing, the most relevant to them and their families! In what universe could the children have been living that they would have grown up without hearing about the greatness of HaShem that they "didn't know Him"?

This is stated explicitly later in the book, during the time of the judge Gideon. As the prophet states (Judges 6:13-15) that at the beginning of his "reign" as the judge of Israel, when he was first approached by the "angel of G-d", (a euphemism for a prophet), at first Gideon was upset about it all. The *Midianites* had conquered the land of Canaan and were terrorizing the Jews (see ibid 6:1-6), and now the prophet comes to tell Gideon to go and save the people. Upon hearing this, Gideon responds:

> *(13) And Gideon said unto him (the "angel of G-d")*
> *"I beg you, my lord, if HaShem is with us – why has*
> *all of this happened to us? And where were all of His*
> *wonders of which our forefathers told us, saying*
> *'Behold! HaShem brought us up from Egypt'? For*
> *now, HaShem has deserted us and He has delivered*
> *us into the grip of Midian."*

Clearly, they were an informed people concerning their own history.

But that's not all. It's not just because of the stories that were told, rather it's because the Torah was taught publicly on a national level as well. This is described by the prophetess Devorah in her "victory song", (Judges 5), in which she sang praises of HaShem after Ehud's victory over the enemy general, *Sisera.*

> *(5) Mountains melted before HaShem – as did*
> *Sinai – before HaShem, the G-d of Israel.*

This refers to the well-known story of the giving of the Torah at Sinai, as is a portion of the rest of the song as well.

*(9) My heart is with the lawgivers of Israel who are devoted to the people, (saying) "Bless HaShem". ... (14) ... From Machir descended lawgivers and from Zebulun those who ply the scribal quill (to write the scrolls of the Torah).*

These refer to the teachers of Israel, whose hearts were with the people at all times to try and teach them to bless HaShem for His bounty and gifts. It also describes the adherents of the tribes of Menashe and Zebulun, from whom great scholars (lawgivers) and Torah scribes came.

### 3.  The Literal Context.

In addition to all the above, this obviously stupid explanation, which was created by evil individuals in order to try and convince others not to follow in G-d's path, totally ignores not only the context of the present story, and not only the story painted in the entire book before and afterward, but even the context that is written in the same paragraph!

Verse 11, which states *"And the children of Israel did evil in the eyes of HaShem"* they explain as being parenthetical. It's not that they *intentionally* did evil in HaShem's eyes, they say. After all, how could they do that if they never knew Him in the first place?! Let's say that we can let this one slide. However, it gets no further than verse 12, which says "And they *left* HaShem, the G-d of their forefathers". Also, in verse 13, it says again "And they *left* HaShem". "Methinks he doth protest too much," I say on reading these verses. Where exactly, O' wise ones, did they leave Him? I'll tell you where! In the garbage bin… along with your stupid interpretation!

The fact that they knowingly and premeditatedly left HaShem is mentioned not once, but twice to show us clearly that this was done *intentionally*. They clearly knew HaShem, they just didn't want to live the life that He described for them in His Torah. Hence the meaning of verse 10 "did not know HaShem" means that they made no effort to get to know Him or to take part in His worship. Like a long-lost great-uncle, that no-one cares about because they never bothered to get to know him. That is the type of "not knowing" that we are talking about in the verse.

Let's go back to the historical context again in order to take note of several very important points.

During the time of the Judges, the *Mishkan* is to be found in the city of *Shilo*, where it remained after moving from *Gilgal*. That was also the resting place of the Ark of the Covenant. The Ark was removed from *Shilo* in the times of Eli, the *Cohen Gadol*, by Eli's sons who wished to bring it to the battle-grounds with the Philistines to bolster the morale of the people of Israel. It was subsequently captured by the Philistines. Because the Ark was no longer present at the *Mishkan*, it ceased to act as the focal point of Jewish National worship.

Eventually, the Ark was returned to the people of Israel by the Philistines under miraculous circumstances, as described in the book of Samuel I (see chapters 4:1 until 7:2). It was later brought, in the times of King David, by King David, to the city of Jerusalem in preparation of the building of the permanent Temple, as described in the book of Samuel II chapter 6. This means that the makeshift Temple, the *Mishkan*, was active for around 350 years from the time that the Jewish people entered the land.

In addition to the actual judges described in the book (of Judges), there were also several hundred, thousands, or tens of thousands of prophets active around the land as well. Their job was to keep the people on track with the Torah and to reproach them if they veered from the Torah. We elaborated on this point in the book in chapter three, *Supernatural*.

The symbol of the people's miraculous crossing of the Jordan and entering the land at HaShem's behest[194], the stones which were erected in the Jordan river as the marker for where the people passed over the Jordan[195], and the other twelve stones that were taken from the Jordan, which were erected in the place of their first encampment site upon entering the land, at *Gilgal*[196], were all still standing. This is evidenced by the fact that the prophet *Shmuel* (Samuel) brought all of the people there at the end of the period of the Judges to both coronate King Saul and to chastise them for choosing a king for the wrong reason. (See Samuel I 11:14-15)

---

194 This was commanded by HaShem to Moshe and recorded in the book of Deuteronomy 27:2-8. The prophet in the book of Joshua records how the people fulfilled this commandment soon after entering the land after their second conquest, the city of HaAy. (See Joshua 8:30-35)

195 See Joshua 4:4-9

196 See Ibid 4:20

These stones were significant for the people, as described in the prophet Joshua (4:20-24):

*(20) And these twelve stones that they had taken from the Jordan, Joshua erected at Gilgal. (21) He spoke to the children of Israel, saying "When your children ask their father tomorrow, saying 'What are these stones?' you should inform your children, saying, 'Israel crossed this Jordan on dry land.'*

In addition, there were also the stones which were erected on *har Eival* (the mount of Eival) upon which the entirety of the Torah was written[197], which were also still standing.

For all of their failings, it is for this reason that the people play the part of the yo-yo during this period of time, alternating between worshiping HaShem and worshiping idols, going back and forth and around again. When calamity strikes, they always immediately go back to the G-d of their forefathers. Obviously, they shouldn't do that, nor would they, if there was a break in the *masorah*.

Throughout the history of the Bible, there is a working *Sanhedrin*, the Jewish Supreme Court, functioning at varying places around the country until the construction of the first Temple in Jerusalem by King Solomon. At that point in time, they took up residence on the premises

---

197 The construction of these stones and the fulfillment of the commandment of the blessings and the curses are described in the book of Joshua (8:30-35).

of the Temple, which is the Torah-mandated place for it. This is clearly described in the book of Deuteronomy (17:8-10)

> *(8) If there is something which eludes your understanding in the judgment between blood and blood, between one ruling and (another) one ruling, or between one (type) of affliction and (another) affliction, or (if there) are words of argument at your gates. And you shall get up and go to it, up to the place which HaShem, your G-d, shall choose. (9) And you shall come to the Cohanim, the Levites, and to the Judges who will be in those days, and you shall ask (of them concerning your dilemma) and they will tell you the (final) word (concerning the) judgment. (10) And you shall do in accordance with the words (i.e. follow the ruling as they tell it to you) which they shall tell you from that place which HaShem will choose, and you shall guard to do in accordance with all that they show you.*

The place "which HaShem will choose" was (and is), of course, Jerusalem.

In any case, it should be clear from all the above that there was a significant amount of religious infrastructure in place during the entire period of the judges and the first prophets, all of which would work on *strengthening* the Torah-identity of the people. Not weaken it.

One more issue before we move on:

## **The Festivals in the Times of the Prophets.**

The above verses speak about the keeping of the festival of Pesach when we commemorate our miraculous release from the bondage of Egypt. The festival of Pesach is mentioned many times throughout the Bible, both in the Torah and in the Prophets as well. There are two other places where the festival of Pesach is mentioned: during the time of Hezekiah, (which we will look at soon), and during the time of Josiah, (which we will look at later). In both cases, the Prophets state that "there was not like this Pesach..." or "there was not like this in Jerusalem..."[198]. Yet, clearly, there *was*, as both of these events happened on Pesach. This is aside from the issue that the festival of Pesach is mentioned MANY times throughout the Prophets: during the times of Joshua[199], during the times of Yechezkel (Ezekiel)[200], during the times of Ezra[201]. All of which is in *addition* to the multiple times that the Pesach is mentioned in the Torah itself.

Another festival that is brought up in this context is that of *Sukkot*, (the festival of Booths). This festival is mentioned in the book of Nehemiah (chapter 8) where a lengthy description of how the people

---

198 In the times of Hezekiah, it can be found at: Chronicles II 30:26 and during the times of Josiah (Kings II 23:22).

199 See Joshua 5:10

200 See Ezekiel 45:21 Even though this was in prophecy this prophecy happened during the time of the exile in Babylonia, as described there in chapter 35.

201 See Ezra 6:20

kept the festival in the times of Ezra is brought. The focus is brought specifically to verse 17, which states:

> *And the entire populace, those who returned from captivity, built Sukkot and they dwelled in the Sukkot, for the children of Israel had not performed (the mitzvah) in this manner since the times of Joshua, son of Nun, until this day. And the rejoicing was exceedingly great.*

Here, also, we must recognize that it is impossible to say that the festival of *Sukkot* was not kept before this time, or that it was in any way "new". Even the "most frum" (most fervent) of the academics agree that the "Cohanim texts" (otherwise known as the book of Leviticus/*Vayikra*) are much older than the book of Nehemiah. In addition, the festival of *Sukkot* is mentioned numerous times in the prophets before the time of Nehemiah (who was at the end of the Babylonian exile/Beginning of the second Temple). During the times of Ezra, ten years previously, the people kept the festival of *Sukkot*[202]. During the times of King Solomon, they kept the festival of *Sukkot*[203]. Sukkot is also mentioned in the prophecies of Zechariah[204] and Ezekiel, as well. SO, it CERTAINLY is nothing new.

---

202 See Ezra chapter 3

203 See Kings I chapter 8, also chronicles 8:13

204 Chapter 14

In addition, there is a verse in Nehemiah (ibid, 14) which states that "they found (*vayimatzeh*) it to be written..." be patient, we'll deal with that later in this appendix!

But let's look at some more tom-foolery, shall we?

## **From the life of King Hezekiah**

The following is brought as a "proof" of the break in the *masorah* as well. It says in Chronicles II 30

*(1) Hezekiah then sent word to all of Israel and Judah, and also wrote letters to Ephraim and Manasseh, to come to the Temple of HaShem in Jerusalem to perform the Pesach-offering to HaShem. ... (5) The established the matter to make an announcement throughout all of Israel, from Be'er Sheba to Dan, to come and perform the Pesach-offering to HaShem, G-d of Israel, in Jerusalem, because for a long time they had not done in accordance with what was written. (6) And the runners went out with their proclamations from the hand of the King and his ministers among all of Israel and Judah, and in accordance with the King's (instructions) they said "Return to HaShem, the G-d of Abraham, Isaac, and Israel, and He will return unto you, the remnant who escaped from the hands*

*of Assyria. (7) And do not continue in the ways of your forefathers and like your brethren, who betrayed HaShem, the G-d of their fathers, and he gave them over to destruction, as you can (plainly) see. ... (13) And there gathered unto Jerusalem a multitude of people to do the Pesach-festival on the fourteenth of the second month, an exceedingly great people.*

From the above, we are told, it is clear that there was a lack of *masorah*, a break in the transmission, as the people are approached and beseeched to return to HaShem as they had left Him. The chapter continues and says:

*(21) And the children of Israel, who were in Jerusalem made the festival of Matzos for seven days with great rejoicing and praising of HaShem each and every day, the Levites and the Cohanim (would play) with instruments with vigor to HaShem. (22) And YeChizkiyahu (Hezekiah) spoke to the hearts of the Levites, who had great understanding (of song in praises) to HaShem, and they ate the (sacrifices of the) festival for seven days, (all the while) sacrificing sacrifices, and admitting to HaShem, the G-d of their forefathers (their iniquities). (23) And the entire people consulted (and decided) to do*

*another seven days. And they did seven days of rejoicing. (24) For Hezekiah, King of Judah raised (for the people) one thousand cows and seven thousand sheep and the ministers raised (for the people) one thousand cows and ten thousand sheep, and there was a multitude of Cohanim who consecrated themselves. (25) And the entire populace of Judah and the Cohanim and the Levites and all of the peoples who came from (the land of) Israel and the converts who came from the land of Israel and those who dwelled in Judah, rejoiced. (26) And it was that the happiness was exceedingly great in Jerusalem, for from the times of Shlomo, son of David, King of Israel there was nothing like this in Jerusalem.*

From the above sources, there are those, wise only in their own minds, who would like to conclude that there was, again, a break in the *masorah*, that the people had not, and did not, know the Torah until it had to be "(re-)introduced" again. Yet like the previous "source", this one suffers from the same maladies. Let's rip this one to shreds too, shall we?

1.  The Meaning of the Words.

"*...because for a long time they had not done in accordance with what was written*" and "*For from the time of Shlomo, son of David, King of Israel there was nothing like this in Jerusalem*" although they *could* imply that nothing was done, the question remains: does it *actually* mean that? As there is nothing concrete within the text to force me to say otherwise I will, therefore, apply the linguistic/numeric rule of our sages, ob"m, "the minimum of a plural is two" and/or "included in two hundred is one hundred."

The meaning of these rules is as follows: If the Torah (or any other document, for that matter) lists a vague amount, whether the amount is a number, a volume, an amount of time, or a number of people, the correct interpretation will always be the sure one, i.e. the minimal amount. Having said that since the smallest number included in a plural is two, and since to have two hundred of anything you first have to have one hundred (unless they come out with a two-hundred-dollar bill) therefore we can say with total confidence that the plural is two and that the person is definitely in possession of, or required to pay one hundred.

The same applies here. To say that the meaning of the above verses, "they had not done" and "there was not", means "not at all" and "there never was" is to jump to the *absolute* conclusion. Which may, or may not, be true. But what the verse is *certainly* saying is that despite the people having performed these mitzvos – they weren't done with the same amount of joy or frequency as the ones described in the verses above.

Is there any way for us to know for sure which one is correct? Of course, there is! But to do that --- you have to know the context!


## 2.  The Historical Context.

Between the times of King Solomon until King Hezekiah there are about 300 years. That's a very long time for there not to have been a Pesach like the one described above! Also, it is clear from the simple text that the people of the Country of Israel (back then) didn't make the sojourn to Jerusalem. As the verse says (7) not to be like their forefathers, who forsake HaShem. Why is that?

Let's start at the beginning.

After the reign of King Solomon began the reign of his son, *Rechavam* (Rehoboam). The prophet (Kings I 12) describes the occurrences at the beginning of his reign, how he was approached by the people to institute some changes in his father's policies, how *Rechavam* rejected them, and how that resulted in the splitting of the kingdom into two: Judah and Israel. The split occurred at 2832 years from creation (+/- 928 BCE).

The first King of Israel was *Yerovam* (Jeroboam) son of *Nabat*. One of Jeroboam's first edicts was to establish golden calves, idols, on the way to Jerusalem near the border with Judah, in order to prevent the people from ascending to Jerusalem three times a year as they had done for centuries. This edict was enforced upon pain of death, and slowly, but surely, the people of the country of Israel stopped coming to Jerusalem on the three-times-a-year pilgrimage. From this time and on it was only the inhabitants of Judah who made the pilgrimage by themselves. This is recorded for posterity in the book of Kings I 12:26, where it says:

> *And Jeroboam said in his heart "Now the kingdom will return to the house of David if this people go up to sacrifice at the house of G-d in Jerusalem. And the hearts of this people will return to their lords, to Rehoboam, King of Judah, and they will kill me, and they will go back to Rehoboam, King of Judah". And the king took advice and he made two golden calves and he said unto them (the peoples of Israel) "It is enough that you have gone up to Jerusalem! Here are your gods, Israel, who have brought you up from the land of Egypt." And he placed the one in Beit El and the one he put in Dan.*

From that point in time and onwards, throughout the reigns of Jeroboam, Nadab, Baasha, Elah, Zimri, Omri, Ahab, Ahaziah, Jehoram, Jehu, Jehoahaz, Jehoash and Jeroboam II, kings of Israel, the people of Israel didn't make the thrice-a-year sojourn to Jerusalem. But then Hezekiah happened, and the above verses transpired. We'll come back to that in a minute.

As a rule, all of the kings of Israel were evil men in the eyes of HaShem. Despite their evil, and despite all of the idol worship going on, there were, during the entire existence of the country of Israel, active prophets going around the country begging and teaching the people to do teshuva. Elijah[205], Elisha, Amos[206], Yonah, Michaya, and Hoshea were all prophets whose main "turf" was the kingdom of Israel. In fact, relative to the time described in Chronicles, the time of Hezekiah that we quoted above, who was king in Judah, happened about 120 years *after* the famous story of Elijah at the Mount of Carmel[207]. (By the way, the story of Elijah shows clearly that there was no break in the *masorah*, rather there was a lot of wishy-washiness, as people were worshiping both HaShem and the Ba'al).

At the same time, in the kingdom of Judah, almost all of the Kings were righteous. One of the Exceptions, however, was Hezekiah's father, Ahaz, who was one of the evil kings of Judah. During the reign of the kings of Judah, the Temple service continued with the Cohanim and the Levites, and prophets walked the land, as in the kingdom of Israel.

However, during the reign of Ahaz things changed. This is because Ahaz installed idolatrous worship in the Temple[208] and was constantly stealing from the Temple in order to send bribes to other nations for treaties or for help against Judah's many enemies. This caused the Temple worship to almost grind to a halt. In the days of Ahaz's son, Hezekiah, who was righteous, things were going to change. This is the point that is told over in the quote from Chronicles above. This was the first time since the days of King Solomon that there was almost unity among the two kingdoms again. This was a re-dedication ceremony of

---

205 See Kings I chapters 17-19
206 See, for example, Amos Chapter 7, where Amos is told to "run away to Judah".
207 See Kings I chapter 18
208 See also Chronicles II chapter 28 see also Chronicles II chapter 28

the Temple, as well, and the people took heart from these two things to rejoice exceedingly.

All of the above is the historical context.

## 3.  The Literal Context.

As opposed to all the above, which may-or-may-not be the way to understand the text, in reality, the text is quite clear in defining its own meaning. Many times, in the above-quoted text the issue of "not being like your forefathers *who abandoned* HaShem" is mentioned. No explanation is given as to *why* there is a need to offer a pascal sacrifice, just some "motivation" to do that which their forefathers ignored doing. No one is recorded as saying "Pascal sacrifice? What's that?" or even expressing any wonderment at such a request. This despite the fact that we are talking about two Jewish kingdoms who were not only ideologically separated, but were at war with each other on and off for many years. The Northern Kingdom (Israel) was in no way influenced by the Southern one (Judah), nor were they subjects of any decree made by Hezekiah. Yet he called --- and they came running!

"Having not done *in accordance with what is written*" never means that *they don't know it*! Just the opposite! It means that they *knew* what was written, they just didn't act in accordance with it.

You can't "betray" someone that you don't know, as well. So how is it that the messengers chastised the people saying:

*(7) And do not continue in the ways of your forefathers and like your brethren, who betrayed HaShem, the G-d of their fathers, and he gave them over to destruction, as you can (plainly) see.*

What I find to be even funnier than all of the above, is the fact that these "wise guys" have the gall to make their statements about "proving" from various verses in the Bible that there are references to the loss of *masorah* etc. while – at the same time – totally ignoring *every other verse in the same prophecies which clearly say the opposite*! How do they answer such a question? "Well, OF COURSE, they couldn't write outright that the people lost it. Who would believe it if that were the case?" they say (in addition to all of the other reasons that we listed in the book not to believe it. For some reason, apparently, this one is the only one that would break the camel's back). "You'll only be able to divine the truth from 'quirks' in the text, that's where they let it slip."

To this I say HA! Hahahahahahahahaha! I've NEVER heard anything quite so funny! Concerning this Shlomo HaMelech says in Mishlei (Proverbs) "A fool will believe everything."

Let's look at one more, supposedly the "real" clincher.

## **From the Times of King Josiah**

This is what the prophet writes in Kings II chapter 22

*(3) And it was during the eighteenth year to the king Josiah, the king sent Shaphan, son of Atzeliahu, son of Meshullam, the scribe to the house of HaShem, saying. (4) "Go to Hilkiyahu, the high-priest, and count the monies which were brought to the House of HaShem, which was collected by the perimeter guards from the nation. (5) And distribute it by means of the artisans, who are responsible for the House of HaShem, and they should distribute it to (among) the working artisans, who are (working) in the House of HaShem, in order to strengthen the House's upkeep." ... (8) And Hilkiyahu, the High-Priest, said to Shafan, the scribe "I have found a sefer Torah (lit. "a book of the Torah") in the House of HaShem" and he gave the Torah scroll to Shafan and he read it. (9) And Shafan, the scribe, came with the scroll to the king, and he brought to the king words (of the job for which he was sent to the House of HaShem). And he said "Your servants have smelted the silver that was found in the House of HaShem, and they distributed it among the managers of the works, who are responsible for the House of HaShem. (10) And Shafan, the scribe, said to the king, as follows "I was*

*given a scroll by Hilkiyahu, the Cohen", and then Shafan read it in front of the king. (11) And it was that when the king heard the words of the Torah that he rent his garments. (12) And the king commanded Hilkiyahu, the Cohen, and Achikam, son of Shafan, and Achboor, son of Michiyah, and Shafan, the scribe, and Assiyah, the servant of the king, as follows. (13) "Go and beseech HaShem for myself and for this nation, and for all of Judah, concerning the words of this book, for great is the anger of HaShem which has been set on us, because our fathers did not listen concerning (al) the words of this book, to do all that is written in it, concerning us".*

Afterward, it continues and says (ibid. chapter 23):

*(3) And the king stood on a pillar and he cut the covenant before HaShem, to follow after HaShem and to guard His commandments and His statutes and His edicts with all (their) heart(s) and with all (of their) soul(s), to establish the words of this covenant, which are written on this book. And all of the people stood for this covenant. (4) And the king commanded of Hilkiyahu, the High-Priest, and the secondary Cohanim, and the guardians of the Saf to*

*remove from the Temple of G-d all of the utensils that were made for the Ba'al and for the Ashera and to all of the heavenly hosts. And they were burned outside of Jerusalem at Shadmot Kidron and their ashes were carried up to Beit El. ... (7) And the houses of the kadeshim (prostitutes) which were in the House of HaShem, the place where the women wove houses for the Ashera (was also destroyed) ... (21) And the king commanded the entire nation, saying "Make the Pesach for HaShem, your G-d, as it is written in this Book of the Covenant." (22) For there has never been like this Pesach since the times of the judges, who judged Israel, and all of the days of the kings of Israel and the kings of Judah. (23) For only on the eighteenth year of King Josiah was this Pesach done for HaShem in Jerusalem.*

What is clear to everyone who reads the above passages is the following:

1.  A sefer Torah is "found" during the reconstruction work at the Temple.

2.  Josiah and all those who read the Torah were "shocked" by what they read.

3.  Josiah immediately began significant reforms around the country as a result of what he read in the Torah.

Now, we are told by the "educated" world that the story is that a new book is "found", one which did not exist previously. "You see," say the academics, "it's here and now that the Torah was introduced. It wasn't really written by Moshe," they say.

Like all of the previous sources, let's take a look at this one using the very same points.

## 1.  The Meaning of the Words.

In addition to the above, there is another verse in the Tanach, in the book of Nehemiah (8:14) which also says something similar:

> *And it was found to be written (vayimatzu) in the Torah, which HaShem commanded to (the children of Israel) by the hand of Moses, that the children of Israel were to sit in sukkot (booths) on the festival in the seventh month.*

Again, another instance of the language "it was found," is used, isn't that indicative of something new?

Clearly the entire "explanation" presented to us by the academics is based on the words (ibid. 22:8) *sefer haTorah matzati*, and *vayimatzu*, because they explain the word *matzati/matzu*, which means "I have found [something]" as "that was not previously known" or "that did not previously exist." The question that we need to ask ourselves is: is that how it is commonly used throughout the prophets? Does it usually mean to find that which was non-existent or unknown? Well, that's something that should not be so difficult to check. Just open a concordance and compare and contrast!

In the New Even-Shushan Concordance, under the root word *matza*, (מצא) we find the following usages of the word:

a) To uncover/acquire. (307 examples. For example, Genesis 19:11 *vayileu limtzo es hapetach*, "and they (the people of Sodom, after they were stricken with blindness by the angels who were by Lot) aspired to discover the doorway")

b) To meet/arrive at (for example Genesis 32:19 *bimetzoachem otoh*, "when you shall find him".)

c) To have enough (for example Leviticus 25:26 *umatzah kedei geulato*, "and he *shall find* enough for his own redemption")

d) Revealed, achieved, was in existence (140 examples. Example: Isiah 55:6 *dirshu HaShem behimatzoh*, "search for HaShem when He is revealed")

e) Occurred, happened (Example: Jeremiah 41:8 *va'asarah anashim nimtzehu bam*, "and there were ten men who happened to be there")

f) There was enough

g) To grant a request

h) To bring, to serve

i) To hand over

In virtually all of the above usages, never do we find that the word *matzah*, in any of its forms carries the modern Hebrew connotation of "discovering that which was entirely unknown." To uncover/acquire, as in example "a" brought above) means that I couldn't find something *that I knew was there*. The revealed/achieved/was in existence (usage d above) also does not carry the connotation of "that which was unknown", but rather the discovery of more about that which was previously known.

So why would we apply this explanation here, exactly? Especially when we consider that modern Hebrew and that of the Bible tend to be, many times, mutually exclusive.

## 2. The Historical Context.

Josiah's story, the one listed above, takes place some ten years into his reign, while he was 18 years old. He became king at the age of eight[209] at the heels of two evil kings, who, for the sum total of their reign of 57 combined years, did everything in their power to spread idolatry and to close down the works of the Temple in Jerusalem. The practices and the attitudes that the kings Manasseh[210] and Amon[211] had towards the worship and the word of HaShem are described in the books of Kings II and Chronicles II, with the pinnacle of their evil happening during the

---

209 See Kings II 22:1, see also Chronicles II 34:1
210 See Kings II 21:1-18
211 See Kings II 21:19-26

reign of Amon, when he burned the *sifrei Torah* of the Temple, as recorded in the Babylonian Talmud, Tractate *Sanhedrin* 103b

> *"(King) Ahaz stopped the workings of the Temple… (King) Manasseh cut out the azkarot (names of HaShem from the scroll of Jeremiah) and destroyed the altar (in the Temple) … (King) Amon [burned the Torah] and (caused the) build-up of cobwebs (on the altar in the Temple)"*

At the age of eighteen, ten years into his reign is when the story of the *sefer Torah* occurs. It seems from the book of Kings that immediately after that he began the process of "cleaning up" the land from the idolatrous practices, which were rampant in those times, and all forms of immorality.  However, the truth is that he began to do so *before* this occurred. This is what we are told in the book of Chronicles II (34:3-12), where this story is paralleled:

> *(3) And during the eighth year of his reign, and he was still a lad, he began to search to the G-d of David, his father, and in the twelfth year (of his reign) he began to purify the (land of) Judah and Jerusalem from the altars (bamot) and the asherim and the idols and the masks.  … (6) … and he purified Judah and Jerusalem. … (12) And during the eighteenth year of his reign, (after he had succeeded) in purifying the land and the House, he*

*sent Shaphan, son of Atzalyahu, and also Ma'aseyahu, Minister of the city, and also Yoach, son of Yoachaz, the secretary, in order to strengthen the house of HaShem, his G-d.*

Meaning, that at the age of 16, eight years into his reign, Josiah began to search for HaShem, and to worship Him. At the age of 20 he began purifying the land, and only at the age of 26, eighteen years into his reign, did he start the process of "strengthening the House of HaShem" when the above story happened. In reality, everything described in the book of Kings after the reading of the *sefer Torah* was the *continued, invigorated process* of cleaning up the idolatry and immorality in the land, *not* the beginning of the process. So really, he didn't start to do anything new as a result of "finding" and reading the *sefer Torah*, rather he resumed the process with greater zest and alacrity.

This, as opposed to the opinion of the academics, who hold that one of the two – conflicting – stories must be true and the other false. They then strive to try and figure out which is the "real" one and … key major confusion call! Our sages, ob"m, however, tell us that the two stories are *complementary*, that the one adds details to the other, as we explained above.

Clearly, this *sefer Torah* is a special one, as it evaded the destruction by fire that all of the other *sifrei Torah* which were in the Temple suffered at the hands of Amon. It also took eighteen years to find it. The apparent reason for this is because it was hidden away in the structure of the

Temple and was subsequently discovered during the reconstruction of the Temple.

## 3. The Literal Context.

It is in this arena that the real picture of the finding of the book begins to emerge. There are several issues that need to be addressed when looking at this *sefer Torah*.

### a)  It's not just any *sefer Torah*

One of the things that jump out at me when I'm reading this portion of the prophets is the fact that this *sefer* is always referred to as *sefer HAbrit*[212], meaning THE book of the Covenant. Alternatively, it is also called *sefer HATorah*[213], THE book of the Torah. Clearly, this isn't just ANY book of the Torah. It's THE book. If all we had was the story as related in the book of Kings II, then we could debate the issue some. However, the truth is, as we mentioned previously, that this story is told not only in the book of Kings but also in the book of Chronicles as well. This is how the story is described here: (Chronicles II 34:15)

> *And as they were taking out the silver (monies)*
> *which was brought to the house of HaShem,*

---

212 See Kings II 23:2,3,21
213 See Kings II 22:8,12

*Hilkiyahu, the High-Priest, found THE sefer Torat HaShem, (written) with the hand of Moses.*

This isn't *a* book of the Torah. This is – truly – *THE* BOOK of the Torah. Written with Moses's own hand! In truth, there were *many* books of the Torah which could be found throughout the land. But there was nothing like this one. It is for this reason that it is always described using language which specifies it's special nature.

b)   It wasn't just hidden away

Why was this book so hard to find? Why did it take eighteen years to find? The answer is because this book had a special resting place: *ba'tzad aron brit HaShem*[214], (on the side of the Ark of the Covenant of HaShem). Unfortunately, apparently during the time of Manasseh, Josiah's father, the Aron HaBrit was removed from the Temple and its whereabouts were unknown. This is clear from the reading of the book of Chronicles II (35:3), which says:

*And he (Josiah) said unto the Levites, they who (teach) understanding to all of Israel, the holy ones to HaShem, "Place the holy Aron (Ark) into the house that was built by Shlomo, son of David, King of Israel. For today there is no more (need to) carry*

---

214 Deuteronomy 31:26

*(the Ark) on the shoulder. Now, worship HaShem,*
*your G-d, and His people Israel".*

This is the last time that the Aron is mentioned in the Bible. Clearly, the Aron was, at this point, missing from the House of HaShem, the Temple. For otherwise, why would Josiah need to command the Levites to place the Aron into the Temple of Solomon? Obviously, it's because it had been removed prior to this point in time. The explanation that is given is that it had been squirreled away by the Levites during the time of Manasseh. Now that they had re-dedicated the Temple, Josiah demanded of them that it be returned. At the very same time that the Aron was hidden away, so, too, was THE Torah of Moses hidden away, as it's permanent place is "on the side" of the Aron. It is not clear if the Torah and the Ark were hidden separately from the start. What is clear, however, is that they were eventually separated, as the Torah was given over to Shafan to read to the king.

c)   It wasn't just any part of the book that was read

How can we know this clearly? It's actually quite simple. After all, if the portion that was read to Josiah was "Understand, O' Israel, the Lord, your G-d, the Lord is One" it wouldn't have caused such an extreme reaction like the one recorded in the prophet! "Wear tefillin?" I wouldn't have a conniption. Yet when Josiah heard the words of the Torah, his initial reaction was "G-d is furious with us!" Why is that?

The answer is because the portion of the Torah that he read is the portion called the Brit, (covenant), which is, actually why it is referred to in the verses as the *sefer ha'brit*, the book of the covenant. When we read the words of the brit, then things get serious. Where is this brit, exactly? It's in the book of Deuteronomy (chapter 28). How do I know this? For two reasons: first, because our sages, ob"m, tell me this explicitly in the Talmud and in the Midrash, and second because the word "brit" is stated there as well. Thusly sayeth the book of Deuteronomy (28:69)

> *These are the words of the BRIT which HaShem commanded Moses to establish with the children of Israel in the land of Moab, in addition to the covenant (brit) which he (Moses) made with them at Horeb (Sinai).*

When we peruse the curses that will befall the children of Israel as laid out in the Torah, we find many things that would (and should) make my hair stand with fear. Our sages, ob"m, tell us that it was specifically this verse which caught Josiah's attention (ibid. 28:36)

> *HaShem will lead you and your king who you will set up over yourself to a nation you never knew – neither you, nor your forefathers – and there you will work for the gods of others, of wood and stone.*

Essentially the words of the brit, the covenant, are clear: if the people of Israel follow the words of HaShem, as laid out in the Torah of Moses things will be super-great in all of the ways that truly matter to a nation:

security, prosperity, peace and more. However, if we fail to follow the ways of HaShem – it will be bad: war, famine, expulsion and more (read it – and weep!). Josiah realized that they were on the precipice of the actualization of these prophecies, he looked into how they were all coming together, and he immediately jumped into action to try and halt them. But he didn't succeed to stop them, only to push them off.

As opposed to the words of the academics who say that a "new" Torah was introduced at this time, (regardless of whether or not we say that it was the whole thing or just the book of Deuteronomy[215]), it was this message that hit home. Our sages, ob"m, tell us that the book, which was in scroll form, not bound like our books, was rolled to this point. Meaning, that as soon as they rolled open the book to read what it said – they were faced with the words of the brit, the words of the covenant, which did not bide well for their future.

## The Real Issue

Here's the real crux of the issue: do we trust the words of the book or not? Jewish tradition was, is, and always will be, that all of the five books were given to us in writing by Moses himself. There never was any doubt of that until the time of the self-proclaimed "enlightenment".

There is a basic rule of all law, which our sages, ob"m, sum-up as "It is incumbent upon he who wishes that the court should take away

---

215 Of course, if you say that it is only the book of Deuteronomy then you kind of shoot yourself in the foot. After all, in Chronicles it says clearly that this book is the work of Moshe's own hands....

something from his friends' possession to bring the proof that we should do so[216]." The Jewish people were in possession of this clear truth for centuries. Never, in all of recorded history, was there anyone who doubted this truth. Not even the Ka'arites, the Sadducees, or any of the other cults that arose from within Judaism, despite the fact that they systematically denied the Divine source of the oral Torah. Yet none of them ever dreamed to say that there were any less than five books given to us by Moses. But all academics are correct, isn't that true?

Nah!

The reality is that the "proof" that they rely on is so flimsy that it would only stand up in an American court, where some of the funniest cases in the world are tried and won. You would have to have a jury of either clowns or fellow (biased) academics as members of the jury in order to accept the proofs brought. I'm not reiterating everything that I said in the book, re-read the book if you need, just the PRACTICAL issues with this argument are insurmountable. I'm also not repeating all of the information in the appendix up until now. What's left?

Basically, the issue of "if Moses wrote the book – how did he write about his own death"? OMG! You've stumped me there! NO ONE in all of recorded history EVER thought of that totally OBVIOUS question! ... Nah! Been there. Done that! This question is addressed explicitly in both the Talmud (Tractate *Bava Batra 16a*) and the Midrash and two opinions are posed:

---

216 In Hebrew hamotzi me'chaveiro alav ha'ra'ayah. See Tractate Bava Metziya 46a, for example.

Either YES, Moses himself wrote about his own death (he DID have prophecy, remember?); OR

Moses didn't write it and it was added, (meaning the last eight lines of the book ONLY), by Joshua after Moses's death.

Do either of these answer the above difficulty? I think so.

So, whose opinion makes more sense?

Think about it.

# About the Author

Rabbi Shlomo Ben Zeev

Born in Boston, Mass. Grew up in Atlanta, Ga. I attended the Hebrew Academy of Atlanta.

1984 Moved to Israel where I attended Neve Shmuel Yeshiva High-School.

1988 Attended Yeshiva Ohr David. Followed by Yeshivas Sha'alvim and Ittri. During my 15 years in ,Sha'alvim I served in the IDF, received rabbinical ordination from the Chief Rabbinate of Israel (*Yoreh-Yoreh*), ordination as a Torah scribe and checker from *Va'ad Mishmereth STA"M* and a BA and MA in Hebrew Letters from Yeshivat Ittri's college program. During this entire time, I taught classes in advanced Talmud studies, Halacha, (the practical application of the oral Talmud), and in many other aspects of Torah learning.

2004 I worked with the Nahal Haredi Project as one of the rabbis. It was there that I began work on the Emunah project, Core Emunah. This book and, with HaShem's help, those that are to follow, are based on the research that I began then and am still working on to this day.

2008 Received ordination as a Certified Mohel (Practitioner of Jewish circumcision).

2014 Finished a degree in Jewish Education (B.Ed.) at the Jerusalem College (Michlala).

Today I am teaching in Yeshivat Ohr David[217] in Jerusalem, (one of my alma maters) and lecturing under the auspices of *Nefesh Yehudi*[218].

I am, with HaShem's help, a lifetime learner. I have been interested in the sciences since I was young and have been an avid reader forever. It is with HaShem's help, the guidance of my teachers and the support of all of my students that I humbly present the reader with this volume and those to follow

---

[217]www.ohrdavid.org

[218]http://www.nefeshyehudi.org/

www.ingramcontent.com/pod-product-compliance
Lightning Source LLC
Chambersburg PA
CBHW021934120726
47992CB00001B/43